Sexual Offending

Sexual Offending

Cognition, Emotion and Motivation

Edited by
Theresa A. Gannon and Tony Ward

Library of Congress Cataloging-in-Publication Data

Names: Gannon, Theresa A., editor. | Ward, Tony, 1954 March 17– editor.
Title: Sexual offending : cognition, emotion and motivation /
    edited by Theresa A. Gannon and Tony Ward.
Description: Chichester, West Sussex, UK : John Wiley & Sons, 2017. |
    Includes bibliographical references and index.
Identifiers: LCCN 2016038232| ISBN 9780470683521 (cloth) | ISBN 9780470683514 (pbk.)
Subjects: LCSH: Sex offenders–Psychology. | Sex offenders–Rehabilitation. |
    Sex crimes–Psychological aspects.
Classification: LCC RC560.S47 .S485 2017 | DDC 616.85/8306–dc23
LC record available at https://lccn.loc.gov/2016038232

A catalogue record for this book is available from the British Library.

Cover image: Grandfailure/Gettyimages

Set in 10/12pt Warnock by SPi Global, Pondicherry, India
Printed and bound in Malaysia by Vivar Printing Sdn Bhd

10 9 8 7 6 5 4 3 2 1

Theresa A. Gannon: For Amy Haskew (1990–2016): A Talented Student.

Tony Ward: To Bill Marshall, friend, mentor, brilliant researcher, and most of all, a great bloke.

Contents

Notes on Editors

Theresa A. Gannon, DPhil, CPsychol (Forensic) is Professor of Forensic Psychology and Director of the Centre for Research and Education in Forensic Psychology (CORE-FP) at the University of Kent, UK. Theresa also works as a Practitioner Consultant Forensic Psychologist specializing in sexual offending and firesetting for the Forensic and Specialist Service Line, Kent and Medway Partnership Trust.

Theresa has published over 100 chapters, articles, books and other scholarly works in the areas of male and female-perpetrated sexual offending. She is particularly interested in research relating to both the treatment needs and overall supervision of individuals who have sexually offended. This includes offence-related cognition and emotion, rehabilitation models (i.e., the Good Lives Model), offence-process models of offending behaviour, polygraph-assisted supervision and truth facilitation, and attitudes towards individuals who have offended. Theresa is lead editor of several books including *Aggressive Offenders' Cognition: Theory, Research, and Treatment* (John Wiley) along with Tony Ward, Anthony Beech and Dawn Fisher, and *Female Sexual Offenders: Theory, Assessment, and Treatment* (Wiley-Blackwell) along with Franca Cortoni. Theresa is also co-editor of several books that discuss or integrate sexual offending with other forensic topics and psychological factors including *Public Opinion and Criminal Justice* (Willan) along with Jane Wood, *Crime and Crime Reduction: The Importance of Group Processes* (Routledge) along with Wood, and *What Works in Offender Rehabilitation: An Evidence-Based Approach to Assessment and Treatment* (Wiley-Blackwell) along with Leam Craig and Louise Dixon.

Theresa serves on the editorial boards of several journals including *Aggression and Violent Behavior, British Journal of Forensic Practice, International Journal of Offender Therapy and Comparative Criminology,* and *Sexual Abuse: A Journal of Research and Treatment.* She is also Editor of *Psychology Crime and Law.*

Tony Ward, PhD, DipClinPsych received his Ph.D. and trained as a Clinical Psychologist at Canterbury University, Christchurch, New Zealand. Tony was the former Director of the Kia Marama Sexual Offenders' Unit at Rolleston Prison in New Zealand and has taught clinical and forensic psychology at Victoria, Deakin, Canterbury and Melbourne Universities. He is currently the Director of Clinical Training at Victoria University of Wellington, New Zealand.

Tony has published over 400 chapters, articles, books and other scholarly works in the areas of male sexual offending and general rehabilitation and practice. He is particularly interested in the critique and generation of theory within forensic psychology as well as the examination of ethical constructs in psychological practice. Tony has made a number of key theoretical contributions to the area of sexual offending and offending behaviour more generally, which include: the *Self-Regulation Model of Sexual Offending* (Ward & Hudson, 2000), the adaptation of the concept of *Implicit Theories to sexual offending* (Ward & Keenan, 1999), the *Good Lives Model of Rehabilitation* (Ward & Stewart, 2003) and the *Integrated Theory of Sexual Offending* (Ward & Beech, 2006). Tony is also lead editor of several books including *Theories of Sex Offending* (Wiley-Blackwell) along with Tony Beech, Sexual Deviance: Issues and Controversies (Sage) along with Richard Laws and Stephen Hudson, and was author of *Rehabilitation: Beyond the Risk Paradigm* (Routledge) along with Shadd Maruna.

Tony serves on the editorial boards of several journals including *Aggression and Violent Behavior, Legal and Criminological Psychology,* and *Psychology Crime and Law.* Tony has served as Associate Editor for *Sexual Abuse: A Journal of Research and Treatment and Legal and Criminological Psychology.*

Notes on Contributors

Ross M. Bartels, PhD, gained his MSc in Forensic Psychology in 2008 from the University of Kent, and was awarded his PhD in 2014 from the University of Birmingham. Ross is currently a Psychology Lecturer and member of the Forensic and Clinical Research Group at the University of Lincoln (UK). He is also an associate editor of 'nextgenforensic'; an online blog for the 'next generation' working in the field of sexual offending research and treatment. Ross's primary research interests focus on adapting indirect measures and socio-cognitive paradigms to gain new insights into the processes underlying (and associated with) sexual thoughts and fantasies, offence-supportive cognition, and attitudes towards people who have sexually offended.

Nicholas Blagden is a Senior Lecturer in Forensic Psychology and the Course Leader for the MSc Forensic Psychology at Nottingham Trent University (NTU). He is a Chartered Psychologist and has worked and researched within the criminal justice system and HM Prison Service for many years. He has taught undergraduate and postgraduate courses in psychology, forensic psychology and criminology. He has also trained police officers. His work has been funded by the National Offender Management Service (NOMS) and he is currently engaged in numerous collaborative forensic projects with NTU and NOMS. Current projects include understanding paedophilic deviant sexual interest, rehabilitative prison climates, religiosity, and denial in relation to sexual offending. He is a trustee of the Safer Living Foundation, a charity that takes a multi-agency approach to reducing sexual (re)offending through rehabilitative initiatives.

Sarah J. Brown is Professor of Forensic Psychology, registered Forensic Psychologist, Chartered Psychologist and Associate Fellow of the British Psychological Society. She is the Deputy Executive Director of the Centre for Research in Psychology, Behaviour and Achievement at Coventry University, Vice Chair of the National Organization for the Treatment of Abusers (NOTA) and a member of the Association for the Treatment of Sexual Abusers (ATSA). She has been conducting research in relation to sexual violence since 1994 and was the Editor of the *Journal of Sexual Aggression (JSA)* from 2008 until 2014. She is currently an Associate Editor of *Child Abuse and Neglect* and Editorial Board member of *JSA* and *Sexual Abuse: A Journal of Research and Treatment*. Brown has published on various topics including sexual aggression, intimate partner violence, engaging individuals who have offended, empathy, risk assessment, evaluation and forensic testing.

Rebecca Lievesley is a Lecturer in Forensic Psychology and part of the Sexual Offences, Crime and Misconduct Research Unit at Nottingham Trent University. She has worked with individuals who have offended since 2008 and is currently engaged in various research projects including an investigation of reoffending and desistance for individuals on short sentences, evaluation of anti-libidinal medication for individuals who have sexually offended, the role of religion in sexual offending and help seeking prior to committing a sexual offence. She is also a trustee and co-founder of the Safer Living Foundation, a charity established to promote sexual offence rehabilitation and the prevention of further victims of sexual crime.

Caoilte Ó Ciardha obtained his PhD from Trinity College Dublin in 2010 for research examining social cognition and the assessment of sexual offending. Since 2011 he has worked at the Centre of Research and Education in Forensic Psychology, part of the School of Psychology at the University of Kent, first as a postdoctoral Research Associate and later as a lecturer. His publications have included both theoretical and empirical research relating to the assessment and treatment of individuals who have committed sexual or firesetting offences. He also conducts research on social cognitive factors in individuals who may be at higher risk of those behaviours but who have not offended.

Geris A. Serran, C. Psych. graduated with a doctoral degree in clinical psychology from the University of Ottawa in 2003. A registered psychologist, Dr Serran is currently employed by Correctional Service Canada providing intervention to men who have offended. Prior to that, she worked with Rockwood Psychological Services, providing intervention to clients who committed sexual offences. Her research interests include therapeutic processes, coping strategies and effective intervention with men who have sexually offended. She has authored several book chapters and journal articles, co-edited and co-authored books, and presented at international conferences.

Jill D. Stinson received a dual doctorate in Clinical Psychology and Psychology, Policy, and Law from the University of Arizona in 2006. She is currently an Assistant Professor and Director of Clinical Training with the Department of Psychology at East Tennessee State University. She has co-authored two books on the aetiology and treatment of problematic sexual behaviour, a third book on motivational interviewing with individuals who have offended, and numerous chapters and articles describing sexual offending in relation to mental illness, self-regulatory problems, and histories of childhood trauma and maltreatment. She is also an Associate Editor for *Sexual Abuse: A Journal of Research and Treatment*.

Jayson Ware graduated with a MA (psychology) in 1997 and then completed a postgraduate diploma in Clinical Psychology in 2000. He is currently the Director of Offender Services & Programs, Corrective Services, New South Wales, Australia. He has worked with individuals who have sexually offended for the past twenty years and has authored over thirty journal articles or book chapters primarily relating to sexual offence treatment. He is currently working toward a doctorate in Psychology at the University of New South Wales, Australia.

Preface

Our initial idea for this book stemmed from a conversation that we had many years ago about the lack of integrative resources available on the topic of sexual offence related cognition, emotion, and motivation (CEM). What became clear to us, as we reflected, was that although the sexual offence field had developed immensely in relation to CEM over the past three decades, more momentum was needed. From this realization, we began to approach a range of internationally esteemed professionals about whether they would be interested in writing a chapter for a book devoted to sexual offence CEM. The response that we received was extremely reassuring; and as editors we feel fortunate to edit a text of special interest to us, with a renowned group of experts. We sincerely hope that this book will promote momentum for theorists, researchers and treatment providers who are working with CEM applied to sexual offending. If readers take only one message from this book we hope it will be that future work on sexual offence related CEM must be expert, integrated and holistic.

Theresa A. Gannon and Tony Ward
May 2016

Acknowledgments

We would like to acknowledge all of the individuals who have made this collection of chapters possible. First of all, thank you to all of the authors who put so much time and effort into writing their chapters. We would also like to thank all those at Wiley-Blackwell who gave expert advice and support on this book. In particular, thank you Clive Hollin for dealing positively with the initial enquiry about this book and for directions about possible avenues for publication. Also, a big thank you to everyone at Wiley-Blackwell for being so patient with us! In particular, thanks must go to Karen Shield for her utter professionalism, Roshna Mohan for her quality checking, and Amy Minshull and Victoria Halliday for dealing with contractual issues. Finally, we would like to thank Jaimee Mallion for helping us with the proofreading of this book and also Alec McAulay for dealing with the copyediting associated with this book.

1

Emotion, Cognition and Motivation

An Enactive Perspective
Tony Ward

A striking feature about emotions in correctional psychology is that they are primarily viewed as problems to be managed. Difficulties with emotional regulation have been identified as a dynamic risk factor in the sexual offending domain, and as a consequence of this are considered to be a critical treatment target (Hanson & Harris, 2000; Thornton, 2013). In the general offending area, impulsive behaviour leading to crime is frequently linked to emotional dyscontrol (Andrews & Bonta, 2010). Theories of sexual offending typically include aetiological pathways or causes that are characterized by emotional instability. For example, in Hall and Hirschman's (1992) Quadripartite Model of child molestation (see Bartels, Chapter 2 in this volume), one group of individuals is defined by their susceptibility to negative affective states and tendency to behave in an impulsive and unplanned manner. Treatment for this group centres on learning how to control and regulate negative emotions. Similarly, according to Ward and Hudson's (1998) self-regulation model, negative emotional states such as anger or anxiety may function as disinhibitors and precipitate reoffending. Finally, a core component of Ross and Fabiano's (1985) influential cognitive skills treatment programme is devoted to preventing emotional arousal from impairing functioning and leading to further offending. One of the core assumptions of cognitive skills programmes is that there are causal relationships between cognition, emotion and motivation. The picture of emotion emerging from these models and theories is a negative one: emotions overwhelm individuals and if unchecked result in antisocial and destructive behaviour. They are problematic, destructive and need to be controlled.

The conceptualization of emotions within correctional psychology as behavioural disrupters, contrasts starkly with the richer and more nuanced characterization evident in contemporary psychological and philosophical theorizing and research (Colombetti, 2009, 2014; Lewis, Haviland-Jones & Barrett, 2008; Solomon, 2007). In this latter body of work, emotions are described as biologically adaptive, essential for sound decision-making, critical elements of interpersonal relationships and conduits to a meaningful engagement with life (Christensen, 2012; Helm, 2002; Maiese, 2011; Sterelny, 2012; Thompson,

2007). Furthermore, a number of emotional phenomena have been identified; ranging from specific emotional states to more enduring moods or personality-based dispositions. Emotions can enhance personal functioning, may be positive or negatively valenced, motivate individuals to pursue goals and function as interpersonal and intrapersonal signals of progress to goal achievement. The distinction between emotion and cognition has been effectively collapsed, and they are no longer considered to be polar opposites (Colombetti, 2014; Pessoa, 2013). Therapy has reflected this renewed interest in emotions as facilitators of behavioural change and specific emotion focused interventions are now routinely part of the repertoire of contemporary clinical practitioners (Greenberg, 2002; Leahy, 2015). For example, learning to focus on the somatic aspects of emotion in order to activate its phenomenological and behavioural components (Greenberg, 2002).

This change in understanding of emotional phenomena and its subsequent enriched role in therapeutic practice has not occurred in correctional psychology. Rather, a more limited understanding of emotions, motivation and cognition and their function in the process of behavioural change is typically the case. Why is this so? I think there are three major reasons for this neglect of emotional theorizing and research by correctional practitioners. First, a preoccupation with risk prediction and management in forensic and correctional practice has resulted in a neglect of desistance processes and emphasis on agency. What I mean by this is that attention to individuals' personal goals and aspirations for living fulfilling and better lives has not occurred (Ward & Maruna, 2007). The process of constructing intervention plans that reflect what is meaningful to individuals necessarily involves consideration of positively valenced emotions – and more generally – well-being related concerns. Second, the fragmentation of treatment programmes into discrete modules, such as emotional regulation, interpersonal functioning, cognitive restructuring and so on, has meant that it is tempting to focus on problem areas rather than processes for facilitating meaningful change. Engaging individuals fully in treatment requires attention to broader values and goals, and a coherent, positive plan for living rather than a disconnected strategy of tackling specific risk factors, or problems. Third, because correctional practice has been driven by pragmatic concerns, there has been a focus only on treatment theories and techniques that have been tested in risk–need–responsivity type studies (Andrews & Bonta, 2010; Marshall, Marshall, Serran & Fernandez, 2006). This is a severe limitation. The desire to effect change in certain problem areas has concentrated efforts on developing specific treatment approaches and, as a result, there has been a lack of awareness of current affective science and its implications for therapy.

In correctional psychology, an artificial distinction between emotion and cognition has been uncritically accepted, and cognition has been favoured as the primary causal process. As we will see later, this has been undermined by theory and research in affective science. In this chapter, I present a view of the interrelationship between cognition, emotion and motivation which challenges the current theoretical status quo in sexual offence treatment and has serious implications for how therapists view and treat the components of emotion, cognition, and motivation. First, I will consider definitional and conceptual issues that are currently under the spotlight of affective science. I will then spend the rest of the chapter detailing the enactive approach to human functioning in general, and emotions, in particular. The enactive view of the mind is that it emerges from the biological process of autopoiesis, or rather, the dynamic processes by which dynamic systems protect, repair and organize their components and actively control their relationship to the environment (Hutto & Myin, 2013; Stewart, Gapenne, & Di Paolo, 2010; Thompson, 2007). It is a relational, dynamic conceptualization of organisms in which affective structures and processes play a significant role in framing salient features of the environment that represent potential benefits or possible threats. In this theory, emotions are at the centre of adaptive functioning and actively support cognition and behaviour. Following a description of enactivisim and its general assumptions, I will discuss its implications for correctional practice. My review of these implications will be brief as my major aim is to present a way of thinking about emotional phenomena that is supported by current research and theory, and that is capable of guiding future practice.

The Concepts of Emotion, Cognition and Motivation

Emotions are complex phenomena involving multiple systems that are loosely associated (Mennin & Farach, 2007) and involve physiological responses (e.g., heart rate, blood pressure), behavioural responses (e.g., facial displays and motor actions such as avoidance or escape) and subjective responses (e.g., feelings, verbally mediated thought). They involve relatively automatic appraisals of internal and external stimuli such as thoughts, interpersonal rejection or physical threats, and ready the organism to respond appropriately. Emotions are organism-wide phenomena and are typically experienced as occurring without volition. There are a range of emotional phenomena that vary in terms of their discreteness, persistence and duration. Specific emotions such as anger, joy and fear emerge readily in response to internal or external cues and serve to alert organisms to sources of threat or well-being. They usually last for a few minutes at most and are intentional in the sense they are directed to specific objects or cues. On the other hand, moods are longer lasting and may be present continually for several days, even weeks. Personality based dispositions are present more or less permanently and causally generate moods. Furthermore, emotions are motivating and direct the person to engage in goal directed actions of a particular kind. The type of goals and related actions reflect the theme or meaning of the affective state. In addition, the meaning of an emotional situation is partly a function of individuals' beliefs and attitudes. For example, fear will generate escape or avoidance goals (based on a threat appraisal) while anger causes retaliatory of self-protective ones (based on a perception of imminent, unjustified harm). Thompson (2007) captures the multi-faceted nature of emotion nicely in the following quote:

> Emotion involves the entire neuroaxis of brain stem, limbic areas, and superior cortex, as well as visceral and motor processes of the body. It encompasses psychosomatic networks of molecular communication among the nervous system, immune system, and endocrine system. On a

psychological level, emotion involves attention and evaluation or appraisal, as well as affective feeling. Emotion manifests behaviorally in distinct facial expressions and action tendencies. (p. 363)

Thus, emotions are organism-wide responses, are initiated without intent, involve evaluations, are motivating (i.e., ready the organism for action), are generally adaptive and have meaning; they are in effect, 'sense-making' (Maiese, 2011). While there is disagreement concerning a number of their features, such as the degree to which specific emotions are discrete, there is consensus on these features (Frijda, 2008).

Conceptual Issues

There are a number of conceptual issues relating to emotions that are currently the focus of research interest in affective science and which will help to elucidate cognition and motivation. These are: (a) the appropriate level of explanation of emotions; (b) the role of emotions in decision-making and rationality; (c) the relationship between cognition and emotion; (d) values and emotion; (e) conceptualization and emotional experience; and (f) emotion, cognition, and motivation.

Level of Explanation

Although affective science researchers agree that emotions are associated with a range of biological, psychological and social/cultural elements, theories vary according to which factors are considered primary (Damasio, 1994; Frijda, 2008; Pessoa, 2013). For some theorists, somatic features such as heart rate, muscle tension or level of respiration are the core emotional phenomena and constrain subsequent evaluation and behavioural responses (Cannon, 1914). While, by way of contrast, cognitive theorists (e.g., Lazarus, 1991) argue that primary appraisal of the personal significance of certain events or stimuli sets the affective tone and, via a causal cascade, activates the other response systems. As I will discuss later, the cognitive model – which has been adopted in correctional psychology – fails to appreciate emotion as an organism-wide, multi-systemic phenomenon characterized by re-entrant and interacting causal processes. There is no such thing as *the* cause or one system that is primary.

Emotions and Decision-Making

Research on the role of emotion in decision-making and judgement contexts suggests that it can have both positive and disruptive effects (Damasio, 1994; Thiele, 2006). Positive effects are arguably due to the way emotions frame salient aspects of a problem task and help to focus attention and subsequent problem-solving efforts on these features. With respect to its disruptive effects, some individuals lack specific emotional competencies, such as emotional awareness or the capacity to manage aversive emotions adaptively, making it harder for them to make good decisions in certain contexts. These problems could be due to the presence of distorted desires (e.g., seeking to dominate others) resulting from impoverished learning histories and opportunities. A study by Damasio and his colleagues provides a good description of the adaptive role of emotions in judgement tasks (Bechara, Damasio, Tranel & Damasio, 1997). In this study participants with bilateral damage of the ventromedial sector of the prefrontal cortex failed to demonstrate galvanic skin responses when engaged in a gambling task. The result was that their judgement was especially poor and they exhibited high levels of inappropriate risk-taking. Somatic markers such as a galvanic skin response (GSR) in normal participants appeared to function as a non-conscious cue that a particular card choice was 'good' or 'bad' and facilitated sound judgement. In other words, emotions can help people to make better judgements in some situations. The diversity of emotions and their association with multiple organism systems mean that they can enhance or obstruct decision-making depending on: (a) type of emotion, their strength, and the specific context in which they occur; (b) where in the decision-making process they exert an influence; and (c) the resources of the person concerned.

Cognition and Emotion

Cognition is an umbrella concept that refers to a range of capacities and processes including attention, decision-making, perception, attention, evaluation, thinking, memory and problem-solving (Maiese, 2011). The relationship between emotion and the different types of cognitive functions is hypothesized to vary from mediation (where emotional processes and cognition are both causally involved in producing an effect) to moderation (where emotion affects the strength of the relationship between cognition and action). In many instances it is not possible to distinguish between the cognitive and emotional components of a psychological process. In fact, neuroscience research has demonstrated that emotion and cognition utilize many of the same neural circuits and, biologically speaking, are closely allied, even fused, processes (Pessoa, 2013). Furthermore, in a recent review of the relationship between cognition and emotion, Pessoa (2013) stated, 'the architectural features of the brain provide *massive* opportunity of cognitive–emotional interactions encompassing *all* brain territories' (p. 257) and 'when we consider the available neuroscientific data, attempts to characterize regions as either "emotional" or "cognitive" quickly break down' (p. 258). For example, in Richard Lazarus's appraisal theory of emotion, (cognitive) appraisal is at the centre of an emotional response, either primarily causing it or, at the very least, is an important associated factor (Lazarus, 1991). Johnson (2007) describes the role of appraisal process in the following quote:

> every emotional response is part of a process in which there is some appraisal of how a given emotionally competent stimulus stands in relation to the potential well-being of the organism. Our emotional responses are based on both our nonconscious and conscious assessments of the possible harm, nurturance, or enhancement that a given situation may bring to our lives. (p. 60).

Thus affective phenomena such as moods, discrete emotion and affective dispositions contain cognitive elements as part of their nature. In addition, with respect to cognitive processes like attention and problem-solving capacities, theorists such as Colombetti (2014), Thompson (2007) and Maiese (2011) have plausibly argued that affective phenomena are essential for their normal functioning. In the case of attention, emotional framing directs attention resources to salient aspects of the internal or external environment for further processing. While, effective problem solving is crucially reliant on affective framing and filtering to help weight options and to arrive at a balanced solution.

Values and Emotion

To grasp the relationship between emotions and values, the pervasiveness of normativity must be examined. Values refer to those aspects of the world that confer benefits to organisms (i.e., help it to survive, flourish, etc.). The influence of values is evident in norms that govern the functioning of different action sequences, such as predator behaviour, workings of biological systems, the application of human moral systems and social relationships. In speaking of the essential roles of norms in biological and social systems, Christensen (2012, p. 104) views normativity as being 'inherent in the organization or form of living systems, specifically in the form that generates their unity and hence explains their existence'. Normative principles are natural since they specify the functional parameters of biological systems and social practices and develop agency in organisms of all types. Norms are reflected in action goals and the strategies selected to further these goals are evaluated against these norms, typically in a fluid, dynamic and immediate manner, in 'real time'. In complex animals such as humans the capacity to flexibly adjust goal-directed strategies and plans in response to changing environmental contingencies is, in part, due to cognitive capacity and to the availability of social and cultural resources (Sterelny, 2012).

Emotions may be viewed as motivational states which function as signals that the organism needs to deal with relevant challenges, whether they are threats, reward opportunities, or physical needs. As I will discuss in the section on enactivism, persons, like all living organisms, are autonomous adaptive systems in which core affective processes direct internal and behavioural processes to protect, repair and advance survival; and in the case of human beings, to achieve greater levels of well-being.

Conceptualization and Emotional Experience

There is current research interest in the neuroevolutionary origin of emotions and their role in animal and human functioning. Panksepp and Biven (2012) argue that empirical evidence supports the existence of seven emotional systems that have evolved in mammals: fear, seeking (desire), rage, lust, care, grief, play and self (feelings related to subjectivity). Each emotional system is thought to have powerful effects on organisms' abilities to respond to their environments and to engage in life-sustaining, enhancing and harm-avoiding behaviours. An important implication of this research is that emotional experience is comparable across mammals, although in human culture it shapes the nature of this experience, and its expression, considerably. The similarity of emotional experience entails that it is non-conceptual, or at the very least, is not necessarily language dependent. This follows from the fact that although animals appear to experience emotions, they do not have language or a conceptual life in the same way that humans do. The possibility of experiencing emotions in the absence of language also applies to babies and young infants given that they also do not appear to possess language or categories. However, it is widely accepted that babies and young infants do have an affective life and are capable of emotionally responding to situations in comparable ways to older children and adults (Colombetti, 2014). In clinical domains, the difficulty that individuals who have offended hold in identifying, managing, or expressing emotions may also indicate problems describing psychological phenomena linguistically (Greenberg, 2002).

Subjective experience constitutes the meaning of the emotional episode for a person (e.g., threat, love, anger or pleasure). It is, therefore, mistaken to assume that because emotions can be expressed in language, a lack of linguistic description implies an absence of the relevant emotional experience. It also suggests that for some individuals therapeutic interventions might need to be relatively non-linguistic, even non-conceptual, and involve purely physical or action based techniques (see below).

Emotion, Cognition and Motivation

As is evident from the above review, emotions motivate organisms to act in ways that promote their goals within certain environments; they are action tendencies evoked automatically by internal and/or external cues. A difficulty with cognitive theories of emotions is that they struggle to account for the immediacy of the call to action. This is because the action, experiential and somatic aspects of emotion are hypothesized to follow an initial appraisal process. It is thought that the meaning of a situation is evaluated in terms of its theme and implications for the welfare of the organism. However, this is doubtful for three major reasons. First, there does not appear to be a delay between an appraisal phase and the other emotional components (Colombetti, 2014). Second, the neuroscientific evidence suggests that emotional and cognitive processes emerge in a coherent way together and, in addition, overlap (Pessoa, 2013). Third, identifying emotionally salient features would be cognitively overwhelming unless there had been some kind of initial affective framing (see below). In other words, without some kind of prior affective and somatic responses, the organism would struggle to evaluate events as well-being related. There would be too many possible ways of interpreting situations. Therefore, cognition must be guided by, or linked to, the other facets of emotion right from the start.

Thus, contemporary theory and research points to a close relationship between emotions, cognition, and motivation. In fact, all three are components or the functional consequences of the experience of emotion. For example, the emotion of anger incorporates a cognitive element (e.g., 'I am under threat'), affective tone element (e.g., 'This feels bad') and a motivational element (e.g., 'I need to remove the threat'). The puzzle is to explain how these components are causally linked. I argue below that the enactive theoretical perspective can answer this question.

An Enactive Approach

The Enactive Mind

In his seminal book, *Mind in Life*, Evan Thompson (2007), building on his earlier work, developed an enactive, phenomenological view of the mind that sought to integrate philosophy, biology, psychology and cognitive neuroscience. In this book he stated that, 'Enaction means the action of enacting a law, but also connotes the performance or carrying out of an action more generally' (p. 13). While Thompson briefly considered the nature of emotion from an enactive perspective, in recent years theorists such as Colombetti (2014) and Maiese (2011) have developed this strand of enactivism in much greater detail. In this chapter I draw heavily on all three theorists. First I will describe the major theoretical assumptions underpinning the general enactive view of the mind that is consistent with contemporary neuroscience, philosophical and psychological research and at odds with current cognitive behavioural therapy (CBT) correctional practice.

From the viewpoint of enactivism, organisms are dynamic, adaptive systems that are self-organizing and inherently purposeful. Natural norms direct the *actions* of dynamic systems to sustain, repair and protect themselves from internal and external threats. The individual components of systems are organized in concert with each other and in response to environmental perturbations and challenges.

The causal relationships within each dynamic system are bidirectional and complex. The overall form and functional integrity of the system is created by the individual parts and their interrelationships, but, in turn, the whole exerts a causal influence on each part and recruits the resources within it, and from the environment, to ensure it is able to function adequately. Any damage is repaired and the physical resources needed to ensure its survival are either created within the organism or extracted from the environment and converted into resources (e.g., energy). Thus, dynamic adaptive systems such as animals are self-sustaining and regulatory.

The above properties give organisms a subjective perspective and create a (proto) self in that all its actions and processes reflect a unique temporal, spatial and functional perspective. It has a point of view because its aim is to sustain and protect itself from external threats. The environment is monitored and evaluated with respect to its needs and interest and in this sense everything it does reflects its singular viewpoint. Consciousness and self-awareness enable organisms to direct attention more effectively to potential benefits and potential harms and to construct longer-term plans for adaptive action. The goal-directed nature of complex systems and the ability to flexibly control one's own activities and actions, causally generates the capacity for agency and a self-conception or sense of identity.

According to enactivism, the mind and its various psychological properties emerge from lower-level biological processes. The development of a mind gives the organism more degrees of freedom with respect to self-regulation and management of needs and core interests. An organism's goal-directed activities can be seen as sense-making, and as a form of cognition. Information about the internal state of the organism and its relationship to the environment is relayed to its internal components and an appropriate response selected. Thus, the mind is not a *thing* but rather an interrelated set of psychological capacities and powers that are essentially dispositions to act in accordance with an organism's needs, interests and respective goals. Mental processes are completely and necessarily embodied in the brain, nervous system and all biological systems. The embodiment conception of human functioning is based on a relatively simple idea: human psychological functioning and sense of meaning is shaped in fundamental ways by bodily experience. Additionally, every bodily system (i.e., sensory, motor, nervous, immune, endocrine, etc.) is either constitutive of, or is causally implicated, in psychological functioning and subjective experience (Gibbs, 2006; Johnson, 2007). The mind and body are interrelated sets of processes. For example, physical gestures have been shown by researchers to provide a non-verbal means of addressing problems of various kinds (e.g., mathematical problems). The research evidence suggests that gestures can foreshadow solutions before a person has consciously solved a problem, and, what is more, such a role is not simply one of emphasis or salience (McNeill, 2005).

Dynamic adaptive systems such as humans always exist in relation to specific environments or contexts, to which they respond and which they shape in ways that increase their chances of survival and enhancement. Cultural resources (e.g., language, norms, institutions, practices, etc.) are simply the contextual aspects of humans' relationship to their social environment. Enactivism proposes that to understand dynamic systems you need to grasp that they always exist with respect to a specific environment, or what has been termed the world around ('*Umwelt*').

The scientific implications of an enactive conception of human functioning are considerable. First, the complexity of multi-faceted human autonomous systems means that explanation needs to be multi-level, dynamic and holistic rather than reductionist. Second, the basic role of sense-making in life and mind means that for humans it is imperative to include subjective experience when seeking to explain social phenomena such as crime. Third, the relational nature of humans as adaptive autonomous systems entails that explanations should take the external environment into account alongside individuals' relevant mental states and biological functioning. Relatedly, explanations should be dynamic and look to identify the causal processes that interact in the production of behaviour. The explanatory picture may change over time, and across contexts, and the relative balance of individual versus environmental explanation will vary accordingly.

An Enactive Model of Emotion, Emotion and Motivation

The enactive model follows conceptually from the general enactive perspective sketched out above. In essence, it accepts a view of human beings as adaptive autonomous systems who are neurobiologically embodied. A variation on the general model is that provided by theorists such as Maiese (2011) and Colombetti (2014), who believe emotion is fundamental to the *sense-making* nature of autonomous systems and operates in tandem with cognition; they are both instances of the sense-making actions of organisms. In this vein, Colombetti (2014) states:

> I have argued that affectivity is a pervasive dimension of the mind, deeper and broader than the emotions and moods of the affective scientist; that emotional episodes are best conceptualized as self-organizing dynamical patterns of the organism (rather than as affect programs, psychological constructions, or component processes driven by a separate process of appraisal); ... that the process of appraisal ... is enacted by the organism in virtue of its organizational properties, including the deep interconnectivity and coregulation of brain and body; ... that the body can enter into an emotion experience in many different ways ... (p. 203)

Primordial or core affectivity is integral to the working of all dynamic autonomous systems and is evident in the basic self-regulating nature of such systems. Based on the core functions of sustaining, repairing, protecting and enhancing the organism, its structures and processes monitor the internal and external environment for cues that indicate goal progress. That is, it is constantly alert to signs indicating possible benefits or potential harms, and modifies its actions accordingly. The orientation towards 'good' outcomes and away from 'bad' is evaluative and involves all the organism's component systems. The feedback is immediate, physically and psychologically experienced, and information is pooled from multiple systems to be able to take immediate advantage of any opportunities for goal success. Maiese (2011) calls this filtering, evaluative system 'affective framing', and states that

> 'affective framing' is the process whereby we interpret persons, objects, facts, states of affairs, images, ourselves, and so on in terms of *embodied desiderative feelings*. ... a frame is a cognitive shortcut that people rely on in order to carve out and highlight features of their surroundings and thereby make sense of the world around them ... carves out the 'starting points' for deliberation, thought, and other cognitive processes. (p. 83)

According to Thompson's (2007) enactive theory of emotions, following a precipitating event its meaning is appraised and affective salience noted. This results in a characteristic feeling tone (positive or negative valence) and motor embodiment with changes in facial expression. Different action tendencies associated with specific emotions may occur, or if the affective state is more diffuse, global intentions for acting on the world are formed. Intentions are cognitive in nature in so far as they are effective plans comprised of beliefs, expectations and goals. Additionally, there will be changes in cardiopulmonary variables, skin conductance, muscle tone and endocrine and immune system activities. The person will have been transformed by the cascading psychological and biological processes and oriented toward anticipated rewards or away from suspected threats. Emotions are in essence *actions* that are directed to aspects of the world or self. The intentionality of emotion is evident in the fact that their associated goals and subsequent actions aim to create greater concordance between goals and internal or external states (self and/or the environment).

According to the enactive conceptualization of affective phenomena, emotional dispositions, moods and discrete emotions develop from these primordial or affective framing actions and reflect the specific types of situations encountered in particular contexts. For example, an individual is born into the world already having a subjective (first person) point of view and is therefore oriented towards rewarding experiences and situations and away from harmful ones. Frequent experience of neglect and harm may result in an anxious, somewhat pessimistic emotional style. A person with this type of emotional disposition is likely to experience more negative, anxious moods and emotions of fear and anger. In addition, social and cultural learning will influence the meaningfulness of the events the person encounters and also modulate the way he or she responds to and manages them.

Emotions provide direct, relatively unmediated access to others' emotional and mental states. This is primarily due to the acute sensitivity individuals have to emotional, contextual, physical and behavioural cues, and the information generated by their own bodies in response to such cues. The perception of emotions in others is as quick, automatic and direct as it is in ourselves. Because many of the major systems of the body are directly activated in emotional episodes (and in fact, constitute emotions), people learn to respond to their patterns rapidly and use them as reliable indicators of goal progress or frustration.

The enactive conceptualization of emotions is essentially a process model where cognitive and emotional causal processes interact and function to orientate organisms to significant personal goals, and to signal to self and others the degree of goal progress. Affective states are strongly evaluative in nature and also involve whole organism systems. The enactive view of affective phenomena, with its strong interpersonal and relational aspects, makes it easier to appreciate its role in generating empathic behaviour. According to Oxley (2011) empathy is 'both an act *and* a capacity' (p. 15). Individuals engage in acts of empathy when they imagine how someone else is likely to be feeling in certain situations, or alternatively, anticipate how they would feel in similar circumstances. In order to act empathically individuals require cognitive and emotional capacities such as the ability to psychologically decentre, emotional knowledge, and the possession of emotional regulation, deliberation and perspective taking skills. Emotions have evolved to provide rapid and often non-verbal evaluations of other people and enable us to quickly identify what they are feeling and experiencing. The natural resonance between different people's emotional states (e.g., facial expressions, body posture, voice tone, etc.) enables us to respond quickly to subtle cues and to pick up on possible goal threats or opportunities for cooperative actions. As Maiese (2011) suggests, emotional responsivity between two people is like a dance: there is a synchronization of expression, body posture, voice inflection and emotional tone.

A final point is that from an enactive viewpoint, emotional experience is sometimes unable to be verbally articulated, and even if it can be, the resulting description is imprecise and arguably a poor substitute for the full body experience, so to speak. A person may be aware of the meaning of an emotionally charged situation and experience the physiological and psychological changes associated with a specific emotion, be motivated to act in ways consistent with this evaluation, but find it difficult to express exactly what they are feeling. Or, they may describe an emotion that is not consistent with their overall response.

Correctional Therapeutic Implications

I would like to now discuss some of the major practice implications suggested by the enactive model of emotion, cognition and motivation. My comments will be preliminary, as the rest of the book will review correctional assessment and therapy in detail. In my view, we need to adopt a broader perspective on emotions in order to more effectively design treatment programmes in line with cutting-edge affective research and theory. Thus, most importantly, we should not prioritize cognition within interventions and dedicate entire modules to this topic (see Ross, Fabiano & Ross, 1989). Instead, the key focus should be on emotion. In some respects this will turn practice on its head and align it more with emerging trends such as strength-based approaches and agency-level explanations of crime.

A first point is that given the grounding of emotions in primordial affectivity and affective framing, they are causally involved in every type of problem experienced by clients. Every treatment module will refer directly or indirectly to affective phenomena of one type or another. For example, individuals with general self-regulation problems are likely to have emotional factors associated with their goals. Additionally, clients who routinely misinterpret interpersonal cues and as a consequence act aggressively are likely to hold dysfunctional core beliefs and values – both linked to problematic affective framing of social encounters. In view of the pervasiveness of affective elements in clients' array of difficulties, it makes sense to think more flexibility about emotional competence and affective framing throughout the whole of treatment. It also raises questions about the usefulness of having treatment modules devoted to problems such as stress management or emotional regulation, rather than working with clusters of interventions that are delivered according to a person's intervention plan.

A second point is that emotions have their evolutionary and developmental origins in the enabling of agency and search for meaning. They are inherently evaluative and reflect what people care most about. The link to desire is evident when you take into account the valenced nature of emotions and their motivational role (i.e., desires for certain outcomes or experiences). The relevance for treatment is that when developing intervention plans for individuals in correctional contexts their core values should be placed at the centre of a treatment plan. Deeply held values are likely to elicit powerful emotions and, conversely, generating emotional states in therapy will make it easier to detect what matters most to them. Going with (rather than against) intense emotional states (using them as indicators of core values) and understanding their relationship to agency and a meaningful life increases the chances of clients investing in treatment.

Third, an important implication of enactivism can be traced to its emphasis on action and, relatedly, the fact that emotions are associated with body-wide systems. Sometimes those who have offended will not be able to verbally express what it is they are fearful of, why they become aggressive in some situations, or why they are feeling lonely. Using emotionally focused techniques and working in an emotional activating and alive way will give therapists an opportunity to clarify these issues (Greenberg, 2002). Relying solely on CBT techniques lessens the chance of this occurring and restricts the range of possibilities for therapists to effect change.

A final point concerns the relationship between dynamic risk factors (criminogenic needs) and emotionally oriented work with clients. Dynamic risk factors are essentially predictive constructs derived from large quantitative studies (Ward, 2014). Recently we developed a model in which dynamic risk factors were broken into their elements and incorporated within an agency model of offending (Durant & Ward, 2015; Heffernan & Ward, in press; Ward & Beech, 2015). In this model, emotions play a central role and are causally linked to individuals' needs and values, action goals, interpersonal strategies and social and cultural contexts. Each dynamic risk factor was hypothesized to be directly or indirectly associated with some kind of affective phenomena and, once conceptually reconstructed, appeared to play a central role in establishing offence meaning and associated benefits. The key point is that the use of dynamic risk factors on their own is unlikely to alert therapists to their emotional significance, while locating them within an agency model of some kind can illuminate their affective relevance and utility.

Conclusions

Emotions and the broader range of affective phenomena have been conceptualized in an impoverished and intervention limiting way in correctional psychology. The stress has primarily been on their potential for disrupting prosocial motivations and for biasing problem solving and impairing individuals' social judgement. Furthermore, cognitive processes have been viewed as having causal priority. In other words, emotions are seen as bad news for both clients and practitioners. This negative and partial view has been paralleled in recent years by attempts to create more positive, constructive environments in correctional faculties and treatment centres (Gannon & Ward, 2014; Ward & Maruna, 2007). As a result of this desire to establish positive therapeutic environments, research attention has been directed to the therapeutic alliance and the attributes effective therapists possess. Interestingly, greater emotional awareness as highlighted in features such as empathy and interpersonal warmth, is a central part of these suggestions.

Therefore, it is timely to think about emotion and its conceptualization in greater depth and to derive what messages we can from contemporary affective science. In my view, one of the most exciting recent developments has been the enactive view of the mind in general, and its application to emotion in particular. It is a rich way of thinking about emotion and psychological functioning and is capable of accommodating many of the conceptual issues and controversies evident in the emotional literature. For one thing, the reciprocal causal links between emotion and cognition and their subsequent impact on motivation are well addressed by enactive theory and related research. My hope is that practitioners will find much of interest in this body of theory and research, which will assist them to deliver more effective treatment. Programmes that, while reducing the risk of further harm to the community, will also help individuals who have committed serious crimes to find more meaningful ways to live.

References

Andrews, D. A., & Bonta, J. (2010). *The psychology of criminal conduct.* New Providence, NJ: Anderson.

Bechara, A., Damasio, H., Tranel, D., & Damasio, A. (1997). Deciding advantageously before knowing the advantageous strategy. *Science, 28,* 1293–1295.

Cannon, W. B. (1914). The interrelations of emotions as suggested by recent physiological researchers. *American Journal of Psychology, 25,* 256–282.

Christensen, W. (2012). Natural sources of normativity. *Studies in the History and Philosophy of Biological and Biomedical Sciences, 43,* 104–112. doi: 10.1016/j.shpsc.2011.05.009

Colombetti, G. (2009). From affect programs to dynamical discrete emotions. *Philosophical Psychology, 22,* 407–425. doi: 10.1080/09515080903153600

Colombetti, G. (2014). *The feeling body: Affective science meets the enactive mind.* Cambridge, MA: MIT Press.

Damasio, A. (1994). *Descartes' error: Emotion, reason, and the human brain.* New York: G.P. Putnam & Sons.

Durrant, R., & Ward, T. (2015). *Evolutionary criminology: Towards a comprehensive explanation of crime and its management.* San Diego, CA: Academic Press.

Frijda, N. H. (2008). The psychologists' point of view. In M. Lewis, J. M. Haviland-Jones, & L. F. Barrett (Eds.), *Handbook of emotions* (3rd ed.) (pp. 68–87). New York: Guilford Press.

Gannon, T., & Ward, T. (2014). Where has all the psychology gone? A critical review of evidence-based psychological practice in correctional settings. *Aggression and Violent Behavior, 19,* 435–436. doi: 10.1016/j.avb.2014.06.006

Gibbs, R. W. (2006). *Embodiment and cognitive science.* New York: Cambridge University Press.

Greenberg, L. S. (2002). *Emotions-focused therapy: Coaching clients to work through their feelings.* Washington, DC: American Psychological Association.

Hall, G. C. N., & Hirschman, R. (1992). Sexual aggression against children: A conceptual perspective of etiology. *Criminal Justice and Behavior, 19,* 8–23. doi: 10.1177/0093854892019001003

Hanson, K., & Harris, A. J. R. (2000). Where should we intervene? Dynamic predictors of sexual offense recidivism. *Criminal Justice and Behaviour, 27,* 2–35. doi: 10.1177/0093854800027001002

Heffernan, R., & Ward, T. (2015). The conceptualization of dynamic risk factors in child sex offenders: An agency model. *Aggression and Violent Behavior, 24,* 250–260.

Helm, B. W. (2002). *Emotional reason: Deliberation, motivation, and the nature of value.* Cambridge: Cambridge University Press.

Hutto, D. D., & Myin, E. (2013). *Radicalizing enactivism: Basic minds without content.* Cambridge, MA: MIT Press.

Johnson, M. (2007). *The meaning of the body: Aesthetics of human understanding.* Chicago: University of Chicago Press.

Lazarus, R. S. (1991). *Emotion and adaptation.* New York: Oxford University Press.

Leahy, R. L. (2015). *Emotional schema therapy.* New York: Guilford Press.

Lewis, M., Haviland-Jones, J. M., & Barrett, L. F. (Eds.). (2008). *Handbook of emotions* (3rd ed.). New York: Guilford Press.

McNeill, D. (2005). *Gesture and thought.* Chicago: University of Chicago Press.

Maiese, M. (2011). *Embodiment, emotion, and cognition.* Basingstoke, UK: Palgrave-Macmillan.

Marshall, W. L., Marshall, L. E., Serran, G. A., & Fernandez, Y. M. (2006). *Treating sexual offenders: An integrated approach.* New York: Routledge.

Mennin, D., & Farach, F. (2007). Emotion and evolving treatments for adult psychopathology. *Clinical Psychology: Science and Practice, 14,* 329–352. doi: 10.1111/j.1468-2850.2007.00094

Oxley, J. C. (2011). *The moral dimensions of empathy: Limits and applications in ethical theory and practice.* London: Palgrave-Macmillan.

Panksepp, J., & Biven, L. (2012). *The archaeology of mind: Neuroevolutionary origins of human emotions.* New York: W. W. Norton & Company.

Pessoa, L. (2013). *The cognitive–emotional brain: From interactions to integration.* Cambridge, MA: MIT Press.

Ross, R.R., & Fabiano, E.A. (1985). Time to think: A cognitive model of delinquency prevention and offender rehabilitation. *Johnson City, TN: Institute of Social Sciences and Arts.*

Ross, R. R., Fabiano, E. A., & Ross, R. D. (1989). *Reasoning and rehabilitation: A handbook for teaching cognitive skills.* Ottawa, Canada: The Cognitive Centre.

Solomon, R. C. (2007). *True to our feelings: What our emotions are really telling us.* New York: Oxford University Press.

Sterelny, K. (2012). *The evolved apprentice: How evolution made humans unique.* Cambridge, MA: MIT Press.

Stewart, J., Gapenne, O., & Di Paolo, E. A. (2010). *Enaction: Toward a new paradigm for cognitive science.* Cambridge, MA: MIT Press.

Thompson, E. (2007). *Mind in life: Biology, phenomenology, and the sciences of the mind.* Cambridge, MA: Belknap-Harvard.

Thiele, L. P. (2006). *The heart of judgment: Practical wisdom, neuroscience, and narrative.* New York: Cambridge University Press.

Thornton, D. (2013). Implications of our developing understanding of risk and protective factors in the treatment of adult male sexual offenders. *International Journal of Behavioral Consultation and Therapy, 8,* 62–65.

Ward, T. (2014). The explanation of sexual offending: From single factor theories to integrative pluralism. *Journal of Sexual Aggression, 20,* 130–141. doi: 10.1080/13552600.2013.870242

Ward, T., & Beech, A. R. (2015). Dynamic risk factors: A theoretical dead-end? *Psychology, Crime & Law, 21*, 100–113. doi: 10.1080/1068316X.2014.917854

Ward, T., & Hudson, S. (1998). The construction and development of theory in the sexual offending area: A metatheoretical framework. *Sexual Abuse: A Journal of Research and Treatment, 10*, 47–63.

Ward, T., & Maruna, S. (2007). *Rehabilitation: Beyond the risk paradigm*. London: Routledge.

2

The Role of Cognition, Emotion and Motivational Goals in Sexual Offending

Multi-Factor Models

Ross M. Bartels

Over the last three decades, a number of major multi-factorial models of sexual offending have been proposed. These include the Four Preconditions Model of Sexual Abuse (Finkelhor, 1984); the Quadripartite Model (Hall & Hirschman, 1991, 1992); the Integrated Theory of the Aetiology of Sexual Offending (Marshall & Barbaree, 1990); the Pathways Model (Ward & Siegert, 2002); and the Integrated Theory of Sexual Offending (ITSO; Ward & Beech, 2006). Previous evaluations of these theories have focused on their ability to explain sexual offending (e.g., Ward, 2001, 2002; Ward & Hudson, 2001; Ward, Polaschek, & Beech, 2006). In this chapter, however, the focus will be on evaluating how each theory conceptualizes cognition, emotion and motivational goals.

Cognition, emotion and motivation are each vastly complex and multi-faceted psychological phenomenon. As Alexandrov and Sams (2005) state 'there are many different definitions for cognition, from simply listing different functions and processes (e.g., memory, language processing, problem solving, thinking) to defining adaptive activities of individuals' (p. 388). In the simplest of terms, cognition represents the processing of information. However, cognition involves both general mental abilities (e.g., working memory, processing speed) and higher-order operations (e.g., attention, beliefs, decision-making). The latter is typically the focus of social cognition, which refers to the mental operations involved in understanding, perceiving and interpreting the social world (Kurtz & Richardson, 2011).

Emotion is also a difficult concept to define (Mulligan & Scherer, 2012). Emotions are often viewed as being brief, target-specific reactions involving cognitive, physiological and behavioural components (Howells, Day & Wright, 2004). As Howells and colleagues (2004) note, emotions are distinct from moods (i.e., more general, enduring affective states), feelings (i.e., the conscious awareness of an emotion) and affect (i.e., the umbrella term for all of the above).

Motivation is essentially the degree to which an individual wants and decides to engage in a specific behaviour. In essence, motivation is hypothesized to energize individuals, invoke volition and direct behaviour. At the core of human motivation is the idea of basic psychological needs (Deci & Ryan, 2008; Maslow, 1943). This is

Sexual Offending: Cognition, Emotion and Motivation, First Edition.
Edited by Theresa A. Gannon and Tony Ward.
© 2017 John Wiley & Sons Ltd. Published 2017 by John Wiley & Sons Ltd.

a defining feature of the Good Lives Model of rehabilitation (Ward & Stewart, 2003). That is, basic human needs (or 'primary goods') are seen as fundamental to understanding what motivates individuals who sexually offend. According to the Good Lives Model, there are nine goods that human beings strive for: *life* (physical satisfaction and health), *relatedness* (i.e., need for relationships), *excellence in agency, excellence in work and play* (including mastery), *inner peace, creativity, happiness, community* and *spirituality*. It is these primary goods that are the 'ultimate underlying motivating factors' in sexual offending (Ward & Gannon, 2006, p. 86). Crucially, however, it is not the goals (goods) that are problematic but rather the means by which they are sought (i.e., offending behaviour).

As Ward (2014) notes, all human action involves cognition, emotion, interpersonal/social relationships and regulation of behaviour. Adaptive functioning within each of these psychological domains will result in a healthy and prosocial lifestyle (Bonta & Andrews, 2007). However, when problems arise in one or more domains, this can lead to maladaptive functioning and, in many cases, offending behaviour. With regards to sexual offending, it has been well documented that sexual recidivism is associated with emotional problems, interpersonal deficits and/or dysfunctional cognitions (Mann, Hanson & Thornton, 2010; Thornton, 2002). As a result, most multi-factor theories of sexual offending have tended to address the role of these psychological problems. However, such theories should also clearly define and conceptualize the fundamental construct/s underlying each problem (Ward & Beech, 2015). Theoretically addressing these fundamental constructs will allow for a deeper understanding of the root causes related to sexual offending; one that is not confined to surface-level symptoms (e.g., cognitive distortions, dysregulated emotion). The aim of this chapter, therefore, is to examine what the existing multi-factor theories of sexual offending tell us about the role of cognition, emotion and motivational goals. For each theory, I will first provide a brief outline to reacquaint the reader with its core assumptions. Then, I will evaluate the theory in terms of how it conceptualizes and accounts for each construct. All of the theories outlined in this chapter focus on males who have sexually offended.

Finkelhor's Precondition Model

In 1984, Finkelhor proposed the first multi-factorial theory of child sexual abuse. On reviewing the literature, Finkelhor argued that child sexual abuse is underpinned by four factors. They were: *emotional congruence* (i.e., sexual activity with children is pursued to satisfy an emotional need); *sexual arousal* (i.e., sexual activity with children is pursued because children are sexually arousing); *blockage* (i.e., sexual activity with children occurs because of a persistent or temporary inability to meet one's sexual and emotional needs with an adult); and *disinhibition* (i.e., sexual activity with a child occurs because a proximal factor, such as intoxication, reduces self-control).

These factors partly formed the basis for what Finkelhor termed the Preconditions Model of Sexual Abuse. Specifically, Finkelhor argued that the first three factors account for why a desire to sexually abuse a child may develop. As a result, he grouped them to formulate the first precondition (motivation to sexually abuse). The fourth factor (*disinhibition*) formed the basis for the second precondition (overcoming internal inhibitors). The third and fourth preconditions focus on how the offence process unfolds. The third (overcoming external inhibitors) involves taking advantage of or creating opportunities that facilitate an offence (e.g., lack of parental supervision), while the fourth (overcoming the resistance of the child) refers to adopting strategies to prevent a child from challenging abusive behaviour. The central tenet of this theory is that these four preconditions must be sequentially met before sexual abuse can occur.

Evaluation

Finkelhor does not provide an explicit definition of cognition but does include the concept within the second precondition. He argues that men who sexually abuse draw upon entrenched societal/cultural attitudes regarding, for example, 'the ideology of patriarchal prerogatives for fathers' (p. 56). Finkelhor only briefly addresses the role that these attitudes play. He argues that they allow individuals to overcome moral concerns about sexual abuse. What is missing is a deeper account of the cognitive processes at work. For example, it is not clear whether these societal attitudes are accommodated into one's existing cognitive structure during early life (e.g., the formation of schema) or whether they are temporarily drawn upon as a self-serving, pre-offence justification. The former would suggest that the prospect of having sex with a child is automatically processed in an offence-supportive manner, thus, overriding inhibitory responses. The latter, however, implies a more explicit and deliberative process, whereby societal norms are consciously used to counter automatic inhibitory responses towards the prospect of engaging in sexual activity with a child. Regardless of the process, there is arguably an implicit link between cognition and motivation akin to the idea of *motivated cognition* (Kunda, 1990). That is, the establishment of an offence-approach motive (precondition 1) has a biasing effect on cognition (precondition 2) in a manner that facilitates meeting this motivational goal.

Finkelhor fails to highlight the cognitive components associated with other aspects of the theory. For example, there is no discussion of the cognitive processes underlying sexual arousal (Przybyla & Byrne, 1984). Finkelhor also fails to acknowledge the cognitive component involved in emotional congruence (McPhail, Hermann & Nunes, 2013). Notably, however, many of these insights were proposed many years after Finkelhor's theory was published.

Emotion is also not directly defined by Finkelhor. However, it is addressed indirectly in the sense that emotion-related problems are seen to play a role in sexual abuse. For example, Finkelhor argues that some individuals who abuse children experience distorted emotional development leading to maladaptive emotional functioning. This maladaptive functioning causes individuals to prefer their emotional needs to be met by children. Similarly, Finkelhor argues that negative emotions related to adult relationships (e.g., fear of rejection) lead children to be viewed as safer sexual partners. These theoretical assumptions suggest an implicit link between emotion and cognition (e.g., fear of rejection leads to a belief that children are safer partners), as well as an emotion–motivation link (i.e., interpersonal relationships with children are sought due to poor emotional functioning). Also, severe stress (e.g., death of a relative) is proposed to be a proximal disinhibitor that impacts the control of one's deviant desires. Lazarus (2006) argues that negative emotions can be regarded as 'stress emotions' as they arise in response to stress (and vice versa). Thus, negative emotions are likely to be essential to the role that stress plays in disinhibiting individuals to sexually abuse. Again, however, Finkelhor did not provide this level of detail.

Precondition 1 is comprised of three factors that motivate an individual to sexually offend. Thus, motivational goals are a core part of Finkelhor's theory. However, the label 'motivation to sexually abuse' is slightly misleading as it suggests there is one motivational goal that is met via three separate means. On examination, the reverse seems more accurate. That is, each factor reflects a distinct motivational goal that can be achieved through sexual abuse. For example, drawing upon the Good Lives Model, emotional congruence involves the goal of safety (good of *inner peace*) or intimacy (good of *relatedness*); sexual arousal involves the goal of physical satisfaction (good of *life*); and blockage (in terms of avoiding rejection from women) reflects the goal of emotional harmony (good of *inner peace*). From this viewpoint, emotional factors can be seen to influence motivational goals. However, the theory is devoid of any reference to the influence of cognition on motivation.

Hall and Hirschman's Quadripartite Model

Hall and Hirschman developed a multi-factor theory for rape (1991) and child abuse (1992) in an attempt to account for the relative prominence of causal factors and heterogeneity among men who have sexually offended. According to Hall and Hirschman, four factors motivate sexual offending: sexual arousal, cognitive distortions, affective dyscontrol and personality problems. The first three are conceptualized as state dependent, while the fourth is seen as enduring or trait-like. Although each individual factor (as well as their synergistic interaction) increases the likelihood to offend, one factor is hypothesized as being most potent. It is this 'primary motivational precursor' that is responsible for causing an individual to exceed their inhibitory threshold and actually offend. Hall and Hirschman also propose that the relative prominence of a particular factor can be used to specify different sexual offending subtypes. In other words, four subtypes of men who rape adults and four subtypes of men who abuse children can be distinguished, each one characterized by a specific primary precursor.

Evaluation

The Quadripartite Model clearly addresses cognition. Although an explicit definition is not provided, Hall and Hirschman (1992) appear to primarily conceptualize cognition as 'elaborate situational appraisal' (p. 19). That is, before sexual arousal is acted upon, it must be cognitively appraised. They argue that distorted cognitions about women (e.g., 'Women are hostile to men and deserve to be raped') or children (e.g., 'Sexual contact with children is a method of educating them about sex') permit individuals to act on their deviant sexual arousal. Implicit in this conceptualization is the idea that cognitive structures (i.e., distorted beliefs about women/children) cause sexual stimuli to be processed in an offence-supportive manner. This corresponds with more contemporary views on offence-supportive social cognition (Gannon, 2009). Interestingly, Hall and Hirschman's implicit inclusion of cognitive structures in their model actually contradicts their view that cognition is solely state dependent. While the appraisal itself would be situational, it would be guided by more enduring beliefs (Ward, 2000). A further issue is that cognitive appraisal of sexual stimuli can be both explicit and implicit (Janssen, Everaerd, Spiering & Janssen, 2000). However, Hall and Hirschman's emphasis on *elaborate* appraisal suggests they view the processing of information as a solely explicit operation.

Hall and Hirschman also state that cognitive appraisal plays a role in the decision to offend, in terms of weighing up the benefits and costs of offending. If the perceived benefits (e.g., sexual gratification) outweigh the perceived threats (e.g., being caught) then a sexual offence is more likely. Again, the appraisal of these costs–benefits is viewed as an elaborate process. As a result, they argue that the role of cognition is linked to the careful planning of an offence. However, they fail to acknowledge the influence of certain automatic cognitive biases, such as the *availability heuristic*. This is when the perceived likelihood of an event is exaggerated when examples come to mind more quickly (Tversky & Kahneman, 1973). Thus, if the benefits of sexual abuse (e.g., sexual gratification) more easily come to mind than the costs, it may tip an individual's decision to be in favour of offending. In addition, despite theorizing that sexual arousal precedes cognitive processing and that 'negative affective states precede cognitive sequences' (Hall & Hirschman, 1991, p. 664), the authors do not address the influence that these visceral experiences would have on the decision-making process (Lerner, Li, Valdesolo & Kassam, 2015). However, emotions can have both disruptive and positive effects on decision-making (see Ward, Chapter 1 in this volume).

The role of emotion is also clearly addressed by the theory as it underpins the affective dyscontrol factor. Although Hall and Hirschman do not provide an explicit definition, they clearly outline what can be regarded as emotion (e.g., depression, anger). They argue that men who abuse children are more likely to experience depression, whereas men who rape adults are more likely to experience anger. Moreover, Hall and Hirschman appear to inadvertently distinguish integral and incidental emotions (Bodenhausen, 1993). Integral emotions are elicited by the current situation and exert an immediate effect (i.e., the state-based effect of emotion). Hall and Hirschman implicitly argue that integral emotions are related to rape offences (e.g., female rejection leads to anger that is directly expressed as sexual aggression). However, incidental emotions are elicited by a prior unrelated situation that may later exert an influence in another context. Hall and Hirschman implicitly propose that incidental emotions are related to child sexual abuse (e.g., loss of a job leads to depression, which later leads an individual to sexually abuse a child in order to feel better).

For both men who sexually abuse adults and men who sexually abuse children, emotions are proposed to only be criminogenic if they are powerful enough to diminish self-regulatory processes. What is not clear in the theory is why powerful negative emotions are not expressed in a non-sexual or non-offensive manner.

Motivational goals are addressed in the Quadripartite Model given its focus on the four primary motivational precursors. However, there are some issues with conceptualization. First, it is not clear whether each factor is a direct motive to offend or whether they are psychological mechanisms that influence the motive to offend. Closer examination suggests a mix of both. For example, sexual arousal is stated as being a motivation to offend, as is the expression of anger in rapists. On the other hand, the affective dyscontrol of depression in men who abuse children is more of an indirect route to offending.

Second, there are issues associated with how some of the factors generate motivational goals. For example, although it can be argued from a Good Lives perspective that the desire to satiate deviant sexual arousal is linked to the goal of physical gratification (*life*), it is not clear which motivational goals are associated with the personality-problem factor. Similarly, the motivational goals associated with distorted cognition are unclear and seemingly contradictory. As Ward (2001) notes, the idea that cognition alone has a motivational function is problematic. Instead, an individual's cognitions about themselves, others and the world exert an influence on personal motives. Interestingly, Hall and Hirschman argue that the motivation to act upon deviant sexual arousal is mediated by distorted beliefs. Thus, they do not actually describe distorted cognition as having a motivating function (despite framing it as a motivational precursor). Instead, the function they describe is one of 'cognitive mediation'.

Marshall and Barbaree's Integrated Theory

In 1990, Marshall and Barbaree introduced the Integrated Theory to the forensic field. This theory identified a number of distal (e.g., biological, developmental, socio-cultural) and proximal (i.e., situational) factors that interact to generate sexual offending. According to the theory, males enter the world with an evolutionarily inherited propensity to sexually aggress. As a result, the developing male must learn to inhibit their capacity to aggress in sexual situations. However, adverse childhood experiences (e.g., poor parenting, physical/sexual abuse) severely impede this capacity and result in poor self-regulatory skills, low self-esteem, insecure attachment and a fusion of sex and aggression.

These deficits become detrimental in adolescence when the male is overcome by a sudden influx of sex hormones and, thus, become sexually aware. When seeking a relationship with a female, adolescent males are likely to be faced with rejection. This worsens their self-esteem and fosters the development of hostile attitudes towards women and the acceptance of patriarchal attitudes within society. To deal with the resulting negative affect, maladaptive coping strategies are employed (e.g., deviant sexual fantasies). Each of these experiences serves to bolster a sense of masculinity. Ultimately, when a male with these vulnerabilities encounters a transient disinhibiting factor (e.g., intoxication, negative emotions) they are likely to sexually offend.

Evaluation

The Integrated Theory is a complex yet elegant account of sexual offending that addresses a number of interacting factors (Ward, 2002). In discussing developmental and socio-cultural factors, Marshall and Barbaree clearly attend to cognition in the form of hostile attitudes towards women. They argue that these attitudes form in childhood and adolescence via two sources. One is by modelling an abusive father's negative attitudes towards women and the other is in response to female rejection. Marshall and Barbaree also state that these attitudes are reinforced by two primary external factors. These include: (1) societal attitudes that support male dominance and foster a hostile view of women (including rape myths); and (2) deviant pornography that reflects these same societal attitudes.

Conceptually, Marshall and Barbaree do not provide an explicit definition of cognition. In fact, they do not use the word 'cognition' but rather the word 'attitude'. Attitudes are summary evaluations (i.e., positive versus negative) of people, situations and behaviour (Fazio, 2007). As Ward (2000) argues, attitudes are cognitive products generated by underlying cognitive structures (i.e., implicit theories) about people and the world. This would suggest that Marshall and Barbaree are talking about cognitive products rather than deeper cognitive constructs. On the other hand, the attention given to the developmental sources of hostile cognitions is in line with how implicit cognitive structures are hypothesized to develop (Rudman, Phelan & Heppen, 2007; Ward, 2000). It is difficult to determine their exact conceptualization given the lack of a definition.

In terms of the role that cognition plays, Marshall and Barbaree argue that negative attitudes about women set the stage for how a male will respond to sexual desires. Apart from stating that such attitudes bolster a sense of masculinity, Marshall and Barbaree do not unpack this statement or offer any insight into the cognitive processes at play. Instead, they refer to research linking negative attitudes towards women with sexual offending; specifically rape. It should be noted, however, that the surrounding literature at the time did not provide the information necessary to give a detailed level of explanation about the specific cognitive processes at work.

Following this point, the theory's exclusive focus on hostile/negative attitudes towards women is problematic. The theory was intended to explain all forms of sexual offending but there is no mention of distorted cognitions about children. This would suggest that Marshall and Barbaree view distorted attitudes about women as being as relevant to child abuse (and other forms of sexual offending) as they are to rape. However, it is not made clear why this is the case, or how such attitudes affect different men who have sexually offended (Ward, 2002).

Marshall and Barbaree address the distal and proximal role of emotion in their discussion on developmental and situational factors, respectively. While a general definition is not offered, they identify a number of negative emotions. These include anger, inadequacy, resentment, rejection, anxiety, emotional loneliness and stress (although many of these would be regarded as moods and/or feelings). The distal role that negative emotions play in Marshall and Barbaree's theory is rather complex and interactive. For example, Marshall and Barbaree argue that – due to poor interpersonal skills – males' sexual advances are often met with female rejection. This results in feelings of resentment, inadequacy and rejection. This inability to experience intimacy creates a sense of emotional loneliness, as well as feelings of anxiety and stress. Also, if a woman is the source of negative emotional state(s), then a male will experience anger towards women. Collectively, these emotions serve to foster negative attitudes about woman. Thus, emotion is involved in the generation of negative attitudes about women and the adoption of maladaptive coping strategies (e.g., sexual fantasizing). The former suggests that negative emotions provide information about females, a phenomenon known as 'affect-as-information' (Schwarz & Clore, 1983). The theory, therefore, embodies an implicit link between emotion and cognition (see also Ward, Chapter 1 in this volume).

The proximal role of emotion is linked to disinhibition. For example, Marshall and Barbaree state that men who have sexually assaulted women often feel angry at the time of their offence, which serves to disinhibit arousal to forced sex. They refer to the woman being the source of this anger, suggesting that anger functions as an integral emotion in relation to their offending. Stress and anxiety are also common in men who have sexually offended, both of which are regarded as disinhibitors for general sexual activity. Thus, if an individual is sexually motivated to offend, the presence of stress or anxiety will increase the likelihood that it will occur. From their discussion of stress and anxiety, it appears Marshall and Barbaree regard them as incidental emotions (i.e., elicited by a prior, unrelated situation).

Unlike the two previous theories, motivational goals are not as clearly outlined. For example, there is no explicit mention of motives or different subtypes of offending behaviour (although see Ward, 2002). However, since a multitude of factors are assumed to result in a vulnerability to offend, some motivational goals are likely to be embedded within the theory. Indeed, when examining the core factors from a Good Lives perspective, a number of motivational goals (or goods) are evident. First, it is argued that males must learn to inhibit their aggressive inclination when pursuing their sexual interests. This suggests that sexual gratification is an underlying motivational goal related to sexual offending (*life*). Second, the focus on males' inability to enter an intimate relationship indicates that the desire for an intimate/romantic relationship is a specific goal (*relatedness*). Third, the use of maladaptive strategies (e.g., sexual fantasies) to cope with negative affect and compensate for feelings of inadequacy implies that emotional harmony and a desire for power are sought after goals (*inner peace* and *mastery*, respectively). Fourth, the expression of anger towards women and the disinhibitory effects of stress and anxiety suggest that freedom from emotional turmoil is a motivational goal (*inner peace*). Finally, it is argued that pornography provides males with distorted information about what women enjoy sexually. Thus, a subtler motivational goal may be the desire to understand 'what women want' (*knowledge*). From these suggestions, the Integrated Theory implicitly includes a number of motivational goals. These suggestions also highlight how emotion and cognition may interact to produce these goals. Unfortunately, Marshall and Barbaree did not explicitly articulate this.

Ward and Siegert's Pathways Model

By knitting together the strongest aspects of the previous theories, Ward and Siegert (2002) developed the Pathways Model; a multi-factor theory of child sexual abuse. This theory states that there are four interacting psychological processes or mechanisms that generate child sexual abuse. These include: intimacy and social deficits; distorted sexual scripts; emotional dysregulation; and cognitive distortions. Each mechanism reflects a vulnerability factor, the structure and functioning of which is influenced by distal (e.g., learning and biology) and proximal (e.g., situational) factors. Ward and Siegert state that, although each mechanism underpins *all* incidences of child sexual abuse, there will be one that functions as a primary causal mechanism. That is, it exerts a greater impact on the other three mechanisms. As a result, Ward and Siegert propose four distinct aetiological pathways that can lead to the sexual abuse of a child, each one defined by one of the aforementioned mechanisms. Ward and Siegert also proposed the Multiple Dysfunctions pathway that involves pronounced deficits in all four mechanisms.

Evaluation

In the Pathways Model, cognitive distortions are identified as a mechanism underlying sexual offending. Thus, cognition is clearly attended to within the theory. Ward and Siegert conceptualize cognitive distortions as cognitive products that originate from the biased processing of social information caused by distorted implicit theories or schema. Thus, it is the distorted cognitive structures that play an aetiological role in child sexual abuse. Within the *multiple dysfunctions pathway*, implicit theories about children as sexual beings interact with deviant sexual preferences and emotional regulation problems to cause child sexual abuse. Within the *intimacy deficit pathway*, Ward and Siegert hypothesize that entitlement and dangerous world beliefs lead children to be viewed as potential (safer) sexual partners. In the *deviant sexual scripts pathway*, Ward and Siegert argue that distorted sexual scripts interact with dysfunctional relationship schemas (i.e., distorted internal working models of relationships caused by an insecure attachment style). Here, sexual cues are misinterpreted as indicating affection and closeness; an example of distorted beliefs leading to faulty processing of sexual and emotional information.

A unique aspect of the Pathways Model is that antisocial (non-sexual) cognitions play a core aetiological role for some men who abuse children. That is, cognition is viewed as the primary psychological mechanism underlying the antisocial cognitions pathway. In this pathway, general pro-criminal beliefs facilitate antisocial behaviour, with child sexual abuse being one manifestation of this general antisociality. Unfortunately, the authors do not unpack the kinds of offence-supportive cognitive processing that these cognitions invoke. For example, Polaschek and Ward (2002) argue that non-sexual implicit theories (e.g., Entitlement, Dangerous World) promote general antisociality. This would suggest that men who have sexually offended and who have higher levels of antisociality hold these beliefs, viewing themselves as being able to do what they want in a world that is hostile and uncertain. Ward and Siegert do state that sexual abuse (by generally antisocial individuals) will be influenced by patriarchal attitudes about children and feelings of superiority. This seems to reflect entitlement beliefs.

Another unique aspect related to cognition is the inclusion of sexual scripts. Scripts are a form of schema that describes the sequence of events that occur in a particular situation (Schank & Abelson, 1977). Thus, scripts are a type of cognitive structure stored in long-term memory, which become activated by certain cues. Ward and Siegert extensively describe the concept of the 'sexual script' (Gagon, 1990) as it is one of the psychological mechanisms underlying child abuse, and defines the distorted sexual scripts pathway. However, apart from stating that they are 'mental representations' and can be researched using cognitive paradigms, Ward and Siegert do not make it clear that scripts are a form of cognition. Nevertheless, the inclusion of scripts extends the theory's conceptual scope with regards to cognition.

Emotions are not explicitly defined but they are clearly addressed in the Pathways Model. This is particularly evident within the intimacy deficits and emotional dysregulation pathways. For example, in the former, distorted internal working models are hypothesized to create intimacy problems leading to loneliness and a fear of rejection. These emotions lead to an avoidance of adult relationships and an increased risk of turning to children for intimacy. From this, an implicit link between cognition and emotion is evident. Within the emotional dysregulation pathway, it is the defective regulation of emotions that plays a role. This includes problems in identifying emotions and the inability to control negative emotions. According to Ward and Siegert, the effect of this emotional dysregulation on offending can be either incidental (e.g., using sex as a coping strategy) or integral (e.g., disinhibition). Maladaptive coping stems from sex and emotional well-being becoming associated during early adolescence, whereby masturbatory activity served to alleviate negative moods and increase self-esteem. What is missing in this theory is an account of how various negative emotions affect the offending pathway. For example, do the effects of anger differ to that of sadness or shame?

Finally, a unique aspect of the Pathways Model is that it addresses positive emotion. Specifically, Ward and Siegert state that individuals following the antisocial cognitions pathway will experience positive integral emotions during their offence. This is because they are gaining pleasure from an activity that they feel entitled to perpetrate. Also, Ward and Siegert explain how individuals' emotions can become more positive as they progress through the offence; a shift that is accompanied by changes in cognition (e.g., perceiving the child as being more willing).

Ward and Siegert do not explicitly delineate any motivational goals within their theory. The four psychological mechanisms do not appear to be motivations but rather causal factors that play a collective role in child sexual abuse. However, employing a Good Lives perspective, certain motivational goals can be seen throughout the theory. For example, within the intimacy deficits, deviant sexual scripts and emotional dysregulation pathways, the goal of having an intimate/romantic relationship is evident (*relatedness*). Within the deviant sexual scripts, multiple dysfunctions and antisocial cognitions pathways, the goal of physical gratification is described (*life*). Within the intimacy deficits and emotional dysregulation, it is clear that freedom from emotional turmoil and mastery is being sought (*inner peace* and *mastery*). Finally, within the antisocial cognitions pathways, self-serving goals are evident (*agency*). From examining the Pathways Model, the offence-supportive strategies adopted to acquire these motivational goals appear to originate from cognitive and emotional problems, highlighting cognitive–motivation and emotion–motivation associations.

Ward and Beech's Integrated Theory of Sexual Offending (ITSO)

The ITSO was proposed by Ward and Beech (2006) in an attempt to explain the deeper causal mechanisms underlying the four surface-level factors associated with sexual offending. The authors argue that certain *biological factors* (i.e., evolutionary and genetic inheritance), in conjunction with proximal and distal *ecological niche factors* (i.e., personal, socio-cultural and physical circumstances), have a significant effect on an individual's brain development. In turn, this affects the three major interlocking neuropsychological systems associated with specific brain structures (Pennington, 2002). These systems include: (a) the *motivation–emotion system* (cortical, limbic and brainstem structures), which is involved in ensuring our perception and actions are influenced by our values and goals; (b) the *action–control* system (frontal cortex, basal ganglia and parts of the thalamus), which is concerned with the planning, implementing and evaluating of a future behaviour designed to achieve high-order goals; and (c) the *perception–memory system* (hippocampal formation and posterior neocortex), which is responsible for processing incoming sensory information and constructing mental representations of the world, which is then fed back to the other two systems. According to Ward and Beech, disruptions in any of these neuropsychological systems can lead to various offence-related vulnerabilities that increase the likelihood of a sexual offence occurring.

Evaluation

As in the previous theories, Ward and Beech do not provide a definition of cognition. They do, however, clearly focus on cognition in terms of higher-order cognitive constructs. For example, they explain that maladaptive beliefs (cognitive structures) act as pre-attentive filters that bias the interpretation of social information (belief/schema-driven processing). These entrenched beliefs, via biased processing, give rise to the cognitive distortions (cognitive products) often reported by men who have sexually offended during therapy. The *perception–memory system* is stated to be responsible for processing sensory information and constructing mental representations of the social world. Thus, Ward and Beech argue that distorted beliefs are the result of problems with this particular neuropsychological system.

In line with the ITSO's main tenet, these problems are seen to arise as a consequence of the interaction between biological and distal ecological factors (i.e., social learning processes). For example, according to Ward and Beech, a male may develop pro-rape beliefs (e.g., women are sexual objects) due to a weak genetic inheritance toward sexual promiscuity interacting with a cultural environment that undermines and devalues women. Ward and Beech argue that, because the *perception–memory system* feeds back to the other two systems, maladaptive beliefs can lead to the activation (and pursuit) of problematic emotions and goals. Thus, the ITSO positions distorted beliefs as the basis from which other offence-related vulnerabilities develop (see Ward, Chapter 1 in this volume for a reconceptualization of the causal priority of cognition).

A potential issue here is that Ward and Beech also state that the *motivation–emotion system* works to ensure goals influence perception. Presumably, the reference to 'perception' here relates to information processing. If so, then it is the opposite of 'faulty processing affecting goals', as described above. This either signifies a contradiction within the theory or implies that cognition and motivation have a bidirectional causal relationship. Unfortunately, the authors do not unpack this particular point so it is difficult to draw any firm conclusions.

One other cognitive aspect evident within the ITSO is the role that cognition plays in guiding action in order to achieve a goal. When deciding upon a plan of action, Ward and Beech argue that the *perception–memory system* is drawn upon for procedural knowledge about how to accomplish the action, as well as declarative knowledge that can help one understand a given situation. Thus, problems with this aspect of the *perception–memory system* are associated with inefficient (or a lack of) planning (i.e., impulsivity). Previous research indicates that problems in planning are linked to deficits in general cognitive abilities such as working memory performance (Ireland, 2008). Unfortunately, this level of detail is not provided within the ITSO.

Emotion is also not defined within this theory. Nevertheless, as with the previous theories, emotion-related issues are seen as a major factor in the aetiology of sexual offending. Ward and Beech argue that emotional problems are clinical (state) symptoms that result from defects in the *motivation–emotion system* (in the form of negative mood) and the *action–control system* (in the form of impulsive behaviour). If this 'impulsive behaviour' is driven by an emotion, then it is possible that the ITSO distinguishes mood from emotion. Indeed, Ward and Beech often refer to emotions and moods separately. Unfortunately, due to the frequent interchange between the terms, it is difficult to know if Ward and Beech conceptually differentiate mood and emotion, or are simply using the two terms to refer to affect more generally (see Ward, Chapter 1 in this volume for a detailed consideration of the difference between emotion and mood).

Ward and Beech state that defects in the *motivation–emotion system* result from problems in an individual's genetic inheritance or cultural/personal upbringing. For example, an emotionally impoverished childhood may lead to an inability to accurately identify one's emotions, leading to confusion during emotionally charged situations. Such confusion may then elicit anger and a subsequent act of antisocial behaviour. From this example, the authors clearly demonstrate how a negative emotion (i.e., anger) can arise and influence offending. In this case, anger has a direct influence on offending behaviour (i.e., it functions as an integral emotion). The two questions here are why anger is experienced in this situation and why it leads to antisocial behaviour. On closer examination of the ITSO, it seems that the other two systems play a role. Addressing the former question, Ward and Beech propose that maladaptive beliefs can activate 'problematic emotions'. Thus, it could be argued that maladaptive beliefs (e.g., women are dangerous) bias the processing of emotionally charged situations (e.g., rejection from a female) leading to anger. Addressing the second question, the authors argue that defects in the *action–control system* (e.g., self-regulatory deficits) cause problems in inhibiting negative emotions, resulting in offensive behaviour (e.g., an explosive outburst).

In addition, the ITSO posits that certain situations can elicit a more enduring negative mood. Here, Ward and Beech argue that ineffective mood management – in conjunction with sexual desire – can increase the likelihood that one will become disinhibited or use sex as a coping strategy. This likelihood is increased further in the presence of certain triggering factors (e.g., anger). This aspect of the ITSO suggests that emotions, such as anger, can also have a more incidental (or indirect) effect on offending. In sum, the ITSO clearly demonstrates how emotion in general can affect sexual offending. What is missing, however, is a discussion of how different types of emotions affect men who have sexually offended (e.g., sadness), including positive emotions.

Ward and Beech clearly address motivational goals within the ITSO through incorporating the idea that human beings have an inherent tendency to seek basic human goods. More specifically, the ITSO states that genetic factors predispose individuals to strive for certain goods (e.g., mastery, relatedness), while learning events (caused by socio-cultural and personal factors) lead individuals to acquire these goods in a certain manner (e.g., sexual promiscuity, use of controlling behaviour in relationships). As discussed in the previous theories, many of these goods will underlie the four clinical risk factors (e.g., the good underlying emotional problems would be *inner peace*).

Ward and Beech state that the goals required to energize (motivate) behaviour are brought about by the *motivation–emotional system*, and are influenced by the *perception–memory system* in terms of how to meet these goals (e.g., by drawing upon procedural knowledge). Thus, problems in the *perception–memory system* (caused by early learning experiences) can lead individuals to, unfortunately, draw upon distorted or offence-supportive knowledge to achieve a goal.

In addition, the ITSO states that problematic goals can be activated by maladaptive beliefs, which also originate from defects in the *perception–memory system*. There seems to be an issue with this statement. If all human beings strive for the same basic human goods/goals, as posited by the ITSO and Good Lives Model (and it is the route taken to acquire them that is of concern in sexual offending), then it is puzzling to know what a problematic goal might be. Arguably, Ward and Beech are referring to 'secondary goods' (e.g., sex with a child to acquire a sense of intimacy); a concept proposed in the Good Lives Model that is synonymous with maladaptive strategies for seeking primary (basic) goods. Unfortunately, however, the authors do not unpack or provide clarification on this point.

Conclusion

In this chapter, the major multi-factorial theories of sexual offending have been evaluated in terms of how they conceptualize cognition, emotion and motivational goals, as well as how these concepts interlink and influence sexual offending. In terms of cognition, each theory primarily focuses on social cognition (e.g., content held in long-term memory that guides interpretation of the world). Little to no attention has been given to general cognitive abilities (e.g., processing speed, working memory). This is problematic, as researchers have shown that impaired cognitive ability can impact on sexual offending behaviour (Becerra-García & Egan, 2014; Ireland, 2008). It is also likely to affect higher-level cognition (e.g., beliefs) in terms of impacting on the processing of social information and decision-making processes. Thus, this aspect of cognition should be incorporated into any future theory of sexual offending or adaptations of existing theory.

Each theory focuses on how emotions are ineffectively regulated. Little weight is given to the more integral effects that emotions can have on offending behaviour. Also, the theories do not explicitly distinguish emotions from other affective constructs, such as mood or feelings. This distinction has been noted by other researchers (e.g., Howells et al., 2004) and should be made within sexual offending theories, as different affective constructs are likely to affect sexual offending in different ways. Importantly, more attention also needs to be attributed to the role of 'positive' emotions (see Ward, Chapter 1 in this volume).

With the exception of the ITSO, the existing multi-factor theories incorporate very little about the development and role of motivational goals. Moreover, there are some conceptual problems evident in the earlier theories in terms of distinguishing motives to offend from more basic motivational goals that are met through offending behaviour. However, a reframing of the core assumptions within each theory, using a Good Lives perspective, allows one to see that various goals are implicitly embedded within each theory. Future theoretical developments should focus more explicitly on motivational aspects of sexual offending, including personal agency.

Despite their various conceptual limitations, each theory clearly addresses how each construct can interact to cause sexual offending, and does so in a manner that highlights the complexity of sexual offending. It should also be noted that these three areas of human nature are themselves multifaceted, highly complex and ever evolving, as researchers continue to uncover deeper insights. Thus, it is a difficult feat for an aetiological theory of sexual offending to comprehensively account for each one. However, given their importance in understanding human behaviour, it is necessary for theorists to appropriately conceptualize and address the role that these constructs play in sexual offending.

Since there are numerous aspects to cognition, emotion and goals, as well as different approaches to understanding each one, theorists should draw upon the soundest theoretical and empirical work within each domain. Ideally, this should involve integrating insights from multiple approaches and perspectives (both non-forensic and forensic) in order to develop a more pluralistic theoretical account of sexual offending (Ward, 2014). This should involve including the aforementioned suggestions associated with each domain (e.g., lower-level cognitive processing, the role of positive emotion, how decisions are affected by state-specific emotions, how goals are influenced by cognitive and affective factors) and knitting them with our contemporary understanding of deviant (and normative) sexual behaviour. Moreover, the appropriate level of detail is required. If not, then we are unlikely to develop a full understanding of why certain factors are empirically associated with (re)offending behaviour (e.g., whether they have a direct or mediated causal relationship).

One final important note is that because all of the theories described in this chapter focus on males, they cannot be applied to females who have sexually offended. Thus, a multifactor theory that sufficiently incorporates all of the points made in this chapter is sorely needed for females. The evaluation outlined in this chapter could not be timelier. It is hoped that it will encourage researchers and clinicians to reflect on the inclusion and appropriate conceptualization of cognition, emotion and motivation within theory in a deeper and more integrative manner.

References

Alexandrov, Y. I., & Sams, M. E. (2005). Emotion and consciousness: Ends of a continuum. *Cognitive Brain Research*, *25*, 387–405. doi: 10.1016/j. cogbrainres.2005.08.006

Becerra-García, J. A., & Egan, V. (2014). Neurocognitive functioning and subtypes of child molesters: Poorer working memory differentiates incestuous from non-incestuous offenders. *Psychiatry, Psychology and Law*, *21*, 585–590. doi: 10.1080/13218719.2013.873974

Bodenhausen, G. V. (1993). Emotions, arousal, and stereotypic judgments: A heuristic model of affect and stereotyping. In D. M. Mackie & D. L. Hamilton (Eds.), *Affect, cognition, and stereotyping* (pp. 13–37). San Diego, CA: Academic Press.

Bonta, J., & Andrews, D. A. (2007). *Risk–need–responsivity model for offender assessment and rehabilitation*. Ottowa: Public Safety Canada.

Deci, E. L., & Ryan, R. M. (2008). Self-determination theory: A macrotheory of human motivation, development, and health. *Canadian Psychology*, *49*, 182–185. doi: 10.1037/a0012801

Fazio, R. H. (2007). Attitudes as object-evaluation associations of varying strength. *Social Cognition*, *25*, 664–703. doi: 10.1521/soco.2007.25.5.603

Finkelhor, D. (1984). *Child sexual abuse: New theory and research*. New York: Free Press.

Gagon, J. H. (1990). The explicit and implicit use of the scripting perspective in sex research. *Annual Review of Sex Research*, *1*, 1–43. doi: 10.1080/10532528. 1990.10559854

Gannon, T. A. (2009). Social cognition in violent and sexual offending: An overview. *Psychology, Crime & Law*, *15*, 97–118. doi: 10.1080/10683160802190822

Hall, G. C. N., & Hirschman, R. (1991). Toward a theory of sexual aggression: A quadripartite model. *Journal of Consulting and Clinical Psychology*, *59*, 662–669. doi: 10.1037/0022-006X.59.5.662

Hall, G. C. N., & Hirschman, R. (1992). Sexual aggression against children: A conceptual perspective of etiology. *Criminal Justice and Behavior, 19,* 8–23. doi: 10.1177/0093854892019001003

Howells, K., Day, A., & Wright, S. (2004). Affect, emotions, and sex offending. *Psychology, Crime and Law, 10,* 179–195. doi: 10.1080/10683160310001609988

Ireland, C. (2008). Cognitive impairment and sex offending: Management during therapy and factors in offending. *The British Journal of Forensic Practice, 10,* 18–25. doi: 10.1108/14636646200800010

Janssen, E., Everaerd, W., Spiering, M., & Janssen, J. (2000). Automatic processes and the appraisal of sexual stimuli: Toward an information-processing model of sexual arousal. *Journal of Sex Research, 37,* 8–23. doi: 10.1080/00224490009552016

Kunda, Z. (1990). The case for motivated reasoning. *Psychological Bulletin, 108,* 480–498. doi: 10.1037/0033-2909.108.3.480

Kurtz, M. M., & Richardson, C. L. (2011). Social cognitive training for schizophrenia: a meta-analytic investigation of controlled research. *Schizophrenia Bulletin, 38,* 1092–1104. doi: 10.1093/schbul/sbr036.

Lazarus, R. S. (2006). *Stress and emotion: A new synthesis.* New York: Springer.

Lerner, J. S., Li, Y., Valdesolo, P., & Kassam, K. S. (2015). Emotion and decision-making. *Psychology, 66,* 799–823. doi: 10.1146/annurev-psych-010213-115043

Mann, R. E., Hanson, R. K., & Thornton, D. (2010). Assessing risk for sexual recidivism: Some proposals on the nature of psychologically meaningful risk factors. *Sexual Abuse: A Journal of Research and Treatment, 22,* 191–217. doi: 10.1177/1079063210366039

Marshall, W. L., & Barbaree, H. E. (1990). An integrated theory of the etiology of sexual offending. In W. L. Marshall, D. R. Laws & H. E. Barbaree (Eds.), *Handbook of sexual assault: Issues, theories, and treatment of the offender* (pp. 257–275). New York: Plenum Press.

Maslow, A. H. (1943). A theory of human motivation. *Psychological Review, 50,* 370–396. doi: 10.1037/h0054346

McPhail, I. V., Hermann, C. A., & Nunes, K. L. (2013). Emotional congruence with children and sexual offending against children: A meta-analytic review. *Journal of Consulting and Clinical Psychology, 81,* 737–749. doi: 10.1037/a0033248

Mulligan, K., & Scherer, K. R. (2012). Toward a working definition of emotion. *Emotion Review, 4,* 345–357. doi: 10.1177/1754073912445818

Pennington, B. F. (2002). *The development of psychopathology: Nature and nurture.* New York: Guilford Press.

Polaschek, D. L. L., & Ward, T. (2002). The implicit theories of potential rapists: What our questionnaires tell us. *Aggression and Violent Behavior, 7,* 385–406. doi: 10.1016/S1359-1789(01)00063-5

Przybyla, D. P. J., & Byrne, D. (1984). The mediating role of cognitive processes in self-reported sexual arousal. *Journal of Research in Personality, 18,* 54–63. doi: 10.1016/0092-6566(84)90038-2

Rudman, L. A., Phelan, J. E., & Heppen, J. B. (2007). Developmental sources of implicit attitudes. *Personality and Social Psychology Bulletin, 33,* 1700–1713. doi: 10.1177/0146167207307487

Schank, D. R., & Abelson, R. (1977). *Scripts, plans, goals and understanding.* Hillsdale, NJ: Lawrence Erlbaum.

Schwarz, N., & Clore, G. L. (1983). Mood, misattribution, and judgments of well-being: Informative and directive functions of affective states. *Journal of Personality and Social Psychology, 45*, 513–523. doi: 10.1037/0022-3514.45.3.513

Thornton, D. (2002). Constructing and testing a framework for dynamic risk assessment. *Sexual Abuse: A Journal of Research and Treatment, 14*, 139–153. doi: 10.1023/A:1014620214905

Tversky, A., & Kahneman, D. (1973). Availability: A heuristic for judging frequency and probability. *Cognitive Psychology, 5*, 207–232. doi: 10.1016/0010-0285(73)90033-9

Ward, T. (2000). Sexual offenders' cognitive distortions as implicit theories. *Aggression and Violent Behavior, 5*, 491–507. doi: 10.1016/S1359-1789(98)00036-6

Ward, T. (2001). A critique of Hall and Hirschman's quadripartite model of child sexual abuse. *Psychology, Crime, and Law, 7*, 333–350. doi: 10.1080/10683160108401799

Ward, T. (2002). Marshall and Barbaree's integrated theory of child sexual abuse: A critique. *Psychology, Crime and Law, 8*, 209–228. doi: 10.1080/10683160208401816

Ward, T. (2014). The explanation of sexual offending: From single factor theories to integrative pluralism. *Journal of Sexual Aggression, 20*, 130–141. doi: 10.1080/13552600.2013.870242

Ward, T., & Beech, A. (2006). An integrated theory of sexual offending. *Aggression and Violent Behavior, 11*, 44–63. doi: 10.1016/j.avb.2005.05.002

Ward, T., & Beech, A. R. (2015). Dynamic risk factors: a theoretical dead-end? *Psychology, Crime & Law, 21*, 100–113. doi: 10.1080/1068316x.2014.917854

Ward, T., & Gannon, T. A. (2006). Rehabilitation, etiology, and self-regulation: The comprehensive good lives model of treatment for sexual offenders. *Aggression and Violent Behavior, 11*, 77–94. doi: 10.1016/j.avb.2005.06.001

Ward, T., & Hudson, S. M. (2001). Finkelhor's precondition model of child sexual abuse: A critique. Psychology, Crime and Law, 7, 291–307. doi: 10.1080/10683160108401799

Ward, T., Polaschek, D., & Beech, A. R. (2006). *Theories of sexual offending.* Chichester, UK: John Wiley & Sons.

Ward, T., & Siegert, R. J. (2002). Toward a comprehensive theory of child sexual abuse: A theory knitting perspective. *Psychology, Crime & Law, 8*, 319–351. doi: 10.1080/10683160208401823

Ward, T., & Stewart, C. A. (2003). Criminogenic needs and human needs: A theoretical model. *Psychology, Crime, & Law, 9*, 125–143. doi: 10.1037/0735-7028.34.4.353

3

Cognitive Explanations of Sexual Offending

Caoilte Ó Ciardha

Cognition is an incredibly broad term incorporating many psychological constructs and processes with the potential to explain sexual offending. *Human cognition* is a general term for the mental processes that allow us to make sense of our environment and how our interpretation of that environment shapes behaviour. These processes include 'attention, perception, learning, memory, language, problem solving, reasoning, and thinking' (Eysenck & Keane, 2010, p. 1). Within an information-processing view, humans perceive and interpret their physical and social environments through the lens of their cognitive abilities or deficits and based on the content of their memory. Simply put, individuals are not passive, unbiased observers. Rather they construct their understanding of the world based on attitudes, heuristics and experiences developed over their lifetime. The manner in which information is processed dictates the resulting behaviour (see Ward, Chapter 1 in this volume, on how emotions and goals form part of this information processing). The study of social cognition examines how individuals' cognitive processes interact with their social context, how they understand other people's social behaviour and how they decide to act in that context. Researchers examining cognition and how it applies to sexual offending can examine neuroscientific, behavioural or physiological data in order to draw conclusions about underlying cognitive structures and processes.

This chapter examines theories of cognition relevant to sexual offending. Primarily I will focus on single factor theories (theories that examine, in detail, single constructs or processes that may contribute to sexual offending) as cognition in multi-factor theories of sexual offending is examined elsewhere in this volume (Bartels, Chapter 2). In approaching this chapter I have taken a deliberately broad view of cognition. Trying to capture such breadth makes it challenging to incorporate all the relevant literature in detail. However, it also lays down the gauntlet for researchers to synthesize disparate literatures into a consolidated pluralistic narrative of the cognitive factors that play a role in sexual offending. Specifically, I advocate an integrative pluralistic approach that means looking not simply at the content of cognitions (i.e., attitudes and beliefs, etc.) but also at the context in which these cognitions emerge and how they relate to a broader

Sexual Offending: Cognition, Emotion and Motivation, First Edition.
Edited by Theresa A. Gannon and Tony Ward.
© 2017 John Wiley & Sons Ltd. Published 2017 by John Wiley & Sons Ltd.

understanding of cognition, its developmental origins and its dependence on factors such as motivation and emotion.

Single Factor Explanations of Cognition in Sexual Offending

Multi-factor theories are necessary to explain behaviour as complex as sexual offending (Ward & Beech, 2006). However, they often lack explanatory depth regarding the specific processes or mechanisms underpinning certain deficits or phenomena highlighted within the theory. Single-factor theories therefore provide an opportunity for more detailed explanation of these deficits or phenomena. Some single-factor theories may be multi-faceted and seek to explain a breadth of clinically relevant phenomena (for example, theories explaining the range of so called *cognitive distortions* observed among individuals who have sexually offended), while others focus on the causal explanations of very specific behaviours (for example theories of paedophilic sexual interest and arousal). Additionally, the processes described by single-factor theories may operate at different levels of analysis (e.g., neurological, psychological, social, etc.) and necessarily interact with one another. As a result, it is important that readers avoid interpreting these theories in a list-like fashion, but rather as an interconnected hierarchy of processes leading to cognitions and behaviours idiosyncratic to the individual. Furthermore, these processes are not robotic operations that function independent of motivation and emotion. While there tends to be general consensus on clinical/cognitive presentation of individuals who have committed sexual offences, a lack of longitudinal research, research on genetics, cohort studies and neuropsychological research has resulted in less clarity regarding the underlying causal mechanisms of those clinical presentations. I first focus on neurodevelopment and deficits in neuropsychological functioning. I then examine single-factor theories relating to social information processing in offending. Finally I outline the key research and theory that has examined possible criminogenic cognitive constructs.

Neurodevelopmental Cognitive Deficits

Examining aggregate data from over 25 000 individuals, Cantor, Blanchard, Robichaud and Christensen (2005) found that adults who had offended sexually scored lower on a measure of IQ than adults who had offended non-sexually, who in turn scored lower than adults who had not offended. IQ scores were lowest among those individuals with the youngest victims. However, while individuals who committed sexual offences had lower IQ scores than individuals who had offended non-sexually and individuals who had not offended, they did not, on average, fall into a range considered indicative of intellectual disability. Findings of lower IQ lend preliminary support to the theory that some risk factors for sexual offending are neurodevelopmental and originate in prenatal life or early childhood (Blanchard et al., 2002). Additional possible indicators of perturbed neurodevelopment include handedness and height. Individuals demonstrating paedophilic sexual interests have been found to have higher rates of non-right handedness (Fazio, Lykins & Cantor, 2014). Cantor and colleagues (2007) examined height in a sample of individuals who had undergone phallometric testing and had committed sexual offences or who had self-referred because of a concern over their own sexual urges. They found that individuals with a sexual interest in (prepubescent and pubescent) children were shorter on average than the population norms for males. Assessed individuals with a sexual interest in adults were also significantly shorter than the population average, though this effect was weaker than for individuals with paedophilic sexual interests. Individuals with paedophilic interests also report more head injuries before the age of 13 (but not after) than those interested in pubescent children, who in turn report more head injuries than individuals with sexual interests towards sexually mature partners (Blanchard et al., 2003). This relationship can be interpreted such that brain injury may increase risk of sexual offending *or* that accident proneness or impulsivity leading to head injury is also found in individuals neurodevelopmentally predisposed to sexual interest in children. Despite this uncertainty, Fazio and colleagues (2014) argue that the combination of evidence based on height, handedness and IQ suggests that for some individuals there may be a neurodevelopmental (prenatal) component in the origin of some paraphilic sexual interests. This relationship appears corroborated by evidence of rape and child molestation clustering in families and evidence suggesting that this clustering is primarily accounted for by genetics rather than shared environment (Långström et al., 2015). Risk of sexual offending therefore appears to be partially explained (Fazio et al., 2014) by prenatal factors that bring about a number of developmental perturbations, including cognitive deficits in the form of lower IQ.

Blanchard, Cantor and Robichaud (2006) carried out a comprehensive review of studies examining the neuropsychological functioning of males who committed sexual offences. They report generally mixed findings, though the limited number of studies with larger sample sizes tended to find males who committed sexual offences to have subnormal scores across a broad range of neuropsychological tests (incorporating reasoning, executive functioning, language and visuospatial skills). Burton, Demuynck and Yoder (2014) found that while adolescent males who sexually offended showed high rates of executive dysfunction, those deficits were predictive of general delinquency but not frequency or severity of sexual crime.

Executive function involves the higher-order cognitive processes involved in the self-regulation of emotions, thoughts and behaviours. Difficulties with emotional regulation and impulse control are a core part of the clinical symptomology associated with sexual offending (Ward & Beech, 2006). It is difficult to assert whether deficits in neuropsychological functioning found among certain people who commit sexual offences are in fact sequelae of neurodevelopmental perturbations with a genetic, prenatal or perinatal origin. For example, being a victim of child abuse and/or neglect, itself a risk factor for sexual offending (Ogloff et al., 2012), may be associated with cognitive deficits in (but not limited to) visual memory, executive functioning, spatial working memory and emotional processing (Gould et al., 2012; Zou et al., 2013).

Social difficulties represent another cluster of clinical symptoms associated with sexual offending including 'emotional loneliness, inadequacy, low self-esteem, passive victim stance, and suspiciousness' (Ward & Beech, 2006, p. 55). In addition, patterns of social information processing, such as the attribution of hostile intent to peer actions (hostile attribution bias) are characteristic of individuals who are generally aggressive (Crick & Dodge, 1994). Lee and Hoaken (2007) argue that while researchers rarely integrate findings on social information processing and executive function, both seem to represent cognitive constructs that overlap to a large degree. While research on cognition in sexual offending is particularly concerned with how individuals interpret the behaviours and intentions of partners and potential victims, especially where (mis) interpretation of social cues may make sexual offending or crime more likely, the literature has not often embedded this in the wider evidence base on social information processing.

Social-Cognitive Development

A comprehensive examination of social learning theory or social cognition in the context of sexual offending is beyond the scope of this chapter. I focus in particular on two mechanisms by which social and contextual factors interact with cognitive processes implicated in sexual offending. These theories and processes should not be seen as mutually exclusive of one another or of the neurodevelopmental processes discussed earlier.

Attachment

Attachment and attachment theory relates to the bond between individuals and significant others and to the beliefs, goals and emotions, and strategies that are utilized to maintain safety. Attachment theory is also concerned with mental representations of emotionally significant others that individuals develop over the lifespan and how these representations shape and interact with cognition and behaviour. Within the literature on sexual offending, poor quality childhood attachments to parents or primary care givers is seen as a critical factor leading to the 'initiation and continuation of sexual offending' (Marshall, 2010, p. 73). Early life stressors such as abuse and neglect may disrupt an individual's development of healthy attachments (Marshall & Barbaree, 1990), which may lead to a greater risk of sexual victimization as well as to greater risk of perpetrating sexual offences (Marshall & Marshall, 2000). Individuals who have sexually offended against children have been found to be characterized by insecure childhood (Smallbone & Dadds, 1998) and adult attachment (Lyn & Burton, 2005; Marsa et al., 2004), though this relationship has not been found in all offending groups (Seto & Lalumière, 2010). Dykas and Cassidy (2011) argue that *securely* attached individuals process attachment-relevant social information fully, regardless of the valence of that information and its potential to cause pain. *Insecurely* attached individuals, however, suppress or exclude social information related to attachment figures or painful childhood experiences. In doing so, they process information using negative schemas that operate on an implicit level possibly reducing the danger of the conscious experience of painful attachment-related content (note the role of emotion and motivation in this process).

Within the attachment system, goal-directed behaviour involves at least three cognitive operations:

> (1) Processing information about the person – environment relationship, which involves monitoring and appraising threatening events in one's own internal state (e.g., distress, security), (2) Monitoring and appraising the attachment figure's responses to one's proximity seeking attempts, (3) Monitoring and appraising the utility of the chosen behaviors in a given context, so that an effective adjustment of these behaviors can be made in accordance with contextual constraints' (Mikulincer & Shaver, 2010, p. 15).

The description of these operations maps well onto Crick and Dodge's (1994) social information processing model of children's social adjustment, suggesting that these may be cognate processes. In Crick and Dodge's model, the processing of social information is cyclical and includes six key steps: encoding of cues, interpretation of cues, clarification of goals, response access or construction, response decision and behavioural enactment. Each of these steps is constantly appraised against a 'database' of memories, acquired rules, social schemas and social knowledge. Peer evaluation and responses to the selected action are then incorporated into the process.

Theory of Mind

Keenan and Ward (2000) proposed a theory of mind perspective on the cognitive, affective and intimacy deficits seen in individuals who committed sexual offences against children. Theory of mind is generally seen as 'the ability to reason about mental states, such as beliefs, desires and intentions, and to understand how mental states feature in everyday explanations and predictions of people's behaviour' (Apperly, 2012, p. 836). Children develop this theory of mind system with which to understand other people's perspectives. Keenan and Ward posited that individuals committing sexual offences have theory of mind deficits that result in impaired perspective taking. They gave the example of research by Hanson and Scott (1995) that showed mixed results on a task measuring perspective taking towards children but showed that people who committed rape or had molested children had difficulty taking the perspective of adult women. Subsequent research found that individuals who sexually offended against children had impaired performance in inferring the mental states of adults but not those of children (e.g., Elsegood & Duff, 2010).

Attachment is a central mechanism for the development of a theory of mind. It follows, therefore, that children may have deficits in theory of mind as a result of the same factors that influence poor attachment. Happé and Frith (1996) proposed that some children with conduct disorder might have intact or relatively intact theory of mind but that this theory is shaped by negative environments into a *theory of nasty minds*. This worldview may be adaptive within an early negative environment, but may lead to later interpersonal difficulties.

Just as emotion and cognition are likely to be inextricably linked (see Ward, Chapter 1 in this volume), rather than discreet systems, it is likely that theory of mind does not constitute a separate system to reasoning or social information processing. Apperly (2011) argues convincingly that not all interactions require cognitively demanding perspective taking. Rather he claims that there are two systems of *mindreading*, or theory of mind, where some mindreading inferences require considerable demands on executive function, are flexible and are used in novel situations or where there is pressure to be accurate. However, there is also a system that works rapidly and without high demand on cognitive resources. This more rapid system must function inflexibly using mindreading modules to perform specific operations. Apperly proposes that some rapid theory of mind operations may be performed by *original modules* that emerge early in development. Additionally, he argues that more complex deliberative operations may become modularized through repetition and learning, such as in the example of a fencer learning to rapidly and automatically interpret and predict their opponents bluff and counter-bluff. The mechanisms of this *downward modularization* do not differ from development of expertise (see Nee and Ward, 2015), nor does the overall two-system model differ from dual-process theories of reasoning and decision-making (see Kahneman, 2011). It is positive that a model of theory of mind should operate in a way that is 'neither unusual nor outlandishly complex' (Apperly, 2011, p. 140) in comparison to other cognitive processes.

The two-system view of theory of mind/mindreading has some interesting implications for the understanding of cognition in those who sexually offend. Individuals may draw on developed views of the world such as the *theory of nasty minds* in interpreting the actions of others, or they may interpret the actions of others as antisocial when they themselves are antisocial (reflecting an egocentric bias in inference). These inferences may result from effortful or automatic appraisal according to the two-system conceptualization. However, Apperly (2011) also argues that schemas and norms may dictate which type of judgment (efficient/inflexible or flexible/effortful) is used by determining what is relevant to the mindreading inference at hand. Therefore, schematic beliefs that treat the intentions of others with suspicion may result in the expenditure of greater cognitive effort in perspective-taking activities, since in the absence of trust towards an agent, a greater amount of additional information must be appraised to determine their intentions. This may result in less cognitive resources available for other aspects of cognitive functioning, such as impulse control.

Theories of Criminogenic Cognitive Constructs

Through various developmental processes, some individuals may already lack some of the protective factors to minimize risk of sexual offending even before any possible distortions of cognitive content are considered. However, it should also be clear from the theory of mind research, for example, that until a greater research base is developed it is not clear yet whether apparent theory of mind challenges arise out of deficits of form or out of the belief content used to make inferences.

Deviant Sexual Interest

It is not surprising that deviant sexual interests would be one of the key criminogenic constructs attributed to perpetrators of sexual aggression (Ward & Beech, 2006). There may be a temptation to treat sexual interest as distinct from cognitive constructs that may be criminogenic in sexual offending. This is likely to be because other cognitive constructs may be more easily conceptualized as relatively self-contained belief systems whereas sexual interests may also involve drives, desires, affective states and physical responses, in addition to multiple phenomena more easily recognized as *cognitive* (Ó Ciardha, 2011).

Almost all multi-factorial theories of sexual offending implicate deviant arousal or deviant sexual interest (see Bartels, Chapter 2 in this volume). This is especially the case for male perpetrators of sexual offences against children. There is a growing body of research suggesting that paedophilic sexual interest or a susceptibility to it may in certain cases be developed early in life or prenatally (Cantor et al., 2008) and that paedophilia may be similar to a sexual orientation (Seto, 2012). However, it is not just individuals with paedophilic interests who appear to hold deviant sexual interests. Individuals who have committed sexual offences against adults show greater arousal to non-consenting sex than controls in laboratory settings, which may also be prenatally influenced (Lalumière, Harris, Quinsey & Rice, 2005).

While sexual arousal *can* occur in individuals to targets that they do not typically find sexually appetitive (especially in women; Chivers et al., 2010), deviant sexual arousal is usually seen as a consequence of an underlying sexual interest (Seto, 2008). Paedophilia, for example, appears to be relatively stable across the lifespan in many cases (Seto, 2012). Sexual interest, deviant or otherwise, can therefore be seen as being made up of structures in, and processes drawing on, explicit and implicit long-term memory (Ó Ciardha, 2011; Spiering & Everaerd, 2007). These include recollections of sexual encounters, fantasies, attitudes about sex, understanding of sexual costs and rewards, innate sexual reflexes, learned sexual scripts, relevant schematic representations and classically conditioned sensations. As a result, assessment measures should be capable of measuring both deviant arousal and the cognitive structures underpinning deviant sexual interest.

Physiological measures, such as penile and vaginal plethysmography, measure the arousal process in a relatively direct manner. Other tasks measure arousal or interest less directly, by measuring related cognitive phenomena. Tasks that measure response times to potentially appetitive stimuli typically show a slowing down of response times consistent with sexual interest. Imhoff and colleagues (2010) attribute these effects to the processing of the stimuli for the purposes of mate selection, and potentially due to the automatic activation of related cognitive structures (e.g., schemas, scripts and sexual fantasies). Other measures of sexual interest appear to be predominantly measuring schematic representations relating to sexual interest from long-term memory. Tasks like the implicit association test (IAT; Greenwald, McGhee & Schwartz, 1998) measure the strength of associations held by individuals between different constructs. Babchishin, Nunes and Hermann (2013) reviewed studies using the IAT to compare individuals who committed sexual offences against children with comparison groups.

The task showed consistent discrimination between groups based on stronger associations between child concepts (e.g., child, boys, children) and sexual attributes (e.g., sexy, erotic, sexually exciting) among individuals who had sexually offended against children compared with controls. Babchishin and colleagues (2013) categorize all these tasks as measures of sexual interest, though some were developed as measures of different cognitive constructs (e.g., Mihailides, Devilly & Ward, 2004). This appears to demonstrate that various cognitive constructs feed into a multi-faceted cognitive architecture of sexual interest (Ó Ciardha, 2011).

Cognitive Distortions

Ó Ciardha and Ward (2013) define cognitive distortions in perpetrators of sexual offences as 'specific or general beliefs/attitudes that violate commonly accepted norms of rationality, and which have been shown to be associated with the onset and maintenance of sexual offending' (p. 6). Since Abel and colleagues introduced the term into the sexual offending literature to refer to belief systems developed by individuals to 'support sexual involvement with children' (Abel, Becker & Cunningham-Rathner, 1984, p. 98), various authors have incorporated minimizing or rationalizing statements into the definition of the term (Bumby, 1996; Neidigh & Krop, 1992). However, at this time, there is no clear evidence that these post-offence statements represent true criminogenic factors (Maruna & Mann, 2006). There is intuitive appeal to the idea that the efforts of certain individuals to reduce perceptions of their culpability are indicative of some pathological cognitive process or structure. However, in most other spheres of behaviour it is seen as quite normal to attempt to diminish responsibility for transgressions (Maruna & Mann, 2006).

Rape Myths

Holding attitudes or beliefs (e.g., cultural myths) that support, trivialize or justify rape (Burt, 1980) and blames victims (usually female) is understood to play a causal role in sexual violence (Bohner, Jarvis, Eyssel & Siebler, 2005). While rape myths are unfortunately widespread in cultural and social discourse around rape and the role of women in society, they can still be considered as violating norms of rationality, as they do not reflect the empirical facts, and therefore fit within Ó Ciardha and Ward's definition of cognitive distortions. By internalizing these beliefs through social learning mechanisms, individuals may use rape myths as cognitive schema to guide their understanding of sexual or social interactions (Bohner et al., 2009).

Schemas and Implicit Theories

Mann and Beech (2003) proposed a schema-based model of cognition in sexual offending. They argued that individuals who sexually offend develop category schemas (stereotypes) or belief schemas (assumptions about the self and the world) to make sense of early life experiences. These dysfunctional schemas are used in response to ambiguous situations or negative life events. Interpretation of these events happens through the lens of these schemas, and schema-relevant cues receive greater focus. This process yields hostile cognitive outputs that may then interact with other dynamic risk factors for sexual offending.

Similarly to Mann and Beech's (2003) model, Ward (2000) proposed that surface level cognitive distortions arise out of *implicit theories* regarding the nature of victims or environment. He explained that these implicit theories 'function like scientific theories and are used to explain empirical regularities (e.g., other people's actions) and to make predictions about the world. They are relatively coherent and constituted by a number of interlocking beliefs and their component concepts and categories' (Ward, 2000, p. 492). He argued that these implicit theories are *schemas* but preferred to avoid that word due to its multiple definitions. A key strength of the implicit theories theory is the fact that it presents a view of these theories or schema as 'interlocking' rather than independent of one another. It is therefore unfortunate that the most salient aspects of the implicit theories theory were the five most common implicit theories detailed in the earlier-published paper by Ward and Keenan (though submitted later; 1999).

The empirical evidence to date does not appear to strongly support the presence of the five implicit theories of individuals who sexually offend against children (the most researched) as distinct measurable cognitive structures. Questionnaire and interview studies do find evidence for themes mapping onto the prototypical implicit theories hypothesized for the different offence types (Gannon, Keown & Rose, 2009; Marziano, Ward, Beech & Pattison, 2006; Polaschek & Gannon, 2004). However, the proposers of the prototypical implicit theories have drawn on questionnaire and interview studies – referred to as cognitive products (Gannon & Polaschek, 2006) – in order to hypothesize the content of these implicit theories. As a result it is not sufficient to demonstrate the validity of these implicit theories using the same data used to devise them. Researchers have instead turned to indirect measures to attempt to demonstrate the presence of concrete cognitive structures corresponding to named implicit theories. Tasks have included implicit association tests (e.g., Mihailides et al., 2004), information-processing tasks (Gannon, Wright, Beech & Williams, 2006), priming tasks (Keown, Gannon & Ward, 2008a) and lexical decision tasks (Keown, Gannon & Ward, 2008b). There is consistent evidence of schematic associations between the concept of children and sexual attributes among individuals who have sexually offended against children (Babchishin et al., 2013), potentially corresponding to a *children as sexual beings* implicit theory but much less for schemas surrounding the other four implicit theories hypothesized to be common among individual who have sexual victimized children. Despite several promising findings (e.g., Mihailides et al., 2004), individuals who have committed sexual offences against children are not typically characterized by consistent cognitive associations between these constructs any more than comparison groups.

Ward and his colleagues attempted to address the evidence that statements made by individuals who have offended do not always appear to reflect underlying stable beliefs (Judgment Model of Cognitive Distortions [JMCD]; Ward, Gannon & Keown, 2006). They argued instead that beliefs and values are key contributing factors in decisions leading to actions, and that when called upon to explain their actions, those explanations will be shaped by an individual's beliefs and values. Ward and colleagues (2006) outlined how implicit theory themes hypothesized for individuals who offended against children (Ward & Keenan, 1999) and perpetrators of rape (Polaschek & Gannon, 2004) can be understood through networks of beliefs, values and the interpretation of actions. While intuitively satisfying, the JMCD lacks empirical evidence in support of it, and indeed suffers from potential difficulties with falsifiability (Ó Ciardha & Ward, 2013). However, taken in combination, the implicit theories theory and the JMCD offer the most detailed explanations of how the statements of perpetrators of sexual offences emerge from their cognitive structures and processing.

Overlapping Constructs within Sexual Offending Cognition

There is a temptation to regard different conceptualizations of offence-related cognition as being independent from one another. For example, IAT findings of schematic associations of children with sex are interpreted by some authors (e.g., Mihailides et al., 2004) as evidence for a *children as sexual beings* implicit theory but by others (e.g., Nunes, Firestone & Baldwin, 2007) as evidence of sexual interest. While researchers may wish to design studies that examine whether one of these explanations of IAT findings has greater support, both may also be accommodated within an interlocking perspective on cognition. In this case, schematic association between children and sex may evidence structures in implicit or explicit memory that form part of a belief about the suitability of children as sexual partners (children as sexual beings), which in turn forms one aspect of the cognitive architecture of a sexual interest in children (Ó Ciardha, 2011).

The example above suggests a relationship between cognitive constructs that are likely to be criminogenic and are idiosyncratic to people who have or are at risk of sexually offending. It is therefore sensible to have a specific theoretical model or models and nomenclature with which to make sense of the cognitive processes involved for that population. There is a risk, however, that we are using different theoretical models to describe the same or similar constructs. This is not in of itself a problem. Ward (2014), for example, argues for an integrative pluralistic approach in which sexual offending is understood by '[building] a patchwork of local theories, each seeking to explain specific phenomena at varying levels of analysis and [linking] them via a conceptual framework' (p. 132). Theories of cognition, whether they look at theory of mind or perception or another phenomenon, simply parse out and reduce neural functioning into manageable processes. However, it is problematic if literature outside the sexual offending domain is offering superior explanations of the cognitive phenomena observed in individuals who sexually offend, or comes with a greater pedigree of empirical research and nuanced experimental probing. I will use the *dangerous world* implicit theory to illustrate how specific phenomena are explained, not just at varying levels of analysis, but also by competing models at similar levels of analysis.

An Example: Dangerous Worlds

Ward and Keenan (1999) proposed that some individuals who molest children perceive the world as dangerous, believing others cannot be trusted. They proposed two subtypes of dangerous world. In the first (referred to for convenience as dangerous world type 1), the individual feels they need to dominate or punish others. If women or children are perceived as threats they may be sexually abused as domination or punishment. In the second version (dangerous world type 2), however, adults are viewed as unreliable while children are viewed as reliable. Thus, children are viewed as loving and able to understand and fulfil sexual needs.

Taken together, there seems to be evidence, from interview-based studies (Beech, Parrett, Ward & Fisher, 2009; Gannon, Hoare, Rose & Parrett, 2010; Polaschek & Gannon, 2004) of increased perceptions of threat across male and female individuals who sexually offend. In fact, Gannon and colleagues (2010) noted that females who had abused children held gender-specific beliefs and relabelled the construct as *dangerousness of men/males*. Evidence is less compelling from studies looking beyond cognitive products. Using an information-processing approach Gannon and colleagues (2006) did not find evidence that individuals distorted their recall of vignettes in a manner consistent with either version of dangerous world (see also Keown et al., 2008b, who failed to find evidence for dangerous world using a lexical decision task). Examining the implicit theories of rape-prone men, Blake and Gannon (2010), again using a lexical decision task, did not find evidence for any implicit theories associated with rape, including dangerous world (see also Keown, Gannon & Ward, 2010).

Only one cognitive experimental approach has found evidence of greater perception of threat among perpetrators of sexual offences. Gannon and Rose (2009) used a paradigm developed by Copello and Tata (1990) to examine perceptions of threat in ambiguous stimuli amongst females who had sexually offended against children. Gannon and Rose (2009) found evidence of implicit beliefs around men being dangerous using this approach.

The most compelling support for a dangerous world implicit theory comes from the interpretive bias task developed as a measure of *hostile attribution bias* (Copello & Tata, 1990). Most of the literature on implicit theories contains references to apparently cognate phenomena. Ward (2000), for example, describes the development of a dangerous world type 1 implicit theory as a child developing an interpretative framework to:

> explain and predict the abusive behavior of his caregivers. In this context, the capacity to make relevant mental state inferences and to anticipate the violent actions of others may prove to be extremely adaptive. However, in an environment where there is a complete absence of interpersonal violence, such implicit theories are likely to result in overly hostile attributions and aggressive behavior toward others (p. 503).

This couches the implicit theories theory in both Theory of Mind (Keenan & Ward, 2000) and Social Information-Processing (Crick & Dodge, 1994) models. Both models have their own nomenclature for the types of beliefs encompassed within a dangerous world implicit theory: *theory of nasty minds* and *hostile attribution bias*. This furnishes researchers with a ready theory of mind mechanism for the acquisition of dangerous world beliefs. However, there is a risk that referring to dangerous world rather than hostile attribution bias, for example, shuts consumers of sexual offending research off from broader relevant literature.

Dangerous world type 2 appears to overlap to a large degree with the *children as sexual beings* implicit theory but also with non-implicit theory constructs such as deviant sexual interest in children as well as emotional congruence with children (see McPhail, Hermann & Nunes, 2013). Indeed Marziano and colleagues (2006) found individuals who offended against male children endorsed higher frequencies of dangerous world beliefs alongside children as sexual beings beliefs. In addition, individuals who have offended against male children tend to demonstrate greater sexual arousal to children (see Elsegood & Duff, 2010, for theory of mind research).

When considered in context, therefore, Ward and Keenan's (1999) dangerous world implicit theory is a conceptualization of cognitive products that may arise from the interaction of hostile attribution biases, entitlement, deviant sexual interest, emotional congruence with children and beliefs regarding children as sexual beings, along with other constructs. The mechanisms through which these constructs are brought to bear on an individual's cognitive processing may include social information processing and neurodevelopment deficits in executive function and may be rooted in early developmental experiences. Taking dangerous world as a small example demonstrates the need for theorists to take an integrative pluralistic approach (Ward, 2014).

Implications for Treatment

There is a risk that modularized treatment programmes that focus on factors such as emotional regulation, deviant sexual interests and offence supportive attitudes as distinct perpetuate a fragmented view of offence-related cognition. Instead, taking an integrative pluralistic approach to research also means doing the same when it comes to individual case formulation. This means both acknowledging the potential causal factors that played a role in that individual's previous offending, and targeting them in treatment, but doing so with an understanding of how those factors may interact with one another. Additionally treatment should be responsive to the developmental factors that may have shaped individual cognition in terms of content and also in terms of the cognitive idiosyncrasies of the individual in terms of cognitive style and neuropsychological functioning.

Conclusions

There is a risk that research on cognition in sexual offending has assumed that there is an otherness about males and females who commit rape or molest children that requires a bespoke account of their cognition. It is comforting to search for the components that make 'sexual offenders' monstrous others, rather than human. Within this approach individuals who have committed sexual offences are sampled as deviant others and indicators of deviance are assumed to be criminogenic. Therefore, appearing to hold deviant sexual interests must be prognostic, and believing in a dangerous world must increase the likelihood someone will aggress against others. In ascribing otherness to people who have committed sexual offences, research loses sight of two important facts. First, individuals are not just sex offenders; they may offend in a number of ways, and they may hold many prosocial qualities. Second, individuals in the community may demonstrate indicators of deviance but may never offend. In demanding a model of cognition underpinning sexual offences, we risk losing touch with the wider literature on cognition in offending, and cognition more broadly. Rather, an integrative pluralism approach is required in which different levels of analysis are knitted together. These levels should include cognitive structures, processes and products that appear unique (or uniquely deficient) among individuals who sexually offend, but these should be couched within a wider knowledge of the development of typical and atypical human cognition.

References

Abel, G. G., Becker, J. V., & Cunningham-Rathner, J. (1984). Complications, consent, and cognitions in sex between children and adults. *International Journal of Law and Psychiatry*, 7(1), 89–103. doi: 10.1016/0160-2527(84)90008-6

Apperly, I. A. (2011). *Mindreaders: The cognitive basis of 'theory of mind'*. Hove, UK: Psychology Press.

Apperly, I. A. (2012). What is 'theory of mind'? Concepts, cognitive processes and individual differences. *The Quarterly Journal of Experimental Psychology*, 65(5), 825–839. doi: 10.1080/17470218.2012.676055

Babchishin, K. M., Nunes, K. L., & Hermann, C. A. (2013). The validity of Implicit Association Test (IAT) measures of sexual attraction to children: A meta-analysis. *Archives of Sexual Behavior*, 42(3), 487–499. doi: 10.1007/s10508-012-0022-8

Beech, A. R., Parrett, N., Ward, T., & Fisher, D. (2009). Assessing female sexual offenders' motivations and cognitions: An exploratory study. *Psychology, Crime and Law*, 15(2–3), 201–216. doi: 10.1080/10683160802190921

Blake, E., & Gannon, T. A. (2010). The implicit theories of rape-prone men: An information-processing investigation. *International Journal of Offender Therapy & Comparative Criminology*, 54(6), 895–914. doi: 10.1177/0306624x09347732

Blanchard, R., Cantor, J. M., & Robichaud, L. K. (2006). Biological factors in the development of sexual deviance and aggression in males. In H. E. Barbaree & W. L. Marshall (Eds.), *The juvenile sex offender* (2nd ed., pp. 77–104). New York: Guilford Press.

Blanchard, R., Christensen, B. K., Strong, S. M., Cantor, J. M., Kuban, M. E., Klassen, P., et al. (2002). Retrospective self-reports of childhood accidents causing unconsciousness in phallometrically diagnosed pedophiles. *Archives of Sexual Behavior*, 31(6), 511–526. doi: 10.1023/A:1020659331965

Blanchard, R., Kuban, M. E., Klassen, P., Dickey, R., Christensen, B. K., Cantor, J. M., et al. (2003). Self-reported head injuries before and after age 13 in pedophilic and nonpedophilic men referred for clinical assessment. *Archives of Sexual Behavior, 32*(6), 573–581.

Bohner, G., Eyssel, F., Pina, A., Siebler, F., & Viki, G. T. (2009). Rape myth acceptance: Cognitive, affective and behavioural effects of beliefs that blame the victim and exonerate the perpetrator. In M. Horvath & J. Brown (Eds.), Rape: *Challenging contemporary thinking* (pp. 17–45). Collumpton, Devon, UK: Willan.

Bohner, G., Jarvis, C. I., Eyssel, F., & Siebler, F. (2005). The causal impact of rape myth acceptance on men's rape proclivity: Comparing sexually coercive and noncoercive men. *European Journal of Social Psychology, 35*(6), 819–828. doi: 10.1002/ejsp.284

Bumby, K. M. (1996). Assessing the cognitive distortions of child molesters and rapists: Developments and validation of the MOLEST and RAPE scales. *Sexual Abuse: A Journal of Research and Treatment, 8*, 37–54. doi: 10.1007/bf02258015

Burt, M. R. (1980). Cultural myths and supports for rape. *Journal of Personality and Social Psychology, 38*(2), 217–230. doi: 10.1037/0022-3514.38.2.217

Burton, D., Demuynck, S., & Yoder, J. R. (2014). Executive dysfunction predicts delinquency but not characteristics of sexual aggression among adolescent sexual offenders. *Sexual Abuse: A Journal of Research and Treatment.* doi: 10.1177/1079063214556357

Cantor, J. M., Blanchard, R., Robichaud, L. K., & Christensen, B. K. (2005). Quantitative reanalysis of aggregate data on IQ in sexual offenders. *Psychological Bulletin, 131*(4), 555–568. doi: 10.1037/0033-2909.131.4.555

Cantor, J. M., Kabani, N., Christensen, B. K., Zipursky, R. B., Barbaree, H. E., Dickey, R., et al. (2008). Cerebral white matter deficiencies in pedophilic men. *Journal of Psychiatric Research, 42*(3), 167–183. doi: http://dx.doi.org/10.1016/j.jpsychires.2007.10.013

Cantor, J. M., Kuban, M. E., Blak, T., Klassen, P. E., Dickey, R., & Blanchard, R. (2007). Physical height in pedophilic and hebephilic sexual offenders. *Sexual Abuse: A Journal of Research and Treatment, 19*(4), 395–407. doi: 10.1177/1079063207019004 05

Chivers, M. L., Seto, M. C., Lalumière, M. L., Laan, E., & Grimbos, T. (2010). Agreement of self-reported and genital measures of sexual arousal in men and women: A meta-analysis. *Archives of Sexual Behavior, 39*(1), 5–56. doi: 10.1007/s10508-009-9556-9

Copello, A. G., & Tata, P. R. (1990). Violent behaviour and interpretative bias: An experimental study of the resolution of ambiguity in violent offenders. *British Journal of Clinical Psychology, 29*(4), 417–428. doi: 10.1111/j.2044-8260.1990.tb00905.x

Crick, N. R., & Dodge, K. A. (1994). A review and reformulation of social information-processing mechanisms in children's social adjustment. *Psychological Bulletin, 115*(1), 74–101. doi: 10.1037/0033-2909.115.1.74

Dykas, M. J., & Cassidy, J. (2011). Attachment and the processing of social information across the life span: Theory and evidence. *Psychological Bulletin, 137*(1), 19.

Elsegood, K. J., & Duff, S. C. (2010). Theory of mind in men who have sexually offended against children: A U.K. Comparison study between child sex offenders and nonoffender controls. *Sexual Abuse: Journal of Research and Treatment*, 22(1), 112–131. doi: 10.1177/1079063209359926

Eysenck, M. W., & Keane, M. T. (2010). *Cognitive psychology: A student's handbook* (6th ed.). London: Taylor & Francis.

Fazio, R. L., Lykins, A. D., & Cantor, J. M. (2014). Elevated rates of atypical handedness in paedophilia: Theory and implications. *Laterality: Asymmetries of Body, Brain and Cognition*, 19(6), 690–704. doi: 10.1080/1357650X.2014.898648

Gannon, T. A., Hoare, J. A., Rose, M. R., & Parrett, N. (2010). A re-examination of female child molesters' implicit theories: Evidence of female specificity? *Psychology, Crime & Law*, 1–16. doi: 10.1080/10683161003752303

Gannon, T. A., Keown, K., & Rose, M. R. (2009). An examination of current psychometric assessments of child molesters' offense-supportive beliefs using Ward's implicit theories. *International Journal of Offender Therapy and Comparative Criminology*, 53(3), 316–333. doi: 10.1177/0306624x07312791

Gannon, T. A., & Polaschek, D. L. L. (2006). Cognitive distortions in child molesters: A re-examination of key theories and research. *Clinical Psychology Review*, 26(8), 1000–1019. doi: 10.1016/j.cpr.2005.11.010

Gannon, T. A., & Rose, M. R. (2009). Offense-related interpretative bias in female child molesters: A preliminary study. *Sexual Abuse: A Journal of Research and Treatment*, 21(2), 194–207. doi: 10.1177/1079063209332236

Gannon, T. A., Wright, D. B., Beech, A. R., & Williams, S. (2006). Do child molesters hold distorted beliefs? What does their memory recall tell us? *Journal of Sexual Aggression*, 12(1), 5–18. doi: 10.1080/13552600500451655

Gould, F., Clarke, J., Heim, C., Harvey, P. D., Majer, M., & Nemeroff, C. B. (2012). The effects of child abuse and neglect on cognitive functioning in adulthood. *Journal of Psychiatric Research*, 46(4), 500–506. doi: 10.1016/j.jpsychires.2012.01.005

Greenwald, A. G., McGhee, D. E., & Schwartz, J. L. K. (1998). Measuring individual differences in implicit cognition: The implicit association test. *Journal of Personality and Social Psychology*, 74(6), 1464–1480.

Hanson, R. K., & Scott, H. (1995). Assessing perspective-taking among sexual offenders, nonsexual criminals, and nonoffenders. *Sexual Abuse: A Journal of Research and Treatment*, 7(4), 259–277. doi: 10.1177/107906329500700403

Happé, F., & Frith, U. (1996). Theory of mind and social impairment in children with conduct disorder. *British Journal of Developmental Psychology*, 14(4), 385–398. doi: 10.1111/j.2044-835X.1996.tb00713.x

Imhoff, R., Schmidt, A. F., Nordsiek, U., Luzar, C., Young, A. W., & Banse, R. (2010). Viewing time effects revisited: Prolonged response latencies for sexually attractive targets under restricted task conditions. *Archives of Sexual Behavior*, 39(6), 1275–1288. doi: 10.1007/s10508-009-9595-2

Kahneman, D. (2011). *Thinking, fast and slow*. London: Penguin Books.

Keenan, T., & Ward, T. (2000). A theory of mind perspective on cognitive, affective, and intimacy deficits in child sexual offenders. *Sexual Abuse: Journal of Research and Treatment*, 12(1), 49–60. doi: 10.1177/107906320001200106

Keown, K., Gannon, T. A., & Ward, T. (2008a). The effects of visual priming on information processing in child sexual offenders. *Journal of Sexual Aggression, 14*, 145–159. doi: 10.1080/13552600802248114

Keown, K., Gannon, T. A., & Ward, T. (2008b). What were they thinking? An exploration of child sexual offenders' beliefs using a lexical decision task. *Psychology, Crime & Law, 14*(4), 317–337. doi: 10.1080/10683160701770112

Keown, K., Gannon, T. A., & Ward, T. (2010). What's in a measure? A multi-method study of child sexual offenders' beliefs. *Psychology, Crime & Law, 16*(1/2), 125–143. doi: 10.1080/10683160802622022

Lalumière, M. L., Harris, G. T., Quinsey, V. L., & Rice, M. E. (2005). *The causes of rape: Understanding individual differences in male propensity for sexual aggression*. Washington, DC: American Psychological Association.

Långström, N., Babchishin, K. M., Fazel, S., Lichtenstein, P., & Frisell, T. (2015). Sexual offending runs in families: A 37-year nationwide study. *International Journal of Epidemiology, 44*(2), 713–720. doi: 10.1093/ije/dyv029

Lee, V., & Hoaken, P. N. (2007). Cognition, emotion, and neurobiological development: mediating the relation between maltreatment and aggression. *Child Maltreatment, 12*(3), 281–298.

Lyn, T. S., & Burton, D. L. (2005). Attachment, anger and anxiety of male sexual offenders. *Journal of Sexual Aggression, 11*(2), 127–137. doi: 10.1080/13552600500063682

Mann, R., & Beech, A. (2003). Cognitive distortions, schemas, and implicit theories. In T. Ward, D. R. Laws & S. M. Hudson (Eds.), *Sexual deviance: Issues and controversies* (pp. 135–153). London: Sage.

Marsa, F., O'Reilly, G., Carr, A., Murphy, P., O'Sullivan, M., Cotter, A., et al. (2004). Attachment styles and psychological profiles of child sex offenders in Ireland. *Journal of Interpersonal Violence, 19*(2), 228–251. doi: 10.1177/0886260503260328

Marshall, W. L. (2010). The role of attachments, intimacy, and loneliness in the etiology and maintenance of sexual offending. *Sexual and Relationship Therapy, 25*(1), 73–85. doi: 10.1080/14681990903550191

Marshall, W. L., & Barbaree, H. E. (1990). An integrated theory of the etiology of sexual offending. In W. L. Marshall, D. R. Laws & H. E. Barbaree (Eds.), *Handbook of sexual assault: Issues, theories, and treatment of the offender.* (pp. 257–275). New York: Plenum Press.

Marshall, W. L., & Marshall, L. E. (2000). The origins of sexual offending. *Trauma, Violence, & Abuse, 1*(3), 250–263. doi: 10.1177/1524838000001003003

Maruna, S., & Mann, R. E. (2006). A fundamental attribution error? Rethinking cognitive distortions. *Legal and Criminological Psychology, 11*(2), 155–177. doi: 10.1348/135532506X114608

Marziano, V., Ward, T., Beech, A. R., & Pattison, P. (2006). Identification of five fundamental implicit theories underlying cognitive distortions in child abusers: A preliminary study. *Psychology, Crime & Law, 12*(1), 97–105. doi: 10.1080/10683160500056887

McPhail, I. V., Hermann, C. A., & Nunes, K. L. (2013). Emotional congruence with children and sexual offending against children: A meta-analytic review. *Journal of Consulting and Clinical Psychology, 81*(4), 737–749. doi: 10.1037/a0033248

Mihailides, S., Devilly, G. J., & Ward, T. (2004). Implicit cognitive distortions and sexual offending. *Sexual Abuse: A Journal of Research and Treatment, 16*(4), 333–350. doi: 10.1023/B:SEBU.0000043327.10168.5b

Mikulincer, M., & Shaver, P. R. (2010). *Attachment in adulthood: Structure, dynamics, and change.* New York: Guilford Press.

Nee, C., & Ward, T. (2015). Review of expertise and its general implications for correctional psychology and criminology. *Aggression and Violent Behavior, 20,* 1–9. doi: 10.1016/j.avb.2014.12.002

Neidigh, L., & Krop, H. (1992). Cognitive distortions among child sexual offenders. *Journal of Sex Education and Therapy, 18,* 208–215.

Nunes, K. L., Firestone, P., & Baldwin, M. W. (2007). Indirect assessment of cognitions of child sexual abusers with the Implicit Association Test. *Criminal Justice and Behavior, 34*(4), 454–475. doi: 10.1177/0093854806291703

Ó Ciardha, C. (2011). A theoretical framework for understanding deviant sexual interest and cognitive distortions as overlapping constructs contributing to sexual offending against children. *Aggression and Violent Behavior, 16*(6), 493–502. doi: 10.1016/j.avb.2011.05.001

Ó Ciardha, C., & Ward, T. (2013). Theories of cognitive distortions in sexual offending: What the current research tells us. *Trauma, Violence, & Abuse, 14*(1), 5–21. doi: 10.1177/1524838012467856

Ogloff, J. R., Cutajar, M. C., Mann, E., Mullen, P., Wei, F. T. Y. et al. (2012). Child sexual abuse and subsequent offending and victimisation: A 45 year follow-up study. *Trends and Issues in Crime and Criminal Justice.* Canberra: Australian Institute of Criminology.

Polaschek, D. L. L., & Gannon, T. A. (2004). The implicit theories of rapists: What convicted offenders tell us. *Sexual Abuse: A Journal of Research and Treatment, 16*(4), 299–314. doi: 10.1023/B:SEBU.0000043325.94302.40

Seto, M. C. (2008). *Pedophilia and sexual offending against children: Theory, assessment, and intervention.* Washington, DC: American Psychological Association.

Seto, M. C. (2012). Is pedophilia a sexual orientation? *Archives of Sexual Behavior, 41*(1), 231–236.

Seto, M. C., & Lalumière, M. L. (2010). What is so special about male adolescent sexual offending? A review and test of explanations through meta-analysis. *Psychological Bulletin, 136*(4), 526.

Smallbone, S., & Dadds, M. R. (1998). Childhood attachment and adult attachment in incarcerated adult male sex offenders. *Journal of Interpersonal Violence, 13*(5), 555–573. doi: 10.1177/088626098013005001

Spiering, M., & Everaerd, W. (2007). The sexual unconscious. In E. Janssen (Ed.), *The psychophysiology of sex.* (pp. 166–184). Bloomington, IN: Indiana University Press.

Ward, T. (2000). Sexual offenders' cognitive distortions as implicit theories. *Aggression and Violent Behavior, 5*(5), 491–507. doi: 10.1016/S1359-1789(98)00036-6

Ward, T. (2014). The explanation of sexual offending: From single factor theories to integrative pluralism. *Journal of Sexual Aggression, 20*(2), 130–141. doi: http://dx.doi.org/10.1080/13552600.2013.870242

Ward, T., & Beech, A. (2006). An integrated theory of sexual offending. *Aggression and Violent Behavior, 11*(1), 44–63. doi: 10.1016/j.avb.2005.05.002

Ward, T., Gannon, T. A., & Keown, K. (2006). Beliefs, values, and action: The judgment model of cognitive distortions in sexual offenders. *Aggression and Violent Behavior, 11*(4), 323–340. doi: 10.1016/j.avb.2005.10.003

Ward, T., & Keenan, T. (1999). Child molesters' implicit theories. *Journal of Interpersonal Violence, 14*(8), 821–838. doi: 10.1177/088626099014008003

Zou, Z., Meng, H., Ma, Z., Deng, W., Du, L. et al. (2013). Executive functioning deficits and childhood trauma in juvenile violent offenders in China. *Psychiatry Research, 207*(3), 218–224. doi: http://dx.doi.org/10.1016/j.psychres.2012.09.013

4

Bridging the Cognitive–Emotion Divide

Empathy and Sexual Offending

Sarah J. Brown

As you begin to read this chapter, you probably have a clear idea as to the characteristics and nature of empathy. Take a moment before you proceed further to *define* empathy, that is, to explain clearly exactly what you think it is. Now think about whether your definition addresses the following questions and in light of these questions whether you wish to modify your definition. Does empathy include thoughts, feelings or both? Do the thoughts and/or feelings of the empathiser have to be identical to those of the empathisee? If yes, what if the empathisee is unconscious or fictional? If no, what is the relationship between the two? Does empathy relate to positive feelings/experiences (i.e., can you have empathy for someone's joy or good fortune?) and/or negative experiences? How does empathy differ from similar concepts such as sympathy, altruism and compassion? To what extent is empathy an automatic response or a response that is managed and/or controlled? Does empathy have to result in a behavioural outcome of some sort? Does empathy vary between individuals? If empathy is a trait, do individuals apply the same levels of empathy to all individuals/situations? If not, what factors lead to the variations in levels of empathy?

If you struggled with this task, you are not alone. Empathy has been the subject of psychological attention since the term 'empathy' was adapted from the German word *Einfühlung* ('in-feeling', or 'feeling-into') by Titchener (1911, see Wispé, 1986) and discussions of the concept appear to date back to early philosophical thought (Stotland, Matthews, Sherman, Hansson & Richardson, 1978). Nevertheless, there remains little consensus about how the construct should be defined and operationalized (Day, Casey & Gerace, 2010). It has been suggested that there are as many definitions of empathy as there are authors in the field (Decety & Jackson, 2004; de Vignemont & Singer, 2006). These definitional difficulties have led to a lack of a shared understanding about the concept that is difficult to resolve.

Sexual Offending: Cognition, Emotion and Motivation, First Edition.
Edited by Theresa A. Gannon and Tony Ward.
© 2017 John Wiley & Sons Ltd. Published 2017 by John Wiley & Sons Ltd.

What is Empathy?

In order to try to identify some consensus in the definitional confusion regarding the concept of empathy, Cuff (see, Cuff, Brown, Taylor & Howat, 2016) reviewed 43 discrete definitions of empathy, identifying eight ways in which definitions varied. The extent to which empirical evidence provided support for the variations was also examined to develop the following definition of empathy:

> Empathy is an emotional response (affective), dependent upon the interaction between trait capacities and state influences. Empathic processes are automatically elicited but are also shaped by top-down control processes. The resulting emotion is similar to one's perception (directly experienced or imagined) and understanding (cognitive empathy) of the stimulus emotion, with recognition that the source of the emotion is not one's own. (p. 7)

The distinction between empathy and sympathy is often not clear but it has been argued that the two concepts are distinct (see Cuff et al., 2016), which is supported by neurological functional magnetic resonance imaging (fMRI) research (Decety & Michalska, 2010). Hein and Singer (2008) suggested that the distinction was 'feeling *as*' in empathy and 'feeling *for* the other' in sympathy (p. 157; emphasis in original). Put simply, observing anger in another would invoke an empathic response of feelings of anger but a sympathetic response of feelings of concern. It is interesting to note that much of the theoretical and empirical work in relation to offending and sexual offending refers almost exclusively to *empathy*; yet in many instances discussions could perhaps refer to terms such as sympathy or other constructs to ensure greater consistency and clarity. For example, Barnett and Mann (2013a, p. 23; see also Barnett & Mann, 2013b, p. 229) stated: 'Even if someone acts in an *empathic manner*, this will not necessarily be motivated by the experience of empathy but could be ethically driven, out of a sense of duty' (emphasis added). Hanson (2003) referred to the conditions required for sympathetic responses in his conceptual model of empathy and stated that: 'Rather than increasing the extent to which offenders absorb and reflect the emotions of others (emotional contagion), most clinicians want offenders to develop feelings of compassion or caring, that is, genuine sympathy' (p. 15). This is an important point to consider in relation to treatment goals (and will be returned to later in this chapter), but the mix between the use of the terms 'empathy' and 'sympathy' is confusing and Hanson's model (see later in the chapter) might be better labelled as a model of sympathy.

Theories of Empathy

It has become common to describe empathy as a process (or model) with a number of interlinked 'sub-processes' or stages. However, this approach is not without its problems since there are disagreements as to the 'sub-processes' that should be included and whether or not 'stages' have to be progressed in a particular linear order.

Multi-Dimensional Model of Empathy: Davis (1994)

This is generally one of the most frequently cited models of empathy. In developing this multi-dimensional model, Davis synthesised previous theory and research and so readers should refer to the original publication to gain a full understanding of the model's complexities. The model has four components: antecedents, processes, intrapersonal outcomes and interpersonal outcomes. These are linked unidirectionally, however, processes and intrapersonal outcomes are not necessarily required. Antecedents relate to the dispositional tendencies of the empathiser (e.g., for perspective taking and emotional responses), the situation (e.g., the emotion valence) and the similarity between the empathiser and empathisee. Davis argued that the level of cognitive activity in which the empathiser engages determines the types of process involved from: 'non-cognitive' (e.g., motor mimicry), 'simple cognitive' (e.g., classical conditioning) to 'advanced cognitive' (e.g., role-taking). Interpersonal outcomes are affective responses that are 'parallel' where the empathiser experiences the same/similar emotions as the empathisee, or 'reactive' where the responses are different from the empathisee. Since the reactive affective outcomes are not the same feelings as those of the empathisee, the model includes empathy *and* sympathy. Non-affective outcomes are also included, such as accuracy in inferences about the empathisee's perspective. Interpersonal outcomes are helping, altruism and aggression.

Four Stage Model: Marshall, Hudson, Jones and Fernandez (1995)

This model was developed specifically to explain the role of empathy (or lack thereof) in sexual offending. The four linear stages are: (1) recognition of another person's emotional state; (2) an ability to perceive the world from that person's point of view; (3) an ability to replicate the emotional state of the other person; and (4) a change in behaviour toward the other person. This model was criticized by Pithers (1999) who reasoned that it could not explain a bystander's response to an endangered person who is unconscious, as the unconscious person would have no emotional response to recognise or replicate. Thus, Pithers argued the bystander would be left feel nothing and would thus do nothing for the person in danger. However, perhaps in such instances it could be argued that sympathy, or simply acting out of a sense of duty or respect for human life (Barnett & Mann, 2013a, b), motivates a positive reaction to this situation. Polaschek (2003) argued that the first stage is unnecessary as we are able to feel empathy for someone who may be masking how they feel, and Barnett and Mann (2013a, b) argued that empathy could be felt retrospectively or for an unseen person.

A Conceptual Model of Empathy Deficits of Sexual Offenders: Hanson (2003)

Hanson pointed out that although we tend to think that it is unusual to take pleasure in the suffering of others, most of us react positively to another's suffering when the other is an enemy (e.g., theatre crowds cheer when bad guys are killed).

We all have different attitudes towards others, or towards the same individual at various times. Thus, Hanson suggested a model of empathy (that overlaps somewhat with sympathy) containing four related components: (1) the *relationship* between the empathiser and empathisee; (2) the empathiser's *perspective taking* ability; (3) the empathiser's ability to *cope* with the perceived distress of the empathisee; and (4) the resulting *response*, which could be 'sympathestic' (i.e., caring or compassionate), unhelpful (e.g., withdrawal or avoidance) or antisocial (anger, vengeance or sexual excitement). Even when the relationship is non-hostile and the suffering has been accurately perceived, Hanson argued that people do not always react with compassion.

Model of the Empathic Process: Barnett and Mann (2013a, b)

Following a review and critique of conceptualizations of empathy, Barnett and Mann (2013a, b) proposed that empathic processing in sexual offending involves (or more accurately fails to involve) five key factors: (1) perspective taking; (2) the ability to experience emotion; (3) a belief that others are worthy of compassion and respect; (4) the application of the previous cognitive and affective processes to a specific situation in which another is distressed; and (5) an ability to manage angry feelings of personal distress. Although Barnett and Mann (2013b) stated that the model was 'non-staged', their diagrams and explanation of how the processes could be disrupted in sexual offending imply a staged process from the situation, through to cognitive processes, then an emotional response and ultimately a behavioural response. Barnett and Mann stressed that all of the factors must be present 'for empathy to prevent someone from offending' (2013a, p. 27) and stated that sexual offending can, in part, be explained by problems in one or more of these factors (2013b).

Theory of Altruism and Empathy: Ward and Durrant (2013)

Hanson (2003) argued that the implicit goal of victim-empathy training should be to increase sympathy, rather than empathy, for others, and he referred to sympathetic responses (compassion, pity tenderness). This argument has similarities with that of Ward and Durrant's (2013): 'In our view, what matters from a treatment perspective is that offenders *act* towards others in an altruistic manner, rather than that they *feel* empathic.' (p. 67, emphasis in original). Ward and Durrant were inspired by the ethical theory of Kitcher (2010, 2011), who posited that *biological altruism* occurs when an individual prioritises his/her own needs. Kitcher contended that an individual engages in *psychological altruism* when he/she adjusts his/her actions to take account of the needs and desires of others. To avoid *altruism failure*, Kitcher argued that ethical norms are important to prompt people to behave altruistically, even if they are disinclined to do so. Accordingly, Ward and Durrant argued that work to reduce sexual offending should be focused on avoiding altruism failure. Underpinned by a multi-dimensional approach, Ward and Durrant reiterated Kitcher's five dimensions, or ways in which individuals act that result in altruism failure: (1) *intensity* – desires are not restrained; (2) *range* – some individuals are not seen as being worthy of altruism; (3) *scope* – cognitive, emotional, social, environmental and physiological factors lead to a lack of altruism in certain contexts; (4) *discernment* – the consequences of actions are not determined; and (5) *empathic skill* – lack of skills in determining the mental states of others. Ward and Durrant argued that the framework they derived from Kitcher's theory could be mapped onto Barnett and Mann's five factors, with the exception of intensity.

Evaluation

All of the above models include interpersonal outcomes or behavioural responses as the final 'stage'. This approach has been criticised by Polaschek (2003) who argued that there are a range of reasons why someone might not act as a result of empathy, such as competing interests and situational factors. As we have seen, there may be a range of motivations for 'positive' responses and it might be difficult to determine the motivation for a particular behaviour. Furthermore, some individuals may be able to accurately identify the suffering of others and yet be indifferent to it, or even attracted to it (e.g., for sadistic reasons; Hanson & Scott, 1995). It has been argued (e.g., de Vignemont & Singer, 2006; Eisenberg et al., 1994) and supported experimentally (Lishner, Batson & Huss, 2011) that behaviour is evoked by empathy only when it is mediated through sympathy, suggesting a more complex link between these two concepts than is captured in the models above.

Empirical Evidence

Link Between Empathy and Negative Behaviours

Although empathy is causally related to prosocial behaviour supporting an empathy–altruism hypothesis (Piliavin & Charng, 1990), the link between empathy and altruism is far from simple, as demonstrated by Kitcher, Ward and Durrant. More importantly in relation to sexual aggression, empathy's role in limiting negative behaviours (i.e., offending) is much less clear. Farrington (2007) argued that people are less likely to victimize others if they can appreciate and/or experience the others' feelings. This has some empirical support in that empathy has been negatively related to aggression and antisocial behaviour (Kaukiainen et al., 1999; Miller & Eisenberg, 1988). However, these studies are generally correlational and so do not demonstrate that low empathy *causes* negative behaviours.

Van Langen, Wissink, van Vugt, Van der Stouwe and Stams (2014) conducted a meta-analysis of 38 studies in which groups of individuals convicted of offences (total $n = 3098$) were compared to individuals with no convictions (total $n = 3533$). The convicted groups had lower levels of cognitive empathy (note that not all studies included assessments of both cognitive and affective empathy) regardless of which type of meta-analytic technique (random or fixed effect) was used and lower levels of affective empathy only when the fixed effect method was used. Given that a random effect analysis is more appropriate for these independent studies, this suggests that affective empathy is not related to offending.

A number of factors (e.g., year of publication, measure of empathy used) were related to the strength and direction of the findings, which limits reliability and validity.

Link Between Empathy and Sexual Offending

In relation to individuals convicted of sexual offences, van Langen and colleagues (2014) found no differences compared to other samples for cognitive empathy. For affective empathy, studies that included individuals convicted of sexual offences specifically produced small negative effect sizes (i.e., the opposite effect to that expected). Furthermore, a link between empathy and sexual offence recidivism has not been supported in meta-analyses (Hanson & Bussière, 1996, 1998; Hanson & Morton-Bourgon, 2004, 2005). However, doubts have been raised about the reliability, validity, quality and variability of the measures of empathy used in empirical studies (see Mann & Barnett, 2013 and the discussion later in this chapter).

Empathy is a complex construct and it could be that individuals who perpetrate sexual offences have difficulties in only some specific areas, for example perspective taking (see Gerace, Day, Casey & Mohr, 2013) or emotion recognition. Hudson, Marshall, Wales and McDonald (1993) discovered that men who had sexually offended were deficient in recognizing emotions in others, especially anger, disgust, surprise and fear (see also Stermac & Segal, 1989). An inability to recognize facial expression (Lisak & Ivan, 1995) and misinterpretation of fear as passivity (McFall, 1990) has been identified in this population. Yet very little attention has been paid to the *recognition* of emotions/distress in others and the development of such deficits (see Covell & Scalora, 2002 for a review). Moreover, this concept has not featured prominently in treatment programmes, perhaps because it is difficult to know how to improve this aspect, or even if it can be improved. Such difficulties might be related to developmental problems and in formulating Theory of Mind (ToM; see Keenan & Ward 2000; Ward, Keenan & Hudson, 2000). ToM deficits have been identified in individuals convicted of child sexual offences or rape (Castellino et al., 2011; Elsegood & Duff, 2010) and it is likely that the identification of the neural networks of cognitive and affective empathy/ToM (e.g., Kalbe et al., 2010; Shamay-Tsoory, Aharon-Peretz & Perry, 2009) will lead to more progress in our understanding of the development of ToM and empathy.

Victim Specific Empathy and Sex Offending

When discussing empathy in relation to offending, we have tended to take a simplistic *trait* view of empathy, in that it is supposed that those committing harmful behaviours towards others have empathy deficits that apply at all times, in all situations and to all people. Early work in relation to sexual offending focused on generalized empathy deficits producing little empirical support to suggest *trait* or generalized empathy deficits in adults or adolescents who have engaged in harmful sexual behaviours (Cohen et al., 2002; Hosser & Bosold, 2006; Marshall, Jones, Hudson & McDonald, 1993; Monto, Zgourides & Harris, 1998; Moriarty et al., 2001). While there may be some individuals who demonstrate such widespread empathy deficits (e.g., psychopaths may have *trait* deficits in affective empathy; Blair, 2005), many individuals display 'normal' levels of empathy towards many people (e.g., members of their family, their peers), but appear to have no empathy towards their victims. This would suggest that empathy is *state* and situation specific; a view in keeping with the models outlined earlier in this Chapter but one that is often overlooked in discussions of individuals who have offended, and particularly those who have offended sexually.

In a small number of studies, researchers have compared levels of empathy for unnamed/unspecified victims of sexual offences between men who have committed sexual offences and a range of comparison groups (Hanson & Scott, 1995; Hennessy, Walter & Vess, 2002; McGrath, Cann & Konopasky, 1998; Rice, Chaplin, Harris & Coutts, 1994; Wood & Riggs, 2008). The findings are inconsistent but in general men who have committed sexual offences demonstrated lower levels of empathy. There is more consistent evidence that such individuals show lower levels of empathy for their own victims, compared to unnamed/unspecified victims and/or other individuals (e.g., victims of car accidents; Buschman et al., 2008; Fernandez & Marshall, 2003; Fernandez, Marshall, Lightbody & O'Sullivan, 1999; Scully, 1988; Teuma, Smith, Stewart & Lee, 2003; Webster & Beech, 2000). Fernandez and colleagues (1999), for example, found that men who had sexually abused children were as empathic as non-offending individuals towards children in general, but reported lower levels of empathy towards their own victims.

These findings may indicate that apparent deficits in empathy are related to cognitions about the individuals and/or situations at the time of the offences (Marshall, Hamilton & Ferdinand, 2001). Evidence shows that individuals convicted of sexual offences frequently fail to appreciate the harm that they have inflicted on their victims, blame their victims for the offences, and interpret victims' behaviour as provocative (see Ó Ciardha, Chapter 3 in this volume). The assumption has been that this is a demonstration of a lack of empathy (Brown, Harkins & Beech, 2012); however, this assumption is problematic. If, for example, an individual believes that another person wishes to engage in sexual behaviour and/or that the sexual behaviour is not harmful, then there is no 'negative' act for which the individual needs to feel empathy (see, Brown, Walker, Gannon & Keown, 2013). Individuals with these thoughts in relation to harmful sexual behaviours might be displaying offence supportive cognitions (see Chapter 3 in this volume) but they are not necessarily displaying empathy deficits. There is some, albeit limited, empirical support for this view. Webster and Beech (2000) found that the total scores derived from the 'victim letters' that were written during treatment programmes correlated with psychometric measures of offence supportive beliefs; yet did not correlate with general measures of empathy. Marshall and colleagues (2001) found that empathy levels towards victims were correlated with offence supportive beliefs. The impact of cognitions on empathy is reflected to some extent in the models discussed earlier in the chapter. These models imply that improving empathy will have no impact on future behaviours if the cognitions remain unchanged.

If empathy is best considered a *state* construct, we need to be able to determine why an individual 'applies' empathy in some situations compared to others.

Further, empathy 'deficits' are most likely to take place when emotional precursors (e.g., anger, anxiety) are present (Pithers, 1999). Yet, research that examines empathy in the presence of different emotions amongst those who have committed sexual offences has not been conducted. The implications of *state* empathy are surprisingly under-researched and the potential 'inhibitor' effects of empathy tend to be considered only in relation to offending. This has resulted in the assumption that the empathic processes of individuals who have committed offences are different to 'normal' populations; yet it is clear that we are all capable of inflicting harm on others in certain circumstances and situations (see for example, Walker & Brown, 2013). Moreover, Pithers (1999) pointed out that recognizing empathy is an inadequate treatment goal if an individual only understands/feels empathy once the offence has been committed. For empathy to have a role in the avoidance of negative behaviours, it is reliant on an individual *anticipating* the pain that the other will feel as a result of his/her actions, or perhaps understanding/feeling empathy at an early stage in the offence process and immediately halting the behaviour. This means that it is difficult to identify when empathy has had an impact on behaviour, as the originally *intended* or *planned* behaviour does not take place, which is clearly not possible to observe.

Evidence for the Efficacy of Interventions to Develop Empathy

Evaluations of programmes that aim to enhance empathy in sex offending populations have produced mixed results (Beech, Fisher & Beckett, 1999; Brown et al. 2012; Marshall, Champagne, Brown & Miller, 1997; Pithers, 1994; Ricci, Clayton & Shapiro, 2006; Schewe & O'Donohue, 1993; Wakeling, Beech & Freemantle, 2013; Wastell, Cairns & Haywood, 2009). Most programmes target a range of goals and it is unusual for specific treatment targets (e.g., increasing empathy) to be evaluated specifically, resulting in a dearth of information about the overall treatment impact of each treatment component. A review of the mean empathy scores of individuals attending interventions aimed at improving empathy in sexually violent offenders (Day et al., 2010) did not demonstrate markedly low empathy levels. Clearly it will be difficult to substantially improve empathy in individuals who do not have empathy problems.

Females

Almost all published studies to date in which the link between empathy and sexual offending has been examined have been conducted on men (see Blagden, Lievesley & Ware, Chapter 5 in this volume, or Gannon & Alleyne, 2013, for descriptions of unpublished studies). Elliott, Eldridge, Ashfield & Beech (2010) used file review to examine whether empathy deficits were present in females. However, the sample numbers were small making conclusions difficult. More generally, van Langen and colleagues (2014) found larger effect sizes in men compared to women in their meta-analysis examining empathy in individuals who had, or had not committed offences, but only four studies included women (some of these included men and women), compared to 26 that only included men; hence, it is not possible to draw conclusions about empathy in females given the extremely limited evidence base.

Assessments

A number of measures of empathy exist that essentially measure different things. Some seem to assess affective empathy (the Impulsiveness–Venturesome–Empathy Scale, Eysenck & Eysenck, 1978; the Index of Empathy for Children and Adolescents/Bryant Empathy Index, Bryant, 1982; the Questionnaire Measure of Emotional Empathy, Mehrabian & Epstein, 1972), while others assess cognitive empathy (the Hogan Empathy Scale, Hogan, 1969). Davis (1980, 1983) developed his Interpersonal Reactivity Index (IRI) in line with his model of empathy with four subscales: perspective-taking (cognitive empathy), empathy concern (affective empathy), fantasy and personal distress. Jolliffe and Farrington (2004) argued that the latter two subscales are not appropriate to measure empathy and it has been difficult to determine whether increases or decreases in these subscales would be expected following successful treatment. The Basic Empathy Scale (Jolliffe & Farrington, 2006) consists of cognitive and affective empathy subscales.

There are a range of other problems with these measures. For example, the reliability and validity of these measures has been challenged (e.g., Blake & Gannon, 2008; Chlopan, McCain, Carbonell & Hagen, 1985; Tierney & McCabe, 2001). Measures also rely on self-report and it is unclear whether individuals are able to reliably report their own empathic abilities. Additionally, measures are very transparent and it might be possible for individuals to identify the 'correct' answers, particularly after intervention (see Webster, 2000; cited in Webster et al., 2004).

A more fundamental issue is that current 'general' measures can only possibly assess a very simplistic construct of 'empathy'. For example, they are premised on the assumption that we apply empathy equally to all people. Consequently, we have no idea how individuals have been responding to measures of empathy and the way in which individuals respond may be dependent on the group that is most salient at the time of responding. Furthermore, individuals respond differently to similar people who are in different situations (see Fernandez et al., 1999), and current measures of empathy do not take into account the range of cognitive factors that influence whether empathy may be applied to an individual or not. A range of factors influence the likelihood of whether someone could be considered to be worthy of empathy, generally, or in a specific context. Cuff (2015) recently developed a tool that includes measures of empathy, sympathy and nine cognition subscales. A number of studies were conducted with students and community samples that revealed a complex interplay of the cognition sub-scales with both empathy and sympathy. Cognitive empathy and similarity had a direct influence on empathy, with morality and self-interest having a direct influence on sympathy. Valuing and perceived need had a direct influence on both empathy and sympathy. These cognitions were in turn influenced by agency, blame and perceived power. This measure requires further development with individuals who have committed offences but should enable us to more clearly understand the role of cognitions on empathy and sympathy.

There is clearly a need in sexual offending research to use and develop methods of assessment that are less transparent than current measures, with good reliability and validity. Ickes and colleagues (see Ickes, 1993, 2003), for example, developed an interpersonal interaction methodology that has been adapted and used in neuroscience research. This method could be used with offending populations, particularly, since it might be possible to produce ethically acceptable recordings that mirror offending type interactions. Measures that have been used to assess ToM could also be considered (see Castellino et al., 2011). For example, the Reading of the Mind in the Eyes Test (Baron-Cohen et al., 2001) in which participants are asked to select a mental state (from a choice of four) from pictures of the eye region of adults' faces. Elsegood and Duff (2010) found that community-based individuals convicted of child sexual offences performed more poorly than community controls on this task. Dael, Mortillaro and Scherer (2012) coded a range of body positions involved in emotional expression, which may enable the development of similar measures not focused solely on the eyes, which might be important in sexual offending.

Practical Implications

Despite all these difficulties, the limited research that has been conducted to explore treatment users' views of interventions appears to indicate that the 'empathy' component is very impactful (Beech et al., 1999; Levenson, Macgowan, Morin & Cotter, 2009; Levenson & Prescott, 2009; Wakeling, Webster & Mann, 2005). Given the equivocal evidence discussed earlier in the chapter, particularly the limited findings in respect of programmes leading to increased empathic capabilities, these findings are difficult to understand and have been the subject of much discussion. One possible explanation is that to date we have not reliably assessed/measured empathy and/or changes have been too subtle to detect with crude self-report measures.

Another plausible explanation is that the tasks completed in the empathy component of interventions have an impact but not on empathy per se. Perhaps the frequent finding that men who have attended treatment find the 'empathy' component most impactful is further evidence that men who commit sexual offences generally do not have empathy deficits, though it is, of course, entirely possible that some men do have such deficits, while others do not. It is possible that appreciating the impact of sexual abuse increases the motivation in men to want to change, and/or helps to engage them in the difficult process of change. Perhaps such activities help to ensure that individuals who are potential victims are viewed as worthy of compassion and respect (as in Barnett and Mann's model) or influence the range and scope of situations in which altruism is applied (as in Ward and Durrant's model). Hence, it could be argued that it is the *cognitions* that are primarily influenced, rather than individuals' abilities to understand or feel others' emotions, although the result is that empathy is applied more widely in future.

Concern has been raised that individuals attending treatment might experience the negative emotions associated with engaging in victim empathy tasks as punishment. Being faced with the negative consequences of their offences could powerfully encourage men to change. Conversely, this might induce or increase feelings of shame and therefore be counter-therapeutic. Shame has been linked to a lack of empathy, aggression and a range of risk factors for criminal recidivism (see Tangney, Stuewig & Hafez, 2011, for a review). The propensity to feel guilt, on the other hand, seems to be a protective factor (Tangney et al., 2011) and so it is important to empirically determine whether efforts to influence empathy induces/increases shame or guilt, and how this impacts on recidivism.

What is clear is that treatment providers have not so far been specific enough in relation to their models of change in respect of empathy. Roys (1997) argued that a lack of understanding of the mechanisms of empathy has resulted in a situation where it is unclear exactly what we are asking people to do when we talk about developing empathy. It is becoming increasingly apparent that we need to be more specific in terms of whether we want individuals to be able to: identify distress in others more effectively; apply empathy to a broader range of individuals; apply it in a broader range of settings; understand others better; feel the emotions of others more effectively; apply empathy regardless of their own moods; predict the feelings of others to ensure that 'risky' situations are avoided and so on. Some of these 'goals' might be easier to influence than others and changes in only some of these might be sufficient to reduce offending. Hence, it is important to investigate these issues further to ensure that interventions are effective and resource efficient.

Currently a one-size-fits-all approach has been applied to empathy interventions and a greater understanding of the precise nature of empathy deficits might reveal that individuals have a diverse range of difficulties, requiring individualized interventions. This necessitates a reliable measure of empathy (and/or ToM and/or potential for altruism failure) and the range of processes/factors that are involved in it.

Conclusion

The role empathy plays in sexual offending is still far from clear. Work in this area has been significantly hampered by a lack of shared agreement as to what exactly empathy is and what factors/processes it does or does not include. The relationship between empathy and other related constructs such as sympathy, compassion, altruism and ToM also need to be clarified and agreed. This has resulted in: (1) a range of theories with no obvious 'agreed' theory to guide work with those who have committed sexual offences; (2) difficultly in comparing findings across studies, particularly when researchers are unclear about the definitions and models they have used; and (3) differences in the way practitioners conceptualize empathy and, therefore, the interventions and therapeutic work delivered on the basis of these (e.g., see Mann & Barnett, 2013).

Currently there is no evidence that empathy interventions are effective; however, this could conceivably be because we have not be able to measure empathy and changes in empathy reliably. Hence, we urgently need to develop reliable measures of empathy and/or the specific elements associated with it. Those who complete programmes seem to find the empathy component powerful but as yet we cannot be clear why this is and whether this has a long-term impact on offending. It might be that empathy components in treatment programmes have had an impact on cognitions such that empathy (or altruism) is applied to a broader range of individuals and/or in a wider range of context/situations but research is needed to determine this. Given that it might be easier to change cognitions than enhance empathy related skills, greater focus is needed on the link between cognitions and empathy, and whether changes in cognition result in greater levels of empathy and lead to reductions in offending.

Decisions that have important consequences are currently made about individuals who have committed sexual offences based on measures of empathy that are unreliable, lack validity and are trait, rather than state, focused. If empathy, or specific aspects of it, are linked to offending, we have yet to identify exactly what the relationship is, and therefore our models of change in interventions are limited. Given the consequences for potential future victims, we urgently need more research, with more specific/precise measurement tools and agreed definitions to enhance our understanding further, such that we can develop interventions and reliably assess their effectiveness.

References

Barnett, G. D., & Mann, R. E. (2013a). Cognition, empathy, and sexual offending. *Trauma, Violence & Abuse, 14*, 22–33. doi: 10.1177/1524838012467857

Barnett, G. D., & Mann, R. E. (2013b). Empathy deficits and sexual offending: A model of obstacles to empathy. *Aggression and Violent Behavior, 18*, 228–239. doi: 10.1016/j.avb.2012.11.010

Baron-Cohen, S., Wheelwright, S., Hill, J., Raste, Y., & Plumb, I. (2001). The 'Reading the Mind in the Eyes' test revised version: A study with normal adults, and adults with Asperger syndrome or high-functioning autism. *Journal of Child Psychology and Psychiatry, 42*, 241–252. doi: 10.1111/1469-7610.00716

Beech, A., Fisher, D., & Beckett, R. (1999). *STEP 3: An evaluation of the Prison Sex Offender Treatment Programme (Home Office Occasional Report).* London: Home Office Publications Unit. Retrieved 15 July 2016 from http://webarchive. nationalarchives.gov.uk/20110218135832/http:/rds.homeoffice.gov.uk/rds/pdfs/ occ-step3.pdf.

Blair, R. J. R. (2005). Responding to the emotions of others: Dissociating forms of empathy through the study of typical and psychiatric populations. *Consciousness and Cognition, 14*, 698–718. doi: 10.1016/j.concog.2005.06.004

Blake, E., & Gannon, T. (2008). Social perception deficits, cognitive distortions, and empathy deficits in sex offenders. *Trauma, Violence and Abuse, 9*, 34–55. doi: 10.1177/1524838007311104

Brown, S., Harkins, L., & Beech, A. R. (2012). General and victim-specific empathy: Associations with actuarial risk, treatment outcome, and sexual recidivism. *Sexual Abuse: A Journal of Research and Treatment, 24*, 411–430. doi: 10.1177/1079063211423944

Brown, S. J., Walker, K., Gannon, T. A., & Keown, K. (2013). Developing a theory of empathy and cognitions in sex offenders. *Journal of Sexual Aggression, 19*, 275–294. doi: 10.1080/13552600.2012.747223

Buschman, J., Wilcox, D., Spreen, M., Marshall, B., & Bogaerts, S. (2008). Victim ranking among sexual offenders. *Journal of Sexual Aggression*, *14*, 45–52. doi: 10.1080/13552600701791271

Bryant, B. K. (1982). An index of empathy for children and adolescents. *Child Development*, *53*, 413–425. Retrieved 15 July 2016 from http://www.jstor.org/stable/1128984

Castellino, N., Bosco, F. M., Marshall, W. L., Marshall, L. E., & Veglia, F. (2011). Mindreading abilities in sexual offenders: Analysis of theory of mind processes. *Consciousness and Cognition*, *20*, 1612–1624. doi: 10.1016/j.concog.2011.08.011

Chlopan, B. E., McCain, M. L., Carbonell, J. L., & Hagen, R. L. (1985). Empathy: Review of available measures. *Journal of Personality and Social Psychology*, *48*, 635–653. doi: 10.1037/0022-3514.48.3.635

Cohen, L. J., McGeoch, P. G., Watras-Gans, S., Acker, S., Poznansky, O., Cullen, K., et al. (2002). Personality impairment in male pedophiles. *Journal of Clinical Psychiatry*, *63*, 912–919.Retrieved from: http://www.psychiatrist.com/jcp/article/Pages/2002/v63n10/v63n1009.aspx.

Covell, C. N., & Scalora, M. J. (2002). Empathic deficits in sexual offenders: An integration of affective, social, and cognitive constructs. *Aggression and Violent Behavior*, *7*, 251–270.Retrieved from: http://www.sciencedirect.com/science/article/pii/S1359178901000465.

Cuff, B. M. P. (2015). *The cognitive antecedents of empathic responding*. Unpublished doctoral dissertation, Coventry University, Coventry, UK.

Cuff, B. M. P., Brown, S. J., Taylor, L., & Howat, D. (2016). Empathy: A review of the concept. *Emotion Review*, *8*(2), 144–153. doi: 10.1177/1754073914558466. Retrieved from: http://emr.sagepub.com/content/early/2014/12/01/1754073914558466.

Dael, N., Mortillaro, M., & Scherer, K. R. (2012). The Body Action and Posture Coding System (BAP): Development and reliability. *Journal of Nonverbal Behavior*, *36*, 97–121. doi: 10.1007/s10919-012-0130-0

Davis, M. H. (1980). A multidimensional approach to individual differences in empathy. *JSAS Catalog of Selected Documents in Psychology*, *10*, 85.

Davis, M. H. (1983). Measuring individual differences in empathy: Evidence for a multidimensional approach. *Journal of Personality and Social Psychology*, *44*, 113–126. doi: 10.1037/0022-3514.44.1.113

Davis, M. H. (1994). *Empathy: A social psychological approach*. Dubuque, IA: Brown & Benchmark.

Day, A., Casey, S., & Gerace, A. (2010). Interventions to improve empathy awareness in sexual and violent offenders: Conceptual, empirical, and clinical issues. *Aggression and Violent Behavior*, *15*, 201–208. doi: 10.1016/j.avb.2009.12.003

Decety, J., & Jackson, P. L. (2004). The functional architecture of human empathy. *Behavioural and Cognitive Neuroscience Reviews*, *3*, 71–100. doi: 10.1177/1534582304267187

Decety, J., & Michalska, K. J. (2010). Neurodevelopmental changes in the circuits underlying empathy and sympathy from childhood to adulthood. *Developmental Science*, *13*, 886–899. doi: 10.1111/j.1467-7687.2009.00940.x de Vignemont, F., & Singer, T. (2006). The empathic brain: How, when and why? *Trends in Cognitive Sciences, 10*, 435–441. doi: 10.1016/j.tics.2006.08.008

Eisenberg, N., Fabes, R. A., Murphy, B., Karbon, M., Maszk, P., Smith, M., et al. (1994). The relations of emotionality and regulation to dispositional and situational empathy-related responding. *Journal of Personality and Social Psychology, 66*, 776–797. doi: 10.1037/0022-3514.66.4.776

Elsegood, K. J., & Duff, S. C. (2010). Theory of mind in men who have sexually offended against children: A UK comparison study between child sex offenders and nonoffender controls. *Sexual Abuse: A Journal of Research and Treatment, 22*, 112–131. doi: 10.1177/1079063209359926

Elliott, I. A., Eldridge, H. J., Ashfield, S., & Beech, A. R. (2010). Exploring risk: Potential static, dynamic, protective and treatment factors in the clinical histories of female sex offenders. *Journal of Family Violence, 25*, 595–602. doi: 10.1007/s10896-010-9322-8

Eysenck, S. B. G., & Eysenck, H. J. (1978). Impulsiveness and venturesomeness: Their position in a dimensional system of personality description. *Psychological Reports, 43*, 1247–1253.

Farrington, D. P. (2007). Child-hood risk factors and risk-focused prevention. In M. Maguire, R. Morgan & R. Reiner (Eds.), *The Oxford handbook of criminology* (pp. 610–640). Oxford, UK: Oxford University Press.

Fernandez, Y. M., & Marshall, W. L. (2003). Victim empathy, social self-esteem, and psychopathy in rapists. *Sexual Abuse: A Journal of Research and Treatment, 15*, 11–26. doi: 10.1177/107906320301500102

Fernandez, Y. M., Marshall, W. L., Lightbody, S., & O'Sullivan, C. (1999). The child molester empathy measure: Description and examination of is reliability and validity. *Sexual Abuse: A Journal of Research and Treatment, 11*, 17–31. doi: 10.1177/107906329901100103

Gannon, T. A., & Alleyne, E. K. (2013). Female sexual abusers' cognition: A systematic review. *Trauma, Violence, & Abuse, 14*, 67–79. doi: 10.1177/1524838012462245

Gerace, A., Day, A., Casey, S., & Mohr, P. (2013). An exploratory investigation of the process of perspective taking in interpersonal situations. *Journal of Relationships Research, 4*, 1–12. doi: 10.1017/jrr.2013.6

Hanson, R. K. (2003). Empathy deficits of sexual offenders: A conceptual model. *Journal of Sexual Aggression, 9*, 13–23. doi: 10.1080/1355260031000137931

Hanson, R. K., & Bussière, M. T. (1996). *Predictors of sexual offender recidivism: A meta-analysis* (user report 96-04). Ottawa, Canada: Department of the Solicitor General of Canada.

Hanson, R. K., & Bussière, M. T. (1998). Predicting relapse: A meta-analysis of sexual offender recidivism studies. *Journal of Consulting and Clinical Psychology, 66*, 348–362. doi: 10.1037/0022-006X.66.2.348

Hanson, R. K., & Morton-Bourgon, K. (2004). *Predictors of sexual offender recidivism: An updated meta-analysis* (Corrections Research user report no. 2004_02). Ottawa, Canada: Public Safety and Emergency Preparedness Canada.

Hanson, R. K., & Morton-Bourgon, K. E. (2005). The characteristics of persistent sexual offenders: A meta-analysis of recidivism studies. *Journal of Consulting and Clinical Psychology, 73*, 1154–1163. doi: 10.1037/0022-006X.73.6.1154

Hanson, R. K., & Scott, H. (1995). Assessing perspective-taking among sexual offenders, nonsexual criminals, and nonoffenders. *Sexual Abuse: A Journal of Research and Treatment, 7*, 259–277. doi: 10.1177/107906329500700403

Hein, G., & Singer, T. (2008). I feel how you feel but not always: The empathic brain and its modulation. *Current Opinion in Neurobiology, 18*, 153–158. doi: 10.1016/j.conb.2008.07.012

Hennessy, M., Walter, J. S., & Vess, J. (2002). An evaluation of the Empat as a measure of victim empathy with civilly committed sexual offenders. *Sexual Abuse: A Journal of Research and Treatment, 14*, 241–251. doi: 10.1177/107906320201400304

Hogan, R. (1969). Development of an empathy scale. *Journal of Consulting and Clinical Psychology, 33*, 307–316. doi: 10.1037/h0027580

Hosser, D., & Bosold, C. (2006). A comparison of sexual and violent offenders in a German youth prison. *Howard Journal, 45*, 159–170.

Hudson, S. M., Marshall, W. L., Wales, D., & McDonald, E. (1993). Emotional recognition skills of sex offenders. *Annals of Sex Research, 6*, 199–211.

Ickes, W. (1993). Empathic accuracy. *Journal of Personality, 61*, 587–610. doi: 10.1111/j.1467-6494.1993.tb00783.x

Ickes, W. (2003). *Everyday mind reading.* New York: Prometheus Books.

Jolliffe, D., & Farrington, D. P. (2004). Empathy and offending: A systematic review and meta-analysis. *Aggression and Violent Behaviour, 9*, 441–476. doi: 10.1016/j.avb.2003.03.001

Jolliffe, D., & Farrington, D. P. (2006). Development and validation of the basic empathy scale. *Journal of Adolescence, 29*, 589–611. Retrieved from: http://www.sciencedirect.com/science/article/pii/S0140197105001090.

Kalbe, E., Schlegel, M., Sack, A. T., Nowak, D. A., Dafotakis, M., Bangard, C., et al. (2010). Dissociating cognitive from affective theory of mind: A TMS study. *Cortex, 46*, 769–780. doi: 10.1016/j.cortex.2009.07.010

Kaukiainen, A., Björkqvist, K., Lagerspetz, K., Österman, K., Salmivalli, C., Rothberg, S., et al. (1999). The relationships between social intelligence, empathy and three types of aggression. *Aggressive Behavior, 25*, 81–89. doi: 10.1002/(SICI)1098-2337

Keenan, T., & Ward, T. (2000). A theory of mind perspective on cognitive, affective, and intimacy deficits in child sexual offenders. *Sexual Abuse: A Journal of Research and Treatment, 12*, 49–60. doi: 10.1177/107906320001200106

Kitcher, P. (2010). Varieties of altruism. *Economics and Philosophy, 26*, 121–148. doi: 10.1017/S0266267110000167

Kitcher, P. (2011). *The ethical project.* Cambridge, MA: Harvard University Press.

Levenson, J. S., Macgowan, M. J., Morin, J. W., & Cotter, L. P. (2009). Perceptions of sex offenders about treatment: Satisfaction and engagement in group therapy. *Sexual Abuse: A Journal of Research and Treatment, 21*, 35–56. doi: 10.1177/1079063208326072

Levenson, J. S., & Prescott, D. (2009). Treatment experiences of civilly committed sex offenders: A consumer satisfaction survey. *Sexual Abuse: A Journal of Research and Treatment, 21*, 6–20. doi: 10.1177/1079063208325205

Lisak, D., & Ivan, C. (1995). Deficits in intimacy and empathy in sexually aggressive men. *Journal of Interpersonal Violence, 10*, 296–308. doi: 10.1177/088626095010003004

Lishner, D. A., Batson, C. D., & Huss, E. (2011). Tenderness and sympathy: Distinct empathic emotions elicited by different forms of need. *Personality and Social Psychology Bulletin, 37*, 614–625. doi: 10.1177/0146167211403157

Mann, R. E., & Barnett, G. D. (2013). Victim empathy interventions with sexual offenders: Rehabilitation, punishment, or correctional quackery? *Sexual Abuse: A Journal of Research and Treatment, 25*, 282–301. doi: 10.1177/1079063212455669

Marshall, W. L., Champagne, F., Brown, C., & Miller, S. (1997). Empathy, intimacy, loneliness and self-esteem in nonfamilial child molesters: A brief report. *Journal of Child Sexual Abuse, 6*, 87–113. doi: 10.1300/J070v06n03_06

Marshall, W. L., Hamilton, K., & Ferdinand, Y. (2001). Empathy deficits and cognitive distortions in child molesters. *Sexual Abuse: A Journal of Research and Treatment, 13*, 123–130. doi: 10.1177/107906320101300205

Marshall, W. L., Hudson, S. M., Jones, R., & Fernandez, Y. M. (1995). Empathy in sex offenders. *Clinical Psychology Review, 15*, 99–113. doi: 10.1016/0272-7358(95)00002-7

Marshall, W. L., Jones, R., Hudson, S. M., & McDonald, E. (1993). Generalized empathy in child molesters. *Journal of Child Sexual Abuse, 2*, 61–68. doi: 10.1300/J070v02n04_04

McFall, R. M. (1990). Assessment modification of cognitive distortions in sex offenders. In W. L. Marshall, D. R. Laws & H. E. Barbaree (Eds.), *Handbook of sexual assault: Issues, theories, and treatment of the offender* (pp. 311–327). New York: Plenum Press.

McGrath, M., Cann, S., & Konopasky, R. (1998). New measures of defensiveness, empathy, and cognitive distortions for sexual offenders against children. *Sexual Abuse: Journal of Research and Treatment, 10*, 25–36. doi: 10.1177/107906329801000104

Mehrabian, A., & Epstein, N. (1972). A measure of emotional empathy. *Journal of Personality, 40*, 525–543. doi: 10.1111/j.1467-6494.1972.tb00078.x

Miller, P. A., & Eisenberg, N. (1988). The relation of empathy to aggressive and externalizing/antisocial behaviour. *Psychological Bulletin, 103*, 324–344. doi: 10.1037/0033-2909.103.3.324

Monto, M., Zgourides, G., & Harris, R. (1998). Empathy, self-esteem, and the adolescent sexual offender. *Sexual Abuse: A Journal of Research and Treatment, 10*, 127–140. doi: 10.1177/107906329801000205

Moriarty, N., Stough, C., Tidmarsh, P., Eger, D., & Dennison, S. (2001). Deficits in emotional intelligence underlying adolescent sexual offending. *Journal of Adolescence, 24*, 743–751. Retrieved from: http://www.sciencedirect.com/science/article/pii/S0140197101904415.

Piliavin, J. A., & Charng, H. (1990). Altruism: A review of recent theory and research. *Annual Review of Sociology, 16*, 27–65. Retrieved 15 July 2016 from http://www.annualreviews.org/doi/abs/10.1146/annurev.so.16.080190.000331

Pithers, W. D. (1994). Process evaluation of a group therapy component designed to enhance sex offenders' empathy for sexual abuse survivors. *Behaviour Research and Therapy, 32*, 565–570.

Pithers, W. D. (1999). Empathy: Definition, enhancement, and relevance to the treatment of sexual abusers. *Journal of Interpersonal Violence, 14*, 257–284. doi: 10.1177/088626099014003004

Polaschek, D. L. L. (2003). Empathy and victim empathy. In T. Ward, D. R. Laws & S. M. Hudson (Eds.), *Sexual deviance: Issues and controversies* (pp. 172–189). Thousand Oaks, CA: Sage.

Rice, M. E., Chaplin, T. C., Harris, G. T., & Coutts, J. (1994). Empathy for the victim and sexual arousal among rapists and nonrapists. *Journal of Interpersonal Violence, 9*, 435–449. doi: 10.1177/088626094009004001

Ricci, R. J., Clayton, C. A., & Shapiro, F. (2006). Some effects of EMDR on previously abused child molesters: Theoretical reviews and preliminary findings. *Journal of Forensic Psychiatry and Psychology, 17*, 538–562. doi: 10.1080/14789940601070431

Roys, D. T. (1997). Empirical and theoretical considerations of empathy in sex offenders. *International Journal of Offender Therapy and Comparative Criminology, 41*, 53–64. doi: 10.1177/0306624X9704100106

Schewe, P. A., & O'Donohue, W. (1993). Sexual abuse prevention with high-risk males: The roles of victim empathy and rape myths. *Violence and Victims, 8*, 339–351. Retrieved from: http://www.ingentaconnect.com/content/springer/vav/1993/00000008/00000004/art00003.

Scully, D. (1988). Convicted rapists' perceptions of self and victim: Role taking and emotions. *Gender and Society, 2*, 200–213. doi: 10.1177/089124388002002005

Shamay-Tsoori, S. G., Aharon-Peretz, J., & Perry, D. (2009). Two systems for empathy: A double dissociation between emotional and cognitive empathy in inferior frontal gyrus versus ventromedial prefrontal lesions. *Brain, 132*, 617–627. doi: 10.1093/brain/awn279

Stermac, L. E., & Segal, Z. V. (1989). Adult sexual contact with children: An examination of cognitive factors. *Behavior Therapy, 20*, 573–584. Available: http://www.sciencedirect.com/science/article/pii/S0005789489801352.

Stotland, E., Matthews, K. E., Sherman, S., Hansson, R. O., & Richardson, B. Z. (1978). *Empathy, fantasy and helping*. Beverly Hills, CA: Sage.

Tangney, J. P., Stuewig, J., & Hafez, L. (2011). Shame, guilt and remorse: Implications for offender populations. *The Journal of Forensic Psychiatry & Psychology, 22*, 706–723. doi: 10.1080/14789949.2011.617541

Teuma, R. T., Smith, D. I., Stewart, A. A., & Lee, J. K. P. (2003). Measurement of victim empathy in intrafamilial and extrafamilial child molesters using the child molester empathy measure (CMEM*). International Journal of Forensic Psychology, 1*, 120–132. Retrieved 15 July 2016 from http://www.uow.edu.au/content/groups/public/@web/@health/documents/doc/uow045102.pdf.

Tierney, D. W., & McCabe, M. P. (2001). The assessment of denial, cognitive distortions and victim empathy among pedophilic sex offenders: An evaluation of the utility of self-report measures. *Trauma, Violence and Abuse, 2*, 259–270. doi: 10.1177/1524838001002003004

Titchener, E. B. (1911). *A text-book of psychology*. New York: Macmillan.

van Langen, M. A. M., Wissink, I. B., van Vugt, E. S., Van der Stouwe, T., & Stams, G. J. J. M. (2014). The relation between empathy and offending: A meta-analysis. *Aggression and Violent Behavior, 19*, 179–189. doi: 10.1016/j.avb.2014.02.003

Wakeling, H., Beech, A. R., & Freemantle, N. (2013). Investigating treatment change and its relationship to recidivism in a sample of 3773 sex offenders in the UK. *Psychology, Crime & Law, 19*, 233–252. doi: 10.1080/1068316X.2011.626413

Wakeling, H. C., Webster, S. D., & Mann, R. E. (2005). Sexual offenders' treatment experience: A qualitative and quantitative investigation. *Journal of Sexual Aggression, 11*, 171–186. doi: 10.1080/13552600412331321323.

Walker, K., & Brown, S. J. (2013). Non sex offenders display distorted thinking and have empathy deficits too: A thematic analysis in non-offender cognitions and application of empathy. *Journal of Sexual Aggression, 19*, 80–100. doi: 10.1080/13552600.2011.618276

Ward, T., & Durrant, R. (2013). Altruism, empathy, and sex offender treatment. *International Journal of Behavioral Consultation and Therapy, 8*, 66–71. Retrieved from: http://www.baojournal.com/IJBCT/IJBCT-8_3-4/A13.pdf.

Ward, T., Keenan, T., & Hudson, S. M. (2000). Understanding cognitive, affective, and intimacy deficits in sexual offenders: A developmental perspective. *Aggression and Violent Behavior, 5*, 41–62. Available: http://www.sciencedirect.com/science/article/pii/S1359178998000251.

Wastell, C., Cairns, D., & Haywood, H. (2009). Empathy training, sex offenders and re-offending. *Journal of Sexual Aggression, 15*, 149–159. doi: 10.1080/13552600902792599

Webster, S. D., & Beech, A. R. (2000). The nature of sexual offenders' affective empathy: A grounded theory analysis. *Sexual Abuse: A Journal of Research and Treatment, 12*, 249–261. doi: 10.1177/107906320001200402

Webster, S. D., Akhtar, S., Bowers, L. E., Mann, R. E., Rallings, M., & Marshall, W. L. (2004). The impact of the prison service sex offender treatment programme on minority ethnic offenders: A preliminary study. *Psychology, Crime and Law, 10*, 113–124. doi: 10.1080/1068316031000093432

Wispé, L. (1986). The distinction between sympathy and empathy: To call forth a concept, a word is needed. *Journal of Personality and Social Psychology, 50*, 314–321. doi: 10.1037/0022-3514.50.2.314

Wood, E., & Riggs, S. (2008). Predictors of child molestation: Adult attachment, cognitive distortion, and empathy. *Journal of Interpersonal Violence, 23*, 259–275. doi: 10.1177/0886260507309344

5

Emotions and Sexual Offending

Nicholas Blagden, Rebecca Lievesley and Jayson Ware

Few would dispute that treatment for individuals who have sexually offended needs to be based on empirical evidence. One important issue for both theory and treatment is whether or not affective or emotional states cause and/or maintain sexual offending (Howells, Day & Wright, 2004). Most clinicians believe that emotions play a critical role in treatment and will, at least anecdotally, attest to instances where emotions have driven sexual offending. Indeed, assisting clients to understand and manage their emotional states is important and may impact upon their engagement with treatment, their treatment progress and the degree to which they are able to benefit from therapy. Yet, despite a growing body of evidence pointing to the central role of affect and emotion in the offence process there is a paucity of work in this area (Day, 2009).

The purpose of this chapter is to critically examine some of the key emotional states related to sexual offending and associated challenges for successful treatment. In line with Chapter 2 (Bartels), we adopt affect as an umbrella term to describe emotions and mood and use the term emotion or emotional state to refer to target-specific reactions incorporating cognition, physiology and behaviour that may or may not be consciously experienced by the individual as an emotion. We discuss positive and negative affect, but will focus primarily on shame and guilt and the interrelationships between affect and the constructs of empathy, self-esteem and offence-supportive beliefs. Given that desistance from crime has both affective and cognitive aspects, understanding these interrelationships in greater detail is critical for treatment professionals.

The Role of Affect in Sexual Offending

Emotions are a central aspect of human experience and play an important role in our everyday life. Not only do they promote interpersonal bonds but they also guide behaviour and the interpretation of behaviour (Elster, 1999; Svensson et al., 2013; Tangney & Dearing, 2002). In terms of sexual offending, research suggests

Sexual Offending: Cognition, Emotion and Motivation, First Edition.
Edited by Theresa A. Gannon and Tony Ward.
© 2017 John Wiley & Sons Ltd. Published 2017 by John Wiley & Sons Ltd.

that individuals who sexually offend experience problems in the regulation of affective states and, furthermore, that this contributes to offending (Gillespie, Mitchell, Fisher & Beech, 2012; Langton & Marshall, 2000). Indeed, the importance of affect is reflected in the fact that 'socio-affective functioning' is one of four risk domains used in the Structured Assessment of Risk and Need (SARN; Webster et al., 2006). Relatedly, a core feature of sexual offence desistance appears to be individuals constructing new narrative identities or prosocial 'changed' selves. Individual identity change consists of affective, cognitive and agentic components, with desisters typically more open to positive emotions and experiences (Göbbels, Ward & Willis, 2012; LeBel, Burnett, Maruna & Bushway, 2008).

Problems in the management of affective states have been associated with offence pathways for clients who have sexually offended against children or adults. In Ward, Louden, Hudson and Marshall's (1995) descriptive model of the offence process, there are nine stages, with three contributing factors that describe the sequence of cognitive, affective and behavioural events that form an offence chain. Three primary offence patterns were found: (1) a positive affect pathway with explicit planning and offence supportive cognitions regarding adult–child sex; (2) a negative affect pathway characterized by implicit planning, neediness and entitlement; and (3) a pathway characterized by a shift between pathways (1) and (2). Interestingly, the nature of the specific affective pathway followed appears related to self-perceptions and lifestyles (Proulx, Perreault & Ouimet, 1999). Most importantly, however, Ward et al.'s model highlighted an offence pathway previously neglected in the research literature: that is, a pathway characterized almost predominantly by positive affect.

Proulx and colleagues (1999) investigated affect across the offending process for 44 men who had sexually assaulted extrafamilial children. Positive and negative affect was reported in all crime phases (i.e., pre-crime, crime and post-crime). Although negative affect was more frequently reported in the pre-crime phase (e.g., loneliness, anxiety), positive affect such as calm mood was also reported. The negative affective state of loneliness was found to be a crucial factor in sexual aggression, with low self-esteem also prominent. The data also supported a positive affect pathway in some child molesters. During the 'crime phase', pleasure and sexual arousal were most frequently reported, though these receded in the 'post-crime' phase where guilt was the most frequently reported emotion. In another offence process study Polaschek, Hudson, Ward and Siegert (2001) constructed a descriptive model of the offence process for men who had raped adults. They found three pathways to rape: (1) men who sought sex to augment positive affect; (2) men who sought sex to alleviate negative affect (the classic avoidance pathway); and (3) men who offended to rectify perceived harm to self. Polaschek and colleagues also found that men reported affective responses consistent with their evaluations. For example, those with a focus on their own gratification often reported both positive evaluations of the offence and positive affect.

While positive affect has been clearly implicated in pathways towards sexual offending, research has primarily focused on negative affect associated with sexual offending. Negative affect has been implicated in theories of the offence and relapse processes, and has been linked to the use of inappropriate sexual fantasies. Proulx and colleagues (1999) found loneliness to be a frequent precursor to the onset of inappropriate sexual fantasies and sexual offending. Looman (1999) also demonstrated a significant association between inappropriate sexual fantasies and negative affect such as loneliness, anxiety and inadequacy. Centrally important to sexual offending is the role that moral emotions or affect, such as shame and guilt, play in guiding behavioural choices.

Shame

The experience of shame and guilt is a quintessential aspect of being human and plays a crucial role in how we relate to others (Clark, 2012). Shame and guilt have been broadly regarded as 'moral emotions' because of their presumed role in inhibiting socially undesirable behaviour and in fostering prosocial behaviour (Tangney, Stuewig & Hafez, 2011). There is now a large body of data derived from a variety of methodologies that attests to the separateness of shame and guilt as affective experiences (Clark, 2012). Shame has been described as representing an important mechanism in crime, justice and rehabilitation (McAlinden, 2007). Harder and Lewis (1987) argue that when experiencing shame, the self is pictured as unable to cope and viewed as a rejected object of scorn and/or disgust. The experience of shame engenders feelings of being worthless and 'often motivates denial, defensive anger and aggression' (Tangney & Dearing, 2002, p. 2). When clients experience shame the self becomes an object of self-scrutiny and the motivation is to externalize blame (Bumby, Marshall & Langton, 1999).

Shame is a discrepancy between what the person wants to be and the way that person is being identified socially. At its core the experience of shame is concerned with one's ideal identity (Lazarus, 2006). There are two types of shame: external and internal. External shame is derived from our perceptions of how others view us, while internal shame is related to how a person judges and feels about themselves (Gilbert, 2003). The experience of shame impairs the ability to experience positive affect, and leads individuals to become self-focused, and by doing so, impairs their ability to engender positive emotions in others. This is an important consideration for rehabilitation and desistance because shame impairs empathetic responses, yet the triggering of positive affect in the self after stimulating positive affect in others is key to positive self-evaluations (Gilbert, 2003). Positive self-evaluations and self-image have also been found to predict successful re-entry upon release from prison (LeBel et al., 2008). The experience of shame has significant consequences for rehabilitation and crime desistance because it triggers depression and powerlessness and can impair the process of rehabilitation (LeBel et al., 2008).

Deterrence theorists argue that formal punishment creates shame and stigmatization, and by doing so may inhibit future offending (Benson, Alarid, Burton & Cullen, 2011). There is, however, a lack of empirical support for this claim since individuals who have offended do not appear to react to the sense of shame in ways that the criminal justice system posits (Benson et al., 2011). Instead, the shaming process appears to lead to offence persistence (Maruna, 2004). Shame and stigmatization are highly associated constructs. Braithwaite (1989) refers to stigmatization as a form of disintegrative shaming, one in which individuals who have offended are rejected as outcasts, with their deviance conceptualized as subsumed as a master status trait. When one considers the vociferous public indignation towards individuals who have sexually offended, it is difficult to find a group who are more stigmatized or publicly denigrated.

Guilt

Whereas shame has a negative focus on the self (i.e., one's core identity), guilt arises from the negative focus on a specific behaviour (Tangney et al., 2011). According to Blackburn (1998), guilt is a special case of empathic distress aroused by the causal attribution of responsibility for another's plight to the self. While the experience of shame is self-focused, experiences of guilt are associated with reparative actions and a desire to put things right rather than the experience of emotional reactions that impair functioning (Proeve & Howells, 2006). The experience of guilt can also promote positive change and allow for positive emotional experiences. Research with individuals in prison has shown that guilt-proneness is positively associated with other-oriented empathy and negatively associated with externalization of blame and hostility (Tangney et al., 2011). While shame has been found to be associated with anger and anti-social attitudes, guilt has been found to be negatively related to antisocial attitudes (Tangney et al., 2011). This has led some to suggest that the experience of guilt may hold protective elements for individuals who have offended.

Gilbert (1998) contends that understanding guilt and shame and their associated differences is crucial for clinical practice because the therapist can often inadvertently become the 'shaming other', which can adversely affect the therapeutic relationship. Shame motivates concealment from others, which inhibits the assimilation of negative information about the self. Thus shame can be a major reason why affective experiences are not integrated into adaptive cognitive-affective experiences (Gilbert, 1998).

Gilbert's arguments regarding shame are important ones for rehabilitation and crime desistance, due to desistance incorporating an affective process (Farrall & Calverley, 2006). Those who desist from crime, including those individuals convicted of a sexual offence, will often experience positive emotions such as hope, trust, self-efficacy and positive affect emanating from a more adaptive self-identity (Farrall & Calverley, 2006; LeBel et al., 2008). The experience of shame, associated with depression, anger, anxiety and disgust, can impair one's ability to experience positive affect and emotions that assist in the change process (Crocker & Quinn, 2003).

Self-Esteem

There is a large body of literature pointing to the importance of self-esteem for healthy psychological functioning (Baumeister, 1993; Marshall, Marshall, Serran & O'Brien, 2009). Self-esteem disturbances have also been found to play a role in sexual offending. For example, researchers have found that low self-esteem is significantly correlated with intimacy deficits and loneliness. Self-esteem has also been associated with inappropriate sexual interests (Marshall, 1997), insecure child and adult attachment styles (Marshall & Mazzucco, 1995) and has been implicated in the aetiology of sexual offending (Marshall, Anderson &

Champagne, 1997). Shine, McCloskey and Newton (2002) identified a difference in self-esteem levels between individuals who had sexually offended against children and those who had sexually offended against adults, with the former having lower personal self-esteem.

Since individuals who sexually offend tend to score high on self-report measures of shame, but low on self-esteem, it is unsurprising that they utilize defensive strategies such as denying guilt and minimizing various aspects of the offence, as well as justifying their behaviour (Marshall, Marshall & Ware, 2009). When faced with stigmatization and punishment, some individuals may not accept their inappropriate sexual acts as a reflection of their true self and may deny or distance themselves from those whom they perceive are the 'real' sexual offenders (Blagden, Winder, Gregson & Thorne, 2014). Finally, interestingly, some research suggests that high self-esteem is also related to offending. Baumeister, Smart and Boden (1996) found that those with inflated, unstable or tentative beliefs in the self's superiority may be most prone to encountering threats to self and thus more likely to act violently.

Empathy, Empathy Deficits and Cognition

Although emphasizing the roles of empathy and empathy deficits in sexual offence treatment has a long tradition, the empirical evidence supporting this focus has been less robust. Indeed, the role of empathy in general offending behaviour has been questioned, with research offering conflicting and inconsistent results (Jolliffe & Farrington, 2004). Jolliffe and Farrington (2004) conclude that there is a need for better measures and more understanding of the role of empathy in offending. Although empathy is not one of the core emotions, it is relevant to emotional distress (Howells et al. 2004; see also Brown, Chapter 4 in this volume).

There is some level of agreement that a useful distinction can be made between cognitive and emotional empathy, and that the experience of empathy involves both cognitive and emotional processes (Jolliffe & Farrington, 2004). Leith and Baumeister (1998) found that guilt was positively correlated with perspective-taking, whereas shame was positively correlated with personal distress. Shame has been found to be negatively related to perspective-taking and empathy, while guilt has been found to be positively associated with other-orientated empathy (Tangney et al., 2011). Supporting these findings Silfver, Helkama, Lönnqvist and Verkasalo (2008) concluded that guilt-proneness is related to empathic concern and perspective-taking, while shame is negatively related to empathy.

There are times where individuals actively avoid meaningful thought and lower levels of empathy in order to reduce negative affect that occurs as a result of their sexual offending. Cognitive deconstruction can occur when individuals are motivated to reduce their level of self-awareness and negative affect in order to avoid negative self-evaluation (Baumeister, 1991). Cognitive deconstruction enables clients who have sexually offended to avoid negative evaluation of themselves and their deviant actions, disrupts empathetic feelings toward the victim, and prevents more adaptive and effective ways of dealing with negative affect/emotions (see Ward, Hudson & Marshall, 1995).

Emotions and Offence Supportive Beliefs

Some individuals who have sexually offended may believe that their actions have not caused any harm to the victim and so will not react empathetically to the victim. This misperception may be the result of implicit theories which bias social information processing (Blake & Gannon, 2008; Ward, 2000). A comprehensive overview of the role of cognitive distortions in sexual offending is beyond the scope of this chapter, but the literature indicates that there are differences between surface cognitions and offence supportive beliefs (See Ó Ciardha, Chapter 3 in this volume for more detailed discussion). While surface cognitions appear to enable individuals to justify and minimize their inappropriate behaviour (Murphy, 1990), offence-supportive beliefs are enduring beliefs that offending behaviour is acceptable and, therefore, represent a psychologically meaningful risk factor for sexual recidivism (Mann, Hanson & Thornton, 2010).

Offence supportive beliefs have been associated with emotion recognition deficits and perspective-taking deficits in individuals who sexually offend (Blake & Gannon, 2008). Given that dysfunctional implicit theories or schema represent global and personal theories of individuals' internal lives and their worlds, it is unsurprising that they give rise to aggressive emotions/emotional responses. For example, Beech, Fisher and Ward (2005) found that individuals who had sexually murdered and who held the 'male sex drive is uncontrollable' implicit theory appeared to feel relatively powerless in their lives. This belief appeared to lead to aggressive emotions that contributed towards sexual murder.

Linking Affect and Key Correlates

There are clear links between affect and other treatment targets. Shame and guilt, for example, are related to empathy but in different ways. Guilt is positively correlated with other-orientated empathy whereas shame disrupts the ability to connect empathetically or respond compassionately to others (Tangney et al., 2011). Shame is associated with anger, hostility, shame-rage loops and the propensity to blame others (Tangney & Dearing, 2002; Tangney et al., 2011). Negative affective states like shame, as previously noted, are related to low self-esteem and high levels of self-distress. Low self-esteem is also linked with low levels of empathy and empathetic responses. However, as Anderson and Dodgson (2002) point out, an apparent observable lack of empathy may be the result of strategies (e.g., denial of harm) that are adopted in order to preserve the self from further blows to low levels of self-esteem. From these observations it would seem that victim empathy deficits reflect self-protective processes (Marshall et al., 2009a). Thus, it is these driving factors (i.e., low self-esteem and shame) that should be addressed (Marshall et al., 2008).

There appears to be clear relationships between negative affect, self-esteem, empathy and offence supportive cognition, which Marshall et al. (2009b) have built into an integrated theoretical framework. They propose that the negative effects of going through the criminal justice process and/or experiencing a lifetime low self-esteem create the conditions for experiences of shame which will lead to inappropriate attributions (e.g., 'I committed offences because I am a bad person'). Shame blocks attempts and beliefs that one can change and this attribution may be worsened by being labelled a 'sexual offender'. An individual low in self-esteem who is experiencing shame will avoid discussing their offending and will distort the offence in order to present a more desirable picture of self. Thus, in Marshall et al.'s (2009b) model, low self-esteem generates shame, which then blocks recognition of harm, which reduces empathy for the victim. Even if a shamed individual acknowledges that he did offend, his self-esteem is so fragile that he is unlikely to feel empathy for his victim. This also has implications for treatment, which are discussed in more detail later in this chapter.

Females who Have Sexually Offended and Affect

Since this area of exploration in females is in its infancy in comparison to the male literature, the available evidence is somewhat limited. Nevertheless, it is possible to identify a number of similarities across the literature as well as some gender specific differences.

Empathy deficits have been identified in some females who sexually offend and are considered to be similar to those of males (Beckett, 2007, as cited in Gannon & Alleyne, 2013). Furthermore, research findings indicate that females who offend alone demonstrate greater deficits in victim empathy than those who have co-offenders (Beckett, 2007, as cited in Gannon & Alleyne, 2013). Many females appear to also experience both guilt and shame as a result of engaging in abusive behaviour (Grayston & Deluca, 1999), with the suggestion that levels of guilt are higher within females who sexually offend relative to males (Ford, 2006).

Similarly to males, evidence suggests that deficits in emotional regulation may play a key role in the sexual offending of some females. Gannon and Rose (2008) suggest that deficits are due to insufficient development of appropriate coping skills. Research supports this, with females who sexually offend reporting higher levels of stressful experiences (Saradijan & Hanks, 1996), low self-esteem (Elliott, Eldridge, Ashfield & Beech, 2010), lack of control over their lives (Beech, Parrett, Ward & Fisher, 2009) and an inability to cope with negative experiences or negative affect (e.g., anxiety, depression, anger) experienced prior to the offence (Elliott et al., 2010; Hislop, 2001). The sexual offending behaviour of females can be viewed as rewarding because of its emotional regulation function, and the fulfilment of intimacy, power and control needs (Gannon, Rose & Ward, 2008, 2010; Grayston & De Luca, 1999; Nathan & Ward, 2002). Research examining positive affect in females who have sexually offended is currently limited, but demonstrates that some experience excitement or satisfaction either prior to or within an offending episode (Gannon et al., 2008, 2010). While positive affect is often associated with inappropriate sexual interests, the extent to which this is true for females who sexually offend is currently unclear (Gannon & Rose, 2008).

While assessment and treatment protocols for females who sexually offend are relatively under developed, recommendations for treatment suggest addressing problematic affect and affect management. For example, helping individuals recognize their emotional needs and how to fulfil these appropriately (Vandiver & Kercher, 2004), increasing empathy (Matthews, 1993), increasing ability to recognize and manage problematic affect and increasing ability to obtain positive affect via appropriate means are all key treatment proposals for this client group (Gannon & Rose, 2008).

Treatment

Affect plays a critical role in treatment for sexual offending and can impact upon successful treatment in a variety of ways. Clients may refuse to participate in, or drop out of, treatment due to strong affect and emotional states (Beyko & Wong, 2005). Given that affect and emotions are causally involved in every type of problem experienced by those who sexually offend, the content of sexual offence treatment programmes should heavily stress coping with problematic negative or positive affect and emotions. An understanding of these issues and acquired skills in emotional regulation is fundamental to treatment success. In terms of treatment process, the expression of emotion has been shown to be a significant predictor of treatment induced change and is, therefore, also a critical goal for treatment providers (Pfäfflin, Böhmer, Cornehl & Mergenthaler, 2005). Treatment providers must use emotionally focused techniques and work in a manner that is emotionally activating (Ware, Frost & Boer, 2015).

Treatment Refusals and Non-Completion

Clients who have sexually offended may experience strong negative reactions at the mere thought of having to experience strong affect within treatment (Mann, Webster, Wakeling & Keylock, 2012). Mann (2009) noted that treatment refusers often report that they had observed others in treatment suffering negative side effects, such as low mood and depression or that they were themselves experiencing anxiety or distress and this led to a reluctance to enter treatment. Serran and Marshall (2006) observed that clients who had sexually offended might also drop out of treatment due to difficulties managing their affect, notably when having to address difficult issues such as victim empathy. Proulx et al. (2004) found that pre-treatment factors relating to affect that were predictive of treatment non-completion included low self-esteem, a lack of empathy and poor coping (see also Ware & Bright, 2008).

As has been discussed in this chapter, individuals who have sexually offended may also experience high levels of shame which can impact upon treatment engagement (Proeve & Howells, 2006). When feeling shamed, individuals who have sexually offended might respond to therapeutic efforts with aggression, withdrawal or externalizations (Tangney & Dearing, 2002). Initial therapeutic attempts to reduce shame are critical, particularly as shame can impair the process of self-change and rehabilitation (Gilbert, 2003; Göbbels et al., 2012; Proeve & Howells, 2006). Indeed, Maruna (2001) has emphasized the importance of cognitive transformations in a person's narrative identity for successful crime desistance. Treatment providers need to be aware of the detrimental role of shame in rehabilitation attempts and ensure that individuals who have sexually offended are given opportunities to construct desirable and adaptive practical identities (Göbbels et al., 2012).

Marshall, Marshall, Serran and O'Brien (2011) propose that the relationship between shame and self-esteem means that, if self-esteem is enhanced, this can lead to reductions in the experience of shame. This assertion is supported by Gilbert (1998), who argues that irrespective of whether the experience of shame is mild or severe the therapist should respond empathically to reported shame experience and, crucially, must make efforts to raise self-esteem if treatment is to be successful.

The point raised by Gilbert is especially relevant for treatment of individuals who have sexually offended since they often, as previously noted, experience severe shame and stigma. Indeed, when faced with stigmatization and punishment, some may not accept their inappropriate sexual acts as a reflection of their true self and may distance themselves from those whom they perceive are the 'real' sexual offenders. Through inoculating themselves in this way such individuals may be less likely to become 'secondary deviants' (Maruna & Copes, 2005). This calls into question one of the core targets for most cognitive-behavioural treatment programmes designed for sexual offending: namely the enhancement of 'offender responsibility' (McGrath et al., 2010; Ware & Mann, 2012). While treatment is beginning to move away from disclosure-based intervention, this approach is still very much the norm for European and North American countries. McGrath et al. (2010) found that 91% of treatment programmes in the United States included 'offender responsibility' as a treatment target. However, while offence disclosure may be seen as a useful precursor of progress (though the evidence for this is largely anecdotal), it may also be a misnomer, since research suggests that full disclosure (particularly when the individual is not ready) can have negative results, particularly for individuals' self-esteem and self-image (Kelly, 2000). Kelly (2000) argues that clients who incorporate desirable images into their self-views are more likely to describe themselves in these ways in the future. There is an argument that sexual offending treatment is too focused on sex which leads to more shame-inducing experiences, feelings of being 'doomed to deviance' and an impaired sense of self-identity (Lacombe, 2008).

Treatment Content

As stated above, emotions are causally involved in almost every type of problem experienced by clients who have sexually offended and therefore the content of treatment ought to reflect this degree of primacy. Ideally, within treatment, clients should be assisted to recognize, monitor, understand and appropriately manage affect *in general* (Ware, 2011). Ware and Mann (2012) argue that this ought to a primary initial focus of treatment, rather than acceptance of responsibility or empathy. They note that although treatment programmes often have modules labelled 'stress management' or 'coping with emotions' these often occur towards the middle or end of treatment at which time a client has already had to cope, seemingly without adequate assistance, with the challenges of acceptance of responsibility or victim empathy work (see also Waldram, 2007).

Recognizing and understanding the relevance of affect at the time of offending is an important treatment goal. If clients are to avoid or manage situations in the future indicative of offending risk they need to understand how to recognize and appropriately manage affect. A deterioration of mood is frequently linked to imminent risk of sexual reoffending (Hanson & Harris, 2000). Individuals also typically report using sex, alcohol or drugs, and other similarly problematic methods of coping with negative mood (Serran & Marshall, 2006). Notably, for certain clients, the offences may be preceded by positive emotional states and the offending is an attempt to enhance or maintain these positive feelings (Ward & Hudson, 2000). The relative importance of an individual's negative or positive emotional states will differ considerably depending on their individual context and situations. For this reason, an individualized case formulation, highlighting the importance of affect for treatment planning is essential (Boer, Thakker, & Ward, 2009). In assisting individuals who have sexually offended to recognize and understand affect relevant to their offending, treatment providers should create emotional contexts within sessions and not rely exclusively upon cognitive tasks.

Assisting a client to effectively regulate their emotions is arguably necessary to effectively address all dynamic risk factors and, more generally, to help individuals strengthen all aspects of their lives (Mann et al., 2010). Sexual preoccupation, relationship conflicts, general self-regulation problems, impulsivity, hostility and emotional congruence with children involve either the under-regulation or dysregulation of affect. Clients may either lack the skills to effectively cope with negative affect or attempt to do so in problematic ways such as through the use of various sexual behaviours, such as pornography or masturbation (Cortoni & Marshall, 2001).

How a treatment programme or provider assists clients to manage their emotions is important. There is now a growing body of literature suggesting that successful treatment needs to focus on engendering positive behaviours and feelings, rather than exclusively attending to the alleviation of negative symptoms (Ryff & Singer, 1996). Whether treatment providers use the Good Lives Model (Ward & Stewart, 2003) or a traditional Relapse Prevention Model to organize their treatment (Gannon & Ward, 2014), it is important to focus on creating a sense of future well-being for the client. Thus, building on the client's existing affect-coping skills in certain contexts is essential.

Treatment must be simple. McGrath and colleagues (2010) reported that 65% of both residential and community-based sexual offence programmes for adults in the United States and Canada included 'emotional regulation' as a core treatment target. We are, however, aware of many programmes where there are different terms and concepts used in each different treatment module to assist clients to manage their emotions. For example, techniques and strategies used within a module on intimacy and relationships may differ from those used within emotional regulation. This can be problematic in that clients may simply get lost in a large list of different techniques and terms (Ware et al. 2015). Arguably, what is needed is one set of clear strategies and techniques that are learnt within the treatment context and rehearsed repeatedly across time and context (Ware, 2011). Importantly, for some clients where the offending appears to have been motivated by a desire to enhance or extend a positive emotional state, treatment must be modified to ensure that this is adequately addressed.

Despite the obvious importance of assisting clients to increase their ability to regulate or cope with emotional states, there is paucity of research examining how this should be done and on the outcomes of this focus. The ability to cope with affect has been examined through coping. Serran, Firestone, Marshall and Moulden (2007) reported that treated clients who had sexually offended against children identified more effective coping strategies in specific high-risk situations and increased their use of task-focused coping strategies. Interestingly, there was no significant decrease after treatment in the use of ineffective emotional coping strategies. More specifically, both Roger and Masters (1997) and Feelgood, Golias, Shaw and Bright (2000) have shown that clients increased their use of task-focused coping and decreased the use of emotion-focused coping following brief specific interventions.

Assisting clients who have sexually offended to manage their affect is often an important target of treatment even if there is no clear link between affect and offending. Typically, there are a number of responsivity factors that may impede an individual's ability to benefit from treatment unless they are addressed and many of these may result in negative affect. For example, whilst low self-esteem (and corresponding low mood or anxiety) has generally not been found to be a dynamic risk factor (Hanson & Morton-Bourgon, 2004), targeting this in treatment may enhance beliefs in capacity to change and reduce low mood (Marshall, Champagne, Sturgeon & Bryce, 1997). Mann et al. (2010) also noted that neither depression nor mental illness have been reliably correlated with increased sex offence recidivism, although they may be risk factors for some individuals but not for others and in some cases will impede treatment engagement without intervention.

Treatment Process

While it is important to understand how affect contributes to sexual offending, clients are likely to benefit most from treatment if they are actually experiencing and expressing emotions within sessions. Using a measure of group climate, Beech and Fordham (1997) and Beech and Hamilton-Giachritsis (2005) found that sexual offence treatment groups with higher scores of emotional expressiveness had greater treatment induced changes in a number of pre- and post-treatment measures. Pfäfflin et al. (2005) also found that emotional expression predicted treatment changes but, importantly, found these benefits to be greatest when the emotional expression was linked to an intellectual understanding of the issue concerned. It has been argued that the quality of the therapeutic relationship is of primary importance in working with the experiences of both shame and guilt in any clinical setting (Clark, 2012). Blagden, Winder, Gregson and Thorne (2013) found that therapists who worked with clients who had sexually offended recognized the importance of negative affect, particularly shame, in treatment. They argued that a therapist's reaction to shame might, in part, determine the level of defence mechanisms utilized by the client. For instance, a therapist who recognizes that offending behaviour is the result of the person looking to pursue the human need/desire for specific experiences (albeit in maladaptive ways), rather than being of 'bad' character, is likely to decrease shame responses in the form of denial and other defence mechanisms (Ward, Vess, Collie & Gannon, 2006). Thus, a collaborative therapeutic alliance built on authentic approach goals is likely to breakdown resistance and facilitate a positive and predictive relationship (Ward et al., 2006). Research has demonstrated a link between the quality of therapeutic alliance and denial (Beyko & Wong, 2005; Wormith & Olver, 2002). The therapist, then, appears key to producing an environment in which emotional expression is welcomed and all such expressions are a further opportunity for understanding, rehearsal and generalization of skills.

Conclusions

This chapter has focused on affect in relation to sexual offending. We have discussed the interrelationships between affect, empathy, self-esteem and offence-supportive beliefs. It is clear that affect plays a significant role in sexual offending and that understanding both positive and negative affect is important for treatment and rehabilitation. In particular, experiences of shame and guilt appear highly important concepts within treatment for sexual offending, and these have previously been under explored. The experience of shame is detrimental to self-reform and positive identity change, yet the experience of guilt gives rise to reparative action which can lead to the facilitation of positive affect. Shame is associated with anger, anxiety, motivates a self-focus and acts as a block in the self-change process. This is important for reform because in order for an individual to change they need to be open to change (i.e., they must possess the cognitive and emotional capacities to capitalize on opportunities to transform themselves and their lives; Göbbels et al., 2012). Sexual offending is, at its core, an affective process. As a result, affect must play much more of a central role in our consideration and treatment of this client group.

References

Anderson, D., & Dodgson, P. G. (2002). Empathy deficits, self-esteem, and cognitive distortions in sexual offenders. In Y. M. Fernandez (Ed.), *In their shoes: Examining the issue of empathy and its place in treatment* (pp. 73–90). Bethany, OK: Wood 'n' Barnes.

Baumeister, R. F. (1991). *Escaping the self.* New York: Basic Books.

Baumeister, R. F. (1993). Understanding the inner nature of low self-esteem: Uncertain, fragile, protective, and conflicted. In R. F. Baumeister (Ed.), *Self-esteem: The puzzle of low self regard* (pp. 201–218). New York: Plenum Press.

Baumeister, R. F., Smart, L., & Boden, J. M. (1996). Relation of threatened egotism to violence and aggression: The dark side of high self-esteem. *Psychological Review, 103,* 5–33. doi: 10.1037/0033-295x.103.1.5

Beckett, R. C. (2007, July). *Female sexual abusers.* Paper presented at the 3rd International Congress of Law and Psychology, Adelaide, Australia.

Beech, A., Fisher, D., & Ward, T. (2005). Sexual murderers' implicit theories. *Journal of Interpersonal Violence, 20,* 1366–1389. doi: 10.1177/0886260505278712

Beech, A., & Fordham, A. S. (1997). Therapeutic climate of sexual offender treatment programmes. *Sexual Abuse: A Journal of Research and Treatment, 9,* 21–9223. doi: 10.1177/107906329700900306

Beech, A. R., & Hamilton-Giachritsis, C. E. (2005). Relationship between therapeutic climate and treatment outcome in group-based sexual offender treatment programs. *Sexual Abuse: A Journal of Research and Treatment, 17,* 127–139. doi: 10.1007/s11194-005-4600-3

Beech, A. R., Parrett, N., Ward, T., & Fisher, D. (2009). Assessing female sexual offenders' motivations and cognitions: An exploratory study. *Psychology, Crime & Law, 15,* 201–216. doi: 10.1080/10683160802190921

Benson, M. L., Alarid, L. F., Burton, V. S., & Cullen, F. T. (2011). Reintegration or stigmatization? Offenders' expectations of community re-entry. *Journal of Criminal Justice, 39,* 385–393. doi: 10.1016/j.jcrimjus.2011.05.004

Beyko, M. J., & Wong, S. C. (2005). Predictors of treatment attrition as indicators for program improvement not offender shortcomings: A study of sex offender treatment attrition. *Sexual Abuse: A Journal of Research and Treatment, 17,* 375–389. doi: 10.1177/107906320501700403

Blackburn, R. (1998). *The psychology of criminal conduct: Theory, research and practice.* Chichester, UK: John Wiley & Sons.

Blagden, N., Winder, B., Gregson, M., & Thorne, K. (2013). Working with denial in convicted sexual offenders: A qualitative analysis of treatment professionals' views and experiences and their implications for practice. *International Journal of Offender Therapy and Comparative Criminology, 57,* 332–356. doi: 10.1177/0306624x11432301

Blagden, N., Winder, B., Gregson, M., & Thorne, K. (2014). Making sense of denial in sexual offenders: A qualitative phenomenological and repertory grid analysis. *Journal of Interpersonal Violence, 29,* 1698–1731. doi: 10.1177/0886260513511530

Blake, E., & Gannon, T. (2008). Social perception deficits, cognitive distortions, and empathy deficits in sex offenders: A brief review. *Trauma, Violence, & Abuse, 9,* 34–55. doi: 10.1177/1524838007311104

Boer, D. P., Thakker, J., & Ward, T. (2009). Sex offender risk-based case formulation. In A. R. Beech, L. A. Craig & K. D. Browne (Eds.), *Assessment and treatment of sex offenders: A handbook* (pp. 77–87). Chichester, UK: Wiley.

Braithwaite, J. (1989). *Crime, shame and reintegration.* Cambridge, UK: Cambridge University Press.

Bumby, K. M., Marshall, W. L., & Langton, C. M. (1999). A theoretical model of the influences of shame and guilt on sexual offending. In B. K. Schwartz (Ed.), *The sex offender: Theoretical advances, treating special populations and legal developments* (Vol. 3, pp. 5–1—5–12). Kingston, NJ: Civic Research Institute.

Clark, A. (2012). Working with guilt and shame. *Advances in psychiatric treatment, 18*(2), 137–143. doi: 10.1192/apt.bp.110.008326

Cortoni, F., & Marshall, W. L. (2001). Sex as a coping strategy and its relationship to juvenile sexual history and intimacy in sexual offenders. *Sexual Abuse: A Journal of Research and Treatment, 13,* 27–42. doi: 10.1177/107906320101300104

Crocker, J., & Quinn, D. M. (2003). Social stigma and the self: Meanings, situations, and self-esteem. In T. F. Heatherton (Ed.), *The social psychology of stigma* (pp. 153–183). New York: Guilford Press.

Day, A. (2009). Offender emotion and self-regulation: Implications for offender rehabilitation programming. *Psychology, Crime & Law, 15,* 119–130. doi: 10.1080/10683160802190848

Elliott, I. A., Eldridge, H. J., Ashfield, S., & Beech, A. R. (2010). Exploring risk: Potential static, dynamic, protective and treatment factors in the clinical histories of female sex offenders. *Journal of Family Violence, 25,* 595–602. doi: 10.1007/s10896-010-9322-8

Elster, J. (1999). *Alchemies of the mind.* Cambridge, UK: Cambridge University Press.

Farrall, S., & Calverley, A. (2006). *Understanding desistance from crime: Theoretical directions in rehabilitation and resettlement.* Maidenhead, UK: Open University Press.

Feelgood, S., Golias, P., Shaw, S., & Bright, D. A. (2000). *Treatment changes in the dynamic risk factor of coping style in sexual offenders: A preliminary analysis.* New South Wales, Australia: N.S.W. Department of Corrective Services Sex Offender Programmes Custody Based Intensive Treatment (CUBIT).

Ford, H. (2006). *Women who sexually abuse children.* Chichester, UK: Wiley.

Gannon, T. A., & Alleyne, E. K. (2013). Female sexual abusers' cognition: A systematic review. *Trauma, Violence, & Abuse, 14,* 67–79. doi: 10.1177/1524838012462245

Gannon, T. A., & Rose, M. R. (2008). Female child sexual offenders: Towards integrating theory and practice. *Aggression and Violent Behavior, 13,* 442–461. doi: 10.1016/j.avb.2008.07.002

Gannon, T. A., Rose, M. R., & Ward, T. (2008). A descriptive model of the offense process for female sexual offenders. *Sexual Abuse: A Journal of Research and Treatment, 20,* 352–374. doi: 10.1177/1079063208322495

Gannon, T., Rose, M. R., & Ward, T. (2010). Pathways to female sexual offending: Approach or avoidance? *Psychology, Crime & Law, 16,* 359–380. doi: 10.1080/10683160902754956

Gannon, T., & Ward, T. (2014). Where has all the psychology gone? A critical review of evidence-based psychological practice in correctional settings. *Aggression and Violent Behavior, 19,* 435–436. doi: 10.1016/j.avb.2014.06.006

Gilbert, P. (2003). Evolution, social roles, and the differences in shame and guilt. *Social Research: An International Quarterly, 70,* 1205–1230.

Gilbert, P. R. (1998). *Counselling for depression.* London: Sage.

Gillespie, S. M., Mitchell, I. J., Fisher, D., & Beech, A. R. (2012). Treating disturbed emotional regulation in sexual offenders: The potential applications of mindful self-regulation and controlled breathing techniques. *Aggression and Violent Behavior, 17,* 333–343. doi: 10.1016/j.avb.2012.03.005

Göbbels, S., Ward, T., & Willis, G. M. (2012). An integrative theory of desistance from sex offending. *Aggression and Violent Behavior, 17,* 453–462. doi: 10.1016/j.avb.2012.06.003

Grayston, A. D., & De Luca, R. V. (1999). Female perpetrators of child sexual abuse: A review of the clinical and empirical literature. *Aggression and Violent Behavior, 4,* 93–106. doi: 10.1016/s1359-1789(98)00014-7

Hanson, R. K., & Harris, A. J. R. (2000). Where should we intervene? Dynamic predictors of sex offense recidivism. *Criminal Justice and Behavior, 27,* 6–35. doi: 10.1177/0093854800027001002

Hanson, R. K., & Morton-Bourgon, K. E. (2004). *Predictors of sexual recidivism: An updated meta-analysis* (Corrections User Report No 2004-02). Ottawa, Canada: Public Safety Canada.

Harder, D. W., & Lewis, S. J. (1987). The assessment of shame and guilt. *Advances in Personality Assessment, 6,* 89–114.

Hislop, J. (2001). *Female sex offenders: What therapists, law enforcement and child protective services need to know.* Ravensdale, WA: Idyll Arbor.

Howells, K., Day, A., & Wright, S. (2004). Affect, emotions and sex offending. *Psychology, Crime & Law, 10,* 179–195. doi: 10.1080/10683160310001609988

Jolliffe, D., & Farrington, D. P. (2004). Empathy and offending: A systematic review and meta-analysis. *Aggression and Violent Behavior, 9,* 441–476. doi: 10.1016/j.avb.2003.03.001

Kelly, A. E. (2000). Helping construct desirable identities: a self-presentational view of psychotherapy. *Psychological Bulletin, 126,* 475–494. doi: 10.1037/0033-2909.126.4.475

Lacombe, D. (2008). Consumed with sex: The treatment of sex offenders in risk society. *British Journal of Criminology, 48,* 55–74. doi: 10.1093/bjc/azm051

Langton, C. M., & Marshall, W. L. (2000). The role of cognitive distortions in relapse prevention programs. In D. R. Laws, S. M. Hudson & T. Ward (Eds.), *Remaking relapse prevention with sexual offenders* (pp. 167–186). London: Sage.

Lazarus, R. S. (2006). *Stress and emotion: A new synthesis.* New York: Springer.

LeBel, T. P., Burnett, R., Maruna, S., & Bushway, S. (2008). The 'chicken and egg' of subjective and social factors in desistance from crime. *European Journal of Criminology, 5,* 131–159. doi: 10.1177/1477370807087640

Leith, K. P., & Baumeister, R. F. (1998). Empathy, shame, guilt, and narratives of interpersonal conflicts: Guilt-prone people are better at perspective taking. *Journal of Personality, 66,* 1–37.

Looman, J. (1999). Mood, conflict and deviant sexual fantasises In B. Swartz (Ed.), *The sex offender* (pp. 3-1–3-11). Kinston, NJ: Civic Research Institute.

Mann, R. E. (2009). Getting the context right for sex offender treatment. In D. Prescott (Ed.), *Building motivation for change in sexual offenders* (pp. 55–73). Brandon, VT: Safer Society Press.

Mann, R. E., Hanson, R. K., & Thornton, D. (2010). Assessing risk for sexual recidivism: Some proposals on the nature of psychologically meaningful risk factors. *Sexual Abuse: A Journal of Research and Treatment, 22,* 191–217. doi: 10.1177/1079063210366039

Mann, R. E., Webster, S. D., Wakeling, H. C., & Keylock, H., (2012). Why do sexual offenders refuse treatment? *Journal of Sexual Aggression, 19*, 191–206. doi: 10.1080/13552600.2012.703701

Marshall, W. L. (1997). The relationship between self-esteem and deviant sexual arousal in nonfamilial child molesters. *Behavior Modification, 21*(1), 86–96. doi: 10.1177/01454455970211005

Marshall, W. L., Anderson, D., & Champagne, F. (1997). Self-esteem and its relationship to sexual offending: Invited Article. *Psychology, Crime & Law, 3*, 161–186. doi: 10.1080/10683169708410811

Marshall, W. L., Champagne, F., Sturgeon, C., & Bryce, P. (1997). Increasing the self-esteem of child molesters. *Sexual Abuse: A Journal of Research and Treatment, 9*, 321–333. doi: 10.1177/107906329700900405

Marshall, W. L., Marshall, L. E., Serran, G. A., & O'Brien, M. D. (2009). Self-esteem, shame, cognitive distortions and empathy in sexual offenders: Their integration and treatment implications. *Psychology, Crime & Law, 15(2–3)*, 217–234.

Marshall, W. L., Marshall, L. E., Serran, G. A., & O'Brien, M. D. (2011). *The rehabilitation of sexual offenders: A strength-based approach.* Washington, DC: American Psychological Association.

Marshall, W. L., Marshall, L. E., & Ware, J. (2009a). Cognitive distortions in sexual offenders: Should they all be treatment targets? *Sexual Abuse in Australia and New Zealand, 2*, 21.

Marshall, W. L., Marshall, L. E., Serran, G. A., & O'Brien, M. D. (2009b). Self-esteem, shame, cognitive distortions and empathy in sexual offenders: Their integration and treatment implications. *Psychology, Crime & Law, 15*, 217–234. doi: 10.1080/10683160802190947

Marshall, W. L., & Mazzucco, A. (1995). Self-esteem and parental attachments in child molesters. *Sexual Abuse: A Journal of Research and Treatment, 7*, 279–285. doi: 10.1177/107906329500700404

Maruna, S. (2001). *Making good: How ex-convicts reform and rebuild their lives.* Washington, DC: American Psychological Association.

Maruna, S. (2004). Desistance and explanatory style: A new direction in the psychology of reform. *Journal of Contemporary Criminal Justice, 20*, 184–200. doi: 10.1177/1043986204263778

Maruna, S., & Copes, H. (2005) Excuses excuses: What have we learnt from five decades of neutralisation research? *Crime and Justice: A Review of Research, 32*, 221–320. doi: 10.1086/655355

Matthews, J. K. (1993). Working with female sexual abusers. In M. Elliot (Ed.), *Female sexual abuse of children: The ultimate taboo* (pp. 61–78). Essex, UK: Longman.

McAlinden, A. M. (2007). *The shaming of sexual offenders: Risk, retribution and reintegration.* Oxford, UK: Hart.

McGrath, R., Cumming, G., Burchard, B., Zeoli, S., & Ellerby, L. (2010). Current practices and emerging trends in sexual abuser management: The Safer Society 2009 North American Survey. Brandon, VT: Safer Society Press.

Murphy, W. D. (1990) Assessment and modification of cognitive distortions in sex offenders. In W. L. Marshall, R. D. Laws & H. Barbaree, *Handbook of sexual* assault: Issues, theory and treatment of the offender (pp. 331–342). New York: Plenum Press.

Nathan, P., & Ward, T. (2002). Female sex offenders: Clinical and demographic features. *Journal of Sexual Aggression, 8,* 5–21. doi:10.1080/13552600208413329

Pfäfflin, F., Böhmer, M, Cornehl, S., & Mergenthaler, F. (2005). What happens in therapy with sex offenders? A model of process research. *Sexual Abuse: A Journal of Research and Treatment, 17,* 141–151. doi:10.1007/s11194-005-4601-2

Polaschek, D. L., Hudson, S. M., Ward, T., & Siegert, R. J. (2001). Rapists' offense processes a preliminary descriptive model. *Journal of Interpersonal Violence, 16,* 523–544. doi: 10.1177/088626001016006003

Proeve, M., & Howells, K. (2006). Shame and guilt in child molesters. In W. L. Marshall, Y. M. Fernandez, L. E. Marshall & G. A. Serran (Eds.), *Sexual offender treatment: Controversial issues* (pp. 125–139). Chichester, UK: Wiley.

Proulx, J., Brien, T., Ciampi, A., Allaire, J. F., McDonald, M., & Chouinard, A. (2004, October). *Treatment attrition in sexual offenders.* Paper presented at the 23rd Annual Research and Treatment Conference of the Association for the Treatment of Sexual Abusers, Albuquerque, NM.

Proulx, J., Perreault, C., & Ouimet, M. (1999). Pathways in the offending process of extrafamilial sexual child molesters. *Sexual Abuse: A Journal of Research and Treatment, 11,* 117–129. doi: 10.1007/bf02658842

Roger, D., & Masters, R. (1997). The development and evaluation of an emotion control training program for sex offenders. *Legal and Criminological Psychology, 2,* 51–64. doi: 10.1111/j.2044-8333.1997.tb00332.x

Ryff, C. D., & Singer, B. H. (1996). Psychological well-being: Meaning, measurement, and implications for psychotherapy research. *Psychotherapy and Psychosomatics, 65,* 14–23. doi: 10.1159/000289026

Saradjian, J., & Hanks, H. G. (1996). *Women who sexually abuse children: From research to clinical practice.* New York: Wiley.

Serran, G. A., Firestone, P., Marshall, W. L., & Moulden, H. (2007). Changes in coping following treatment for child molesters. *Journal of Interpersonal Violence, 22,* 1199–1210. doi: 10.1177/0886260507303733

Serran, G. A., & Marshall, L. E. (2006). Coping and mood in sexual offending. In W. L. Marshall, Y. M. Fernandez, L. E. Marshall & G. A. Serran (Eds.), *Sexual offender treatment: Controversial issues* (pp. 109–124). Chichester, UK: Wiley.

Shine, J., McCloskey, H., & Newton, M. (2002). Self-esteem and sex offending. *Journal of Sexual Aggression, 8,* 51–61. doi: 10.1080/13552600208413332

Silfver, M., Helkama, K., Lönnqvist, J. E., & Verkasalo, M. (2008). The relation between value priorities and proneness to guilt, shame, and empathy. *Motivation and Emotion, 32,* 69–80. doi: 10.1007/s11031-008-9084-2

Svensson, R., Weerman, F. M., Pauwels, L. J., Bruinsma, G. J., & Bernasco, W. (2013). Moral emotions and offending: Do feelings of anticipated shame and guilt mediate the effect of socialization on offending? *European Journal of Criminology, 10,* 22–39. doi: 10.1177/1477370812454393

Tangney, J. P., & Dearing, R. L. (2002). *Shame and guilt.* New York: Guilford Press.

Tangney, J. P., Stuewig, J., & Hafez, L. (2011). Shame, guilt, and remorse: Implications for offender populations. *Journal of Forensic Psychiatry & Psychology, 22,* 706–723. doi: 10.1080/14789949.2011.617541

Vandiver, D. M., & Kercher, G. (2004). Offender and victim characteristics of registered female sexual offenders in Texas: A proposed typology of female sexual offenders. *Sexual Abuse: A Journal of Research and Treatment, 16,* 121–137. doi: 10.1023/b:sebu.0000023061.77061.17

Waldram, J. B. (2007). Narrative and the construction of 'truth' in a prison-based treatment program for sexual offenders. *Ethnography, 8,* 145–169. doi: 10.1177/1466138107078631

Ward, T. (2000). Sexual offenders' cognitive distortions as implicit theories. *Aggression and Violent Behavior, 5,* 491–507. doi: 10.1016/s1359-1789(98)00036-6

Ward, T., & Hudson, S. M. (2000). A self-regulation model of relapse prevention. In D. R. Laws, S. M. Hudson & T. Ward (Eds.), *Remaking relapse prevention with sex offenders: A sourcebook* (pp. 79–101). Thousand Oaks, CA: Sage.

Ward, T., Hudson, S., & Marshall, W. (1995). Cognitive distortions and affective deficits in sex offenders: A cognitive deconstructionist approach. *Sexual Abuse: A Journal of Research and Treatment, 7,* 67–83. doi: 10.1007/bf02254874

Ward, T., Louden, K., Hudson, S. M., & Marshall, W. L. (1995). A descriptive model of the offense chain for child molesters. *Journal of Interpersonal Violence, 10*(4), 452–472. doi: 10.1177/088626095010004005

Ward, T., & Stewart, C. A. (2003). Criminogenic needs and human needs: A theoretical model. *Psychology, Crime, & Law, 9,* 125–143. doi: 10.1037/0735-7028.34.4.353

Ward, T., Vess, J., Collie, R. M., & Gannon, T. A. (2006). Risk management or goods promotion: The relationship between approach and avoidance goals in treatment for sex offenders. *Aggression and Violent Behavior, 11,* 378–393. doi: 10.1016/j.avb.2006.01.001

Ware, J. (2011). The importance of contextual issues within sexual offender treatment. In D. P. Boer, R. Eher, L. A. Craig, M. H. Miner & F. Pfäfflin (Eds.), *International perspectives on the assessment and treatment of sexual offenders: Theory, practice and research* (pp. 299–312). Chichester, UK: Wiley.

Ware, J., & Bright, D. A. (2008). Evolution of a treatment program for sex offenders: Changes to the NSW Custody Based Intensive Treatment (CUBIT). *Psychiatry, Psychology, and Law, 15,* 340–349. doi: 10.1080/13218710802014543

Ware, J., Frost, A., & Boer, D. (2015). Working with sex offenders. In K. Sullivan, A. King & T. Nove (Eds.), *Group work in Australia* (pp. 252–267). Sydney, Australia: Institute of Group Leaders.

Ware, J., & Mann, R. E. (2012). How should 'acceptance of responsibility' be addressed in sexual offending treatment programs? *Aggression and Violent Behavior, 7,* 279–288. doi: 10.1016/j.avb.2012.02.009

Webster, S. D., Mann, R. E., Carter, A. J., Long, J., Milner, R. J., O'Brien, M. D., et al. (2006). Inter-rater reliability of dynamic risk assessment with sexual offenders. *Psychology, Crime & Law, 12,* 439–452. doi: 10.1080/10683160500036889

Wormith, J. S., & Olver, M. E. (2002). Offender treatment attrition and its relationship with risk, responsivity, and recidivism. *Criminal Justice and Behavior, 29,* 447–471. doi: 10.1177/0093854802029004006

6

Motivators, Self-Regulation and Sexual Offending

Jill D. Stinson

Self-regulation, broadly viewed as the ability to modulate and control emotion, cognition and behaviour, has gained increasing prominence in the aetiology and treatment of psychopathology and behavioural problems. Research highlighting the role of self-regulatory functioning in problematic sexual behaviour has spurred the introduction of several theoretical conceptualizations and related treatment approaches for individuals with a history of sexual offending. A fundamental assumption underlying these emergent ideas is that self-regulation plays a critical role in the motivation to sexually offend against children and/or adults.

Within this chapter, three models will be explored to facilitate a greater understanding of the connection between self-regulation and the sexual offence process: relapse prevention (Laws, 1989; Pithers, 1990; Pithers, Marques, Gibat & Marlatt, 1983); self-regulation (Ward & Hudson, 1998; Ward, Hudson & Keenan, 1998); and the multi-model self-regulation theory (Stinson, Sales & Becker, 2008). With each model, important theoretical concepts, empirical support, treatment methodologies and critical limitations will be discussed. Finally, the chapter concludes with implications for diverse subgroups of people who have sexually offended (i.e., women and those experiencing major mental illness).

Relapse Prevention

First introduced in the 1980s by Alan Marlatt (1982; Marlatt & Gordon, 1985), relapse prevention (RP) represented a dramatic departure from treatment-as-usual for clients with problematic alcohol and drug use. RP was initially conceptualized as a means of identifying precursors to substance use, including behavioural, interpersonal, cognitive and emotional contingencies. The overall aim was to develop a comprehensive skills plan to circumvent behaviours likely to lead to substance use relapse (Marlatt, 1982; Marlatt & Gordon, 1985). RP was applied to the sexual offence process by Pithers, Laws and colleagues (Laws, 1989; Pithers, 1990; Pithers et al., 1983), who argued that an important goal of

Sexual Offending: Cognition, Emotion and Motivation, First Edition.
Edited by Theresa A. Gannon and Tony Ward.
© 2017 John Wiley & Sons Ltd. Published 2017 by John Wiley & Sons Ltd.

understanding and treating individuals who sexually offend was identifying specific precipitants of problematic sexual behaviour.

Theoretical Conceptualization

Critical to the RP model (Marlatt, 1982; Marlatt & Gordon, 1985) are the concepts of *lapse* and *relapse*. A lapse, within the context of illicit substances, is a singular event in which the individual who is striving to abstain takes a sip of alcohol or uses prohibited drugs but goes no farther. This is differentiated from a relapse, when the individual reverts to a previous pattern of addictive behaviour or repeated substance abuse. Applied to those who sexually offend (Laws, 1989; Pithers, 1990; Pithers et al., 1983), a lapse involves purposeful involvement in offence-supportive sexual fantasy or other risky behaviours (e.g., a man who has sexually abused a child agreeing to babysit small children or a man who has raped an adult woman engaging in masturbatory fantasies of past victims), whereas relapse occurs when a new sexual offence is committed.

The RP model focuses on high-risk situations, or situations in which the person is at significant risk of committing a sexual offence. An important assumption is that prior to the high-risk situation, the person is in a state of abstinence (i.e., free from sexual thoughts or intention to offend), rendering them less able to objectively evaluate potential risk.

The original model (Marlatt, 1982; Marlatt & Gordon, 1985) proposed three pathways to a high-risk situation. First, the individual might find themselves unexpectedly exposed to risk (e.g., a recovering alcohol abuser being offered a drink). Second, acute stressors may challenge the person's limited coping, leading them to rely on previous maladaptive strategies (e.g., a person who has stopped smoking finding it easier to deal with increased work stress by having a cigarette). Third, a person may engage in seemingly unimportant decisions – termed SUDs – that increase risky behaviours. These decisions might seem reasonable in the moment or go overlooked by others, and may be beyond the person's immediate awareness (e.g., driving home past a favourite bar or agreeing to have dinner with a friend who continues to use drugs).

The description of RP for sexual offending put forth by Pithers et al. (1983) and Laws (1989; Laws, Hudson & Ward, 2000) focuses primarily on the latter two pathways, though unexpected exposure to risk is addressed within the context of a RP plan. Acute or unrelenting periods of stress may challenge adaptive coping and lead to offence-related sexual fantasy or behaviours, as these have served as coping mechanisms in the past. Similarly, individuals may engage in a series of SUDs, such as a man who has abused children finding low-cost housing in a neighbourhood with a nearby community playground, or a man with a rape conviction obtaining employment as a bouncer in a club involving routine contact with intoxicated female patrons. In each of these situations, such decisions may not seem immediately related to a plan to sexually re-offend, but we can clearly anticipate resulting risks that may precipitate lapse and later relapse.

In a high-risk situation, the individual may face momentary surrender to risky behaviour (i.e., lapse). Marlatt and Gordon (1985) described the problem of immediate gratification (PIG) that contributes to a decision to go forth with risky behaviour despite potential consequences. The individual may fail to cope with the risky situation or succumb to the PIG, resulting in a lapse. Pithers, Laws and colleagues more thoroughly described a predictable sequence of events following a lapse (Laws, 1989; Laws et al., 2000; Pithers, 1990; Pithers et al., 1983). First, the individual experiences the abstinence violation effect (AVE). This realization that a lapse has occurred precipitates associated cognitive and affective responses. The individual recognizes failure. Cognitive responses include attributions regarding the controllability, origin and pervasiveness of the lapse. One who believes the lapse to be externally motivated, or not reflective of his or her treatment success (e.g., 'That was only a minor setback. I can use my coping skills to get past it.'), is more likely to succeed in circumventing relapse. However, for one who views the lapse as indicative of treatment failure or personal weakness (e.g., 'I knew I couldn't do this.'), there is a high likelihood of relapse. Affective responses may include guilt, shame, hopelessness or disappointment, and these emotions, in combination with attributions of personal weakness or treatment failure, influence likelihood of relapse or re-offence.

The RP model of sexual offending was designed to explain two primary components of the offence process: (1) how individuals find themselves in risky situations; and (2) how the individual handles that risk in an adaptive versus maladaptive way (Laws et al., 2000). The self-regulation component of this model is largely concerned with the latter and presupposes past struggles with maladaptive coping, particularly in the form of sexualized coping. Consequently, development of more adaptive coping is a salient need.

Empirical Evidence and Treatment Implications

Teasing apart the evidence for RP as an aetiological model from the evidence that evaluates its effectiveness as a treatment proves difficult. RP was introduced as an intervention approach and explains the process of preventing reoffending rather than the initial offence. The treatment has been presented in many forms, most of which involve describing the individual's offence cycle (e.g., specific situational, cognitive and affective responses that build upon one another related to lapse and relapse) and developing a comprehensive RP plan that identifies necessary coping skills or avoidance strategies to prevent relapse.

The longevity of RP in both correctional and community sexual offender treatment programmes (McGrath et al., 2010) has prompted extensive research examining its impact on sexual re-offence. The initiation of the Sex Offender Treatment Evaluation Project (SOTEP; Marques, Day, Nelson & Miner, 1989) led to a long-term examination of the impact of RP on sexual offence recidivism in males receiving two years of intensive RP programming, in comparison with two untreated control groups. Preliminary results suggested treatment success, in that treated individuals showed improved ability to describe strategies for coping with high-risk situations, and rates of sexual recidivism were significantly reduced for men who had completed treatment (i.e., 8% vs. 20–21% for two untreated control groups; Miner, Marques, Day, & Nelson, 1990). However, final results found that although participants who met the programme's treatment goals demonstrated a lesser rate of sexual reoffending than controls after eight-years' follow-up, differences were not significant (Marques et al., 2005).

Critique and Future Implications

The literature examining sexual offending is replete with conceptual and practical critiques of RP. In particular, Hudson, Ward and colleagues (e.g., Hudson, Ward & Marshall, 1992; Laws et al., 2000; Ward, 2000; Ward & Hudson, 1996; Ward, Hudson & Siegert, 1995) have identified several areas of concern. The first involves definitions of lapse and relapse, as applied to treatment for individuals who have sexually offended. Such concepts were originally described in the context of substance abuse, and it is vital for us to question their applicability to a process as disparate as sexual offending. A lapse defined as taking a sip of champagne at a party is qualitatively different from a lapse defined as engaging in masturbatory fantasies of children. A second concern noted by these authors is that the PIG and AVE must simultaneously occur to transition from lapse to relapse, but that they conceptually conflict with one another. The theory presupposes that the excitement and need for offending (i.e., PIG) exists in equal measure with the fear or distress about failing to abstain from offending (i.e., AVE). The need for offending must, therefore, work together with the fear of offending to propel the individual closer to relapse, which is difficult to reconcile. Third, SUDs imply that individuals implicitly plan offences without conscious awareness of it, a finding which has not been borne by research (e.g., Ward, Hudson & Siegert, 1995).

A broader concern, however, is the scope of RP in explaining initial sexual offending (e.g., Polaschek, 2003). The model begins with re-offence, inherently presuming that previous offences have occurred. It does not describe important developmental mechanisms precipitating early offending, nor does it provide evidence or theoretical hypotheses as to how those early mechanisms overlap with the more immediate self-regulatory processes associated with re-offence. This and the related concern that it may not fully or accurately describe the reported mechanisms of re-offence (e.g., Polaschek, 2003; Ward & Hudson, 1998), as well as a lack of support in the literature, has led to a shift away from using RP in sexual offence work. Future research should continue to examine aspects of the RP model showing promise (e.g., Marques et al., 2005), and to relate these findings to other evidence of self-regulatory functioning in the sexual offence process.

Self-Regulation Model

First developed to clarify the role of self-regulation in the relapse process, Ward and Hudson (1998) and Ward, Hudson and Keenan (1998) introduced the self-regulation model. This approach targets the sequence of internal and external events most proximal to lapse or relapse and expands upon mechanisms of sexual offending to include multiple regulatory pathways. The self-regulation model includes pathways explaining not only the inhibition or suppression of behaviour, but also enhancement, maintenance and elicitation of behaviour (Ward & Hudson, 1998), recognizing differing motivators for each. Ward and colleagues posited that for some, planning or committing a sexual offence represents a deliberate self-regulatory approach goal.

This model adopts a functional-contextual definition of self-regulation, with self-regulation occurring through internal and external processes that facilitate movement toward goal-directed behaviour (Baumeister & Heatherton, 1996; Karoly, 1993). Goals are paramount – all self-regulatory functioning serves established goals. These may be categorically divided into acquisitional/approach goals and inhibitory/avoidance goals (Cochran & Tesser, 1996), existing as hier-archical structures with associated behavioural scripts, reactive and reciprocal feedback loops, and a sequence of emotional responses, all of which are both consciously and unconsciously controlled over time (Carver & Scheier, 1981, 1990). These combined processes operate to direct responses to changing environmental and interpersonal contingencies and facilitate learning toward the achievement of identified goals.

Theoretical Conceptualization

Sexual offending occurs within the context of self-regulating approach and avoidance goals. Ward and Hudson (1998) and Ward, Hudson and Keenan (1998) describe five core features of the self-regulation model. First, it contains varied offence pathways, each accounting for changes or individual differences in affect and the degree of planning involved in distinct behaviours. Second, it integrates cognitive, affective and behavioural components of the self-regulatory and offence processes. Third, it describes fluid and dynamic regulatory processes proximal to offending. Fourth, the model is part of a comprehensive theoretical framework, with proximal factors distinctly relating to behavioural outcomes. Finally, the model relates to specific phases or aspects of the offence process identified in the empirical research. Such features promote the integration of complex and changing conditions that may precipitate a sexual offence.

Self-regulatory problems are described in three ways. The first reflects failure to control emotions and behaviours; for those who have sexually offended, this may be the failure to control sexual offence supportive intentions or desires, or the under regulation of negative affect that leads to disinhibited behaviour. For example, someone overwhelmed by negative affect or sexual urges may become disinhibited or less able to manage impulses in the moment. The second involves misregulation, when attempts to regulate thoughts, emotions or behaviours are ineffective or unintentionally decrease self-control. This is demonstrated, for example, by an individual coping with stress by drinking alcohol, which may instead disinhibit sexual impulse control.

These two features of self-regulatory dysfunction were included in the original RP model (Ward & Hudson, 1998; Ward, Hudson & Keenan, 1998). However, the third is unique to the self-regulation model and reflects specific approach goals. Here, the individual's ability to self-regulate is intact, but they choose to commit a sexual offence. Thus, the problem is the selected goal rather than self-regulation. The goal's origin is varied and complex. Any chosen goal is influenced by personality, development and characteristics of the individual's learning and environment. This is no different for persons whose goals relate to sexual offending, whether they be avoidance or approach goals. Factors like impulsivity, need for immediate gratification, early learned experiences and beliefs about sexuality all play a role (Ward, Hudson & Keenan, 1998).

First is the salience of the individual's goal. Distal factors like developmental experiences, or proximal factors, such as life events or affective states that trigger familiar patterns of thought, sexual interest or behavioural scripts, contribute to the formation and recognition of important approach and avoidance goals (Ward, Hudson & Keenan, 1998). Recognizing that important goals are not being met, the individual experiences an associated affective state and cognitive self-appraisal, prompting identification of ways to correct the situation. This initiates implicit or explicit planning behaviour, and the particular self-regulatory pathway instigated depends on the nature of the goal and the individual's ability to develop and implement self-regulatory strategies.

Implicit planning requires little conscious awareness of true intentions or motives – perhaps related to SUDs as described in RP – and activates habitual behavioural scripts or automatic cognitive processes. Such sequences of thinking and behaviour may be more strongly associated with self-regulatory failure and avoidance goals. Explicit planning, on the other hand, reflects intact self-regulatory systems motivated by a specific goal as well as the individual's ability to effectively execute self-regulatory strategies.

The self-regulation model proposes four regulatory pathways through which implicit and explicit planning are evident, any of which may prompt a sexual offence (Ward & Hudson, 1998). The first is the avoidant-passive pathway, in which the individual wants to avoid a sexual offence but fails to do anything to prevent it. For example, situational events or affective states may remind the individual of past offences, past inadequacies or emotional states associated with previous self-regulatory failure. Implicit planning occurs when the individual begins a sequence of unconscious thought or behavioural patterns that increase risk of offending.

A second is the avoidance-active pathway, in which the individual wishes to avoid sexual offending but selects ineffective strategies that have the paradoxical effect of increasing sexual offending (i.e., misregulation; Ward & Hudson, 1998). Use of alcohol, drugs, pornography or masturbation would characterize this hypothesized pathway.

The third pathway, approach-automatic, results from a goal that facilitates sexual offending and involves behaviours that are overlearned, automatic or habitual (Ward & Hudson, 1998). Thus, the individual may not be consciously planning an offence but does not act to avoid offending. Here, a male who seeks sexual gratification or attention from a female partner may go to a bar to meet women. As he has engaged in coercive sexual behaviour in the past, some implicit planning may influence his behaviour. He does not intend to victimize anyone, though he is also not avoiding contextual cues linked to offending. He therefore may be at increased risk of acting in inappropriate ways to satisfy his sexual desires.

Finally, the fourth pathway – approach-explicit – involves harmful goals and effective and deliberate self-regulatory functioning (Ward & Hudson, 1998; Ward, Hudson & Keenan, 1998). This is best exemplified by an individual who: (1) desires sexual contact with a victim; (2) develops a plan that facilitates contact with a chosen victim and minimizes the possibility of detection or failure; and (3) commits a sexual offence.

Self-regulatory mechanisms then drive further action. Self-evaluation and information processing comparing the current situation to proximal and distal goals, interpersonal feedback and immediate affective state, and other contextual factors allow the individual to appraise the situation, interact with or avoid potential victims, devote necessary cognitive effort to appropriate versus offence-supportive coping strategies and so on. For those with avoidance goals, contextual factors may foretell impending failure, whereas those with approach goals may view such contextual factors as indicative of success (Ward & Hudson, 1998). Following sexual offence or relapse, the self-regulation model posits that individuals experience something akin to the AVE component of RP, in that the affective response and cognitive appraisal of that response will be integrated into future goal-orienting behaviours, either contributing to further offence-supportive planning or strengthening the desire to avoid sexual relapse.

Empirical Evidence

Emerging empirical research supports a number of underlying conceptual features of the self-regulation model. The initial model, emphasizing nine phases and four distinct pathways, relied on qualitative empirical evidence described by Ward, Louden, Hudson and Marshall (1995). Two types of child molesters were identified that corresponded to approach versus avoidance offence goals, a distinction subsequently demonstrated by Bickley and Beech (2003) in a larger sample. Webster (2005) differentiated avoidance-active, approach-automatic and approach-explicit pathways in a sample of men who had sexually recidivated following treatment (see also Yates, Kingston & Hall, 2003). Specifically, approach pathways of either type were more common among individuals with female victims, whereas those with male victims were more likely to exhibit an approach-explicit pathway. Men characterized by incest offences were likely to follow approach pathways, though some also exhibited an avoidance-passive style (Yates, Kingston & Hall, 2003).

The relationship between offending and the four proposed self-regulatory pathways has been supported in a sample of individuals with intellectual disability who have sexually offended, with some differentiation on the basis of overall level of intellectual and adaptive functioning (Ford, Rose & Thrift, 2009). Using a similar sample, Lindsay, Steptoe and Beech (2008) found that approach pathways are predominant and may be more associated with offence-supportive thoughts and beliefs (Langdon, Maxted, Murphy & SOSTEC-ID Group, 2007). Finally, other research (Kingston, Yates & Firestone, 2012; Yates & Kingston, 2006) indicates that the four pathways are differentially associated with indicators of static and dynamic risk, with those in the approach pathways not surprisingly evidencing the highest rates of risk and criminality overall.

Treatment Implications

The self-regulation model was developed in tandem with the Good Lives Model (GLM), a treatment approach emphasizing approach goals and fundamental human strivings. Though a great deal has been written elsewhere regarding the implementation and efficacy of the GLM with regard to improving outcomes for persons with a history of sexual offending (see Ward & Brown, 2004; Ward & Gannon, 2006; Ward, Mann & Gannon, 2007), it is worth noting that the self-regulation model provides direction in developing treatment-related attainment goals. Using approach pathways, the GLM seeks to modify or activate individuals' approach goals to prosocial and appropriate ones. This is in contrast to other treatment models that address specific deficits or offence-supportive attitudes and beliefs, or encourage avoidance strategies that lend themselves to a higher degree of self-regulatory failure.

Critique and Future Implications

The self-regulation model of the relapse process was introduced as a means of improving the RP approach that preceded it, yet there are still areas of need for future research. First, the self-regulation model presumes the existence of offence-related approach or avoidance goals without examining the origin or development of such goals. While noting that early developmental events, including exposure to violence or sexual abuse (Ward, Hudson & Keenan, 1998), as well as personality variables, play a role in the formation of offence-related goals, the model does not elaborate further, as it is intended to explain factors most proximal to offending. Future research, however, could assist in understanding important personality, developmental or other individual characteristics linked with each pathway so as to understand these from a wider aetiological perspective. Relatedly, it is important to learn how individuals select sexual offending or offence-supportive behaviours as an approach goal, particularly in the absence of obvious antecedents (e.g., sexual victimization, modelling of offence-supportive attitudes and behaviours from important others), or in spite of other, more prosocial goals.

A great strength of the self-regulation model is its use of an established definition of self-regulation that applies broadly across behaviours and has been evaluated in multiple contexts. Further, empirical research has established a relationship between proposed pathways and offence behaviours among a variety of individuals, including persons with intellectual disability. However, this research has predominantly identified approach pathways as those most associated with offending, and additional research is needed to determine if this is the reality for most individuals, or if these instead reflect the goals of those who have been caught. It is also possible that after having participated in treatment, these individuals are more likely to indicate approach goals through some expectancy bias (e.g., equating 'taking responsibility' with admitting to approach goals). Such research would help clarify the role, if any, of avoidance goals, and would also more accurately describe underregulation and misregulation.

Multi-Modal Self-Regulation Theory

The multi-modal self-regulation theory (Stinson, Sales & Becker, 2008) examines the role of self-regulation from a developmental perspective. Self-regulation is defined as the individual's ability to modulate thoughts, emotions and behaviours in order to maintain a comfortable homeostasis. The drive for such homeostasis is assumed, presupposing a unique, idiosyncratic 'set point' for an individual's emotions, interpersonal interactions, thoughts and behaviours. Deviation from the set point results in dysregulation, activating the drive to self-regulate. How people self-regulate depends on their ability to use functional regulatory skills. Functional skills work to alleviate dysregulation, whereas dysfunctional skills fail to restore homeostasis. Self-regulatory skills are further adaptive or maladaptive, signifying the extent to which skills present potential harm to self or others. Self-regulatory skills are reinforced over time and become patterns of self-regulatory behaviour. Such definitions stem from the larger clinical literature examining persons with pervasive difficulties with emotion regulation and borderline personality disorder (see Linehan, 1993) and have been used to examine maladaptive self-regulatory behaviours in those with a range of problems, including self-harm and suicidality (e.g., Claes, Vertommen, Smits & Bijttebier, 2009; Linehan, 1993), substance use problems (Hull & Slone, 2004) and aggression (Hirschi, 2004).

Theoretical Conceptualization

The multi-modal self-regulation theory examines the development of self-regulatory ability among persons who have committed sexual offences. Sexual offending behaviours are viewed as maladaptive self-regulatory strategies, used by some to modulate extreme states of dysregulation. This occurs over time and through a combination of factors.

Biological vulnerabilities impact the individual's self-regulatory ability, particularly with regard to aspects of brain functioning related to emotionality and behavioural inhibition. The amygdala and associated components of the limbic system have implications for the individual's ability to express, modulate and learn from emotional experiences, while the prefrontal cortex plays a role in inhibiting behavioural impulses associated with strong emotion. Persons with problematic self-regulation have been shown to exhibit a combination of overactivation in the amygdala and underactivation in the prefrontal cortex, suggesting high emotionality with low impulse control (Hazlett et al., 2005; Heatherton, 2011; Hill et al., 2009; Minzenberg et al., 2007, 2008; Siegle, 2007). The proposed origin of such characteristics may range from early developmental adversity and trauma (e.g., Beers & DeBellis, 2002; Bremner,

2003a, b) to genetic predisposition (Linehan, 1993). Such vulnerabilities may be exhibited through easily-observed temperamental characteristics, including increased sensitivity to environmental cues, heightened response to distress, prominent negative affect and difficulty returning to baseline following dysregulation (see Linehan, 1993; Stinson & Becker, 2012; Stinson, Sales & Becker, 2008).

Biological vulnerabilities alone, however, do not explain pervasive self-regulatory problems. Also important are socialization and interactions with peers and caregivers, many of whom serve as models for self-regulatory coping. Some caregivers may ameliorate the impact of biological vulnerability among those who experience more extreme and negative emotionality, exhibiting adaptive, functional self-regulatory skills they use themselves. Not all caregivers are able to do this. Hostile parenting, abuse and inconsistent or unresponsive parenting result in continuing distress and fail to teach adequate, effective coping. This may lead to a cycle of heightened distress, desperate behaviours to solicit assistance (e.g., temper tantrums, crying) and resulting harshness and punitive responses from others. Further, caregivers who lack the ability to self-regulate themselves may model inappropriate regulatory behaviours (e.g., substance abuse, violence or manipulative behaviours).

The individual with biological vulnerabilities and adverse developmental experiences may exhibit problematic or maladaptive self-regulatory skills during times of emotional (e.g., anger, anxiety, sadness), cognitive (e.g., judgment, rumination, blame) or interpersonal (e.g., isolation, arguing, hostility) dysregulation (Stinson & Becker, 2012; Stinson, Sales & Becker, 2008), and successful relief from distress or dysregulation will result in reinforcement of these behaviours over time. Here, dysregulation is a normative experience, though the intensity, frequency and duration of dysregulation is individual and contextually dependent. For persons lacking functional regulatory coping skills (i.e., they never learned them or the skills they learned failed to sufficiently work), or for those who learned maladaptive responses through modelling or other environmental cues, the drive to reduce dysregulation is paramount. Such persons seek regulatory strategies that are effective, immediate and relatively effortless. This unfortunately favours a number of maladaptive strategies that are highly reinforcing and that also artificially and temporarily change mood or other internal states, such as consuming alcohol or drugs, aggression or violence, or sexual behaviour. In particular, the multi-modal self-regulation theory emphasizes sexual behaviour as a maladaptive coping strategy, as sexual fantasy and behaviour are highly reinforcing, present a range of opportunities for gratification and may be readily available, depending on perceived opportunities in the immediate environment. Reinforcement is key, as immediate gratification of desires or reduction of dysregulation may outweigh the longer-term consequences of detection, punishment and shame.

Finally, certain personality characteristics have long been associated with increased propensity toward sexually acting out and are linked to self-regulatory problems (see Stinson, Sales & Becker, 2008). For example, impulsivity, entitlement, egocentricity and traits of sadism or psychopathy may be particularly implicated in this process. Associated cognitions like believing that the world owes them something, or that their needs are more important than others' may greatly predispose these individuals to specific types of maladaptive behavioural responses.

Pragmatically, this approach conceptualizes a range of persons with sexual behaviour problems. Because the model emphasizes individualized patterns of dysregulation and behavioural reinforcement, it focuses less on types of victims or offences and instead on how dysregulation manifests itself. The theory describes development of sexual behaviour problems within the context of emotional, cognitive, interpersonal and behavioural dysregulation and also considers the extent of self-regulatory deficits and reinforced patterns of maladaptive regulatory strategies across the lifespan.

Empirical Evidence

Growing evidence supports the hypothesis that sexual behaviours emerge as coping skills for some individuals (e.g., Burk & Burkhart, 2002; Cortoni & Marshall, 2001; Feelgood, Cortoni & Thompson, 2005), and that self-regulatory problems are predictors of sexual recidivism (e.g., Hanson & Harris, 1998; Hanson, Harris, Scott & Helmus, 2007). Pilot research with this model used path analysis in a sample of civilly-committed sexually violent predators (SVPs) to demonstrate that those with greater affective instability, negative emotionality and mood disorders evidenced greater sexual pathology, more frequent sexual offending and more indiscriminate sexual and criminal offending (Stinson, Becker & Sales, 2008). A second study in a sample of psychiatric inpatients with sexual behaviour problems used factor analysis to categorically identify subtypes of dysregulation and then relate these to specific behavioural outcomes, including suicidal/self-injurious behaviours, sexual offending and aggressive or criminal behaviours (Stinson, Robbins & Crow, 2011).

Continued research examining domains of self-regulation and further delineating relationships between early childhood adversity, self-regulatory deficits and maladaptive regulatory behaviours is underway. More is needed to clarify the role of distinctive personality traits and their interaction with self-regulatory abilities, and also to better understand the process of reinforcement with regard to self-regulatory skills development.

Treatment Implications

Treatment applications of the multi-modal self-regulation theory include a manualized treatment programme designed for those with pervasive self-regulatory problems, mental illness and/or intellectual disabilities (Stinson & Becker, 2012), though treatment has been applied to those with varying degrees of these impairments. This treatment, called Safe Offender Strategies (SOS) is aimed at identifying existing difficulties with self-regulation in multiple domains and addresses these deficits with self-monitoring protocols and adaptive skills training. SOS stresses the importance of understanding individualized precipitants of a sexual offence and associated client vulnerabilities that lead to dysregulation and maladaptive behaviour. This approach additionally includes aspects of motivational interviewing (Miller & Rollnick, 2013) and validation (e.g., Linehan, 1993) to foster client responsivity.

Two pilot studies have thus far demonstrated early empirical support for the use of SOS in inpatient psychiatric samples characterized by histories of mental illness, intellectual impairment and self-regulatory problems. Stinson, McVay and Becker (2015) evaluated the impact of weekly SOS groups on hospitalized adult men receiving treatment for their sexual offending behaviour, using a year of pre-treatment data and two years of data while participants were engaged in treatment. The percentage of SOS groups attended and time in treatment were significantly predictive of decreases in charted incidents of verbal and physical aggression, sexual offending and team-rated treatment engagement, in comparison with pre-treatment baseline. The second study examined outcomes for a group of similar psychiatric patients who had received RP during an inpatient stay in comparison with a group who had received SOS (Stinson, McVay & Becker, in press). They were tracked for up to three years post-release, and those who had received SOS were significantly less likely to be arrested (no arrests versus 9% arrested in the RP group) or psychiatrically re-hospitalized during the follow-up (5% versus 55% re-hospitalized), suggesting a broader impact of self-regulatory skills training on post-release behaviour (Stinson, McVay & Becker, in press).

Critique and Future Directions

The multi-modal self-regulation theory and SOS remain comparatively new. A clear limitation of the model is the paucity of empirical evaluation and the need for further examination. At present, it is difficult to ascertain the accuracy of certain components of the model, including the impact of reinforcement and the validity of dysregulation as a construct, as used here.

A second critique relates to the theory's assumptions of diversity – one comprehensive framework explains not only varied sexual behaviours, but other maladaptive behaviours as well. While this is not inherently problematic given the overlap between sexual offending and other maladaptive behaviours (see Stinson, Sales & Becker, 2008), it goes against other, more established conceptual models and traditional clinical practice.

Third, the development of sexual offending behaviour as described by the multi-modal self-regulation theory leaves gaps which may not be easily resolved through further research. For example, we do not yet know the exact contingencies that cause one person to self-harm in response to extreme dysregulation, whereas another sexually molests a child. Because such individuals are only identified after the behaviour has occurred, we must rely on self-report to reach our conclusions. Such self-report is plagued by post-hoc justification, bias and lack of insight into prompting events or contingencies precipitating the behaviour. Similarly, we do not fully understand the environmental contingencies that lead some to perceive sexual activity with a child as a potential regulatory opportunity.

Finally, the multi-modal self-regulation theory emphasizes deficits in self-regulatory capacity, while the literature increasingly acknowledges the importance of strengths-based work. Although self-regulatory and other deficits remain relevant indicators of risk (e.g., Hanson & Harris, 1998; Hanson et al., 2007), we need to develop and foster protective factors in intervention programmes for persons who have sexually offended. Relatedly, we must remember that the precipitants of maladaptive sexual behaviour described herein (e.g., dysregulation and self-regulatory deficits) are common to many who do not commit sexual offences. Future research should consider the role of protective factors, as well as factors that assist in adaptive self-regulatory development among persons who have not committed sexual crimes.

Unique Populations and Self-Regulation Models

Self-regulation and its impact on motivation to sexually offend may be particularly relevant for some minority populations who sexually offend, including females and persons with serious mental illness. These groups often remain under-addressed in traditional conceptualizations of the sexual offence process and may exhibit features suggestive of self-regulatory problems.

Females Who Sexually Offend

Early causal theories regarding women who have committed sexual offences relied on societal biases, limited research sampling and understudied assumptions of females who offend (e.g., Gannon & Cortoni, 2010). However, more recent and thorough analyses have revealed common characteristics of women who have sexually offended and precursors to offending that significantly overlap with evidence from self-regulatory models (e.g., Gannon, Rose & Ward, 2008).

Women who have sexually offended often come from households characterized by instability, chaos and violence (e.g., Levenson, Willis & Prescott, 2015). Recent meta-analysis (Colson, Boyer, Baumstarck & Loundou, 2013) demonstrated that developmental histories of women who had sexually offended were marked by poverty, parental mental illness, trauma, familial substance use and learning disabilities, incest and other abuse, and a lack of closeness among family members. Such findings extended to nearly two-thirds of the women in the studies reviewed and are consistent with many of the models of self-regulation described within this chapter. Chaotic, violent, and unstable homes have implications for long-term self-regulatory problems and poor self-regulatory skills development, as well as selection of goals consistent with one's learned expectations of the environment and interpersonal relationships.

Women who have sexually offended display increased rates of mood and other disorders, personality pathology, decreased self-esteem, emotional and social dependence on others, anger problems, substance abuse, continued victimization and emotional instability (e.g., Colson et al., 2013; Gannon & Cortoni, 2010). Such features are characteristic of persons with self-regulatory problems and are represented in the varying self-regulation frameworks associated with sexual offending. Women who have sexually offended may disproportionately exhibit both distal and proximal precursors to offending described by these models, including the selection of important interpersonal goals. Though not explicitly causal, such characteristics may be over-represented in samples of women who sexually offend and merit further research.

Individuals with Serious Mental Illness

A small body of literature describes those who have sexually offended who have been diagnosed with serious mental illness. Among this subpopulation, high rates of trauma and familial dysfunction in early childhood, problems with relationships and community functioning, and evidence of impulsivity and aggression, affective instability, pervasive thought disorder, personality pathology and substance abuse are common (see Stinson & Becker, 2011). As is true for women who have sexually offended, such characteristics are often associated with problems in self-regulatory functioning. For those who experience mental illness, self-regulation models may provide additional insight into the nature of their sexual offending and formation of offence-related goals.

Developmental experiences of trauma or familial disorganization, paired with significant psychiatric symptoms, may interfere with the ability to effectively modulate emotions and behaviour and could additionally compromise learning appropriate self-regulatory goals and coping mechanisms. Some evidence suggests that persons with serious mental illness who have committed sexual offences may be responsible for a greater rate of sexual offending than those who do not experience mental illness (Alden, Brennan, Hodgins & Mednick, 2007; Fazel, Sjostedt, Långström & Grann, 2007), perhaps indicating more pervasive or chronic self-regulatory problems for this particular group.

Conclusions

Aetiological theories incorporating self-regulation as a motivator in the sexual offence process offer a rich conceptual framework for understanding a very complex behaviour. RP, the self-regulation model and the multi-modal self-regulation theory offer a unique perspective on sexual offence behaviour. Additional research is needed to further refine and evaluate these theoretical concepts and to inform future prevention and intervention efforts. Finally, some subpopulations of individuals who have sexually offended, including females and those with serious mental illness, exhibit characteristics suggestive of increased self-regulatory problems, making self-regulation models particularly relevant for these groups.

References

Alden, A., Brennan, P., Hodgins, S., & Mednick, S. (2007). Psychotic disorders and sex offending in a Danish birth cohort. *Archives of General Psychiatry, 64*(11), 1251–1258. doi: 10.1001/archpsyc.64.11.1251

Baumeister, R. F., & Heatherton, T. F. (1996). Self-regulation failure: An overview. *Psychological Inquiry, 7*(1), 1–15. doi: 10.1207/s15327965pli0701_1

Beers, S. R., & De Bellis, M. D. (2002). Neuropsychological function in children with maltreatment-related posttraumatic stress disorder. *American Journal of Psychiatry, 159*(3), 483–486. doi: 10.1176/appi/ajp.159.3.483

Bickley, J. A., & Beech, A. R. (2003). Implications for treatment of sexual offenders of the Ward and Hudson model of relapse. *Sexual Abuse: A Journal of Research and Treatment, 15*(2), 121–134. doi: 10.1177/107906320301500203

Bremner, J. D. (2003a). Long–term effects of childhood abuse on brain and neurobiology. *Child & Adolescent Psychiatric Clinics North America, 12*, 271–292. doi: 10.1016/S1056-4993(02)00098-6

Bremner, J. D. (2003b). *Does stress damage the brain? Understanding trauma–based disorders from a neurological perspective.* New York: Norton.

Burk, L. R., & Burkhart, B. R. (2002). Disorganized attachment as a diathesis for sexual deviance: Developmental experience and the motivation for sexual offending. *Aggression & Violent Behavior, 8*(5), 487–511. doi: 10.1016/S1359-1789(02)00076-9

Carver, C. S., & Scheier, M. F. (1981). *Attention and self-regulation.* New York: Springer-Verlag.

Carver, C. S., & Scheier, M. (1990). *Principles of self-regulation: Action and emotion.* New York: Guilford Press.

Claes, L., Vertommen, S., Smits, K., & Bijttebier, P. (2009). Emotional reactivity and self-regulation in relation to personality disorders. *Personality and Individual Differences, 47*(8), 948–953. doi: 10.1016/j.paid.2009.07.027

Cochran, W., & Tesser, A. (1996). The 'what the hell' effect: Some effects of goal proximity and goal framing on performance. In L. L. Martin & A. Tesser (Eds.), *Striving and feeling: Interactions among goals, affect, and self-regulation* (pp. 99–120). New York: Lawrence Erlbaum.

Colson, M.-H., Boyer, L., Baumstarck, B. K., & Loundou, A. D. (2013). Female sex offenders: A challenge to certain paradigms. Meta-analysis. *Sexologies, 22*, 109–117. doi: 10.1016/j.sexol.2013.05.002

Cortoni, F., & Marshall, W. L. (2001). Sex as a coping strategy and its relationship to juvenile sexual history and intimacy in sex offenders. *Sexual Abuse: A Journal of Research and Treatment, 13*(1), 27–43. doi: 10.1177/107906320101300104

Fazel, S., Sjostedt, G., Långström, N., & Grann, M. (2007). Severe mental illness and risk of sexual offending in men: A case-control study based on Swedish national registers. *Journal of Clinical Psychiatry, 68*(4), 588–596. doi: 10.4088/JCP.v68n0415

Feelgood, S., Cortoni, F., & Thompson, A. (2005). Sexual coping, general coping, and cognitive distortions in incarcerated rapists and child molesters. *Journal of Sexual Aggression, 11*(2), 157–170. doi: 10.1080/13552600500073657

Ford, H. J., Rose, J., & Thrift, S. (2009). An evaluation of the applicability of the self-regulation model to sexual offenders with intellectual disabilities. *Journal of Forensic Psychiatry & Psychology, 20*(3), 440–457. doi: 10.1080/14789940802638317

Gannon, T. A., & Cortoni, F. (Eds.). (2010). *Female sexual offenders: Theory, assessment and treatment.* John Wiley & Sons. doi: 10.1002/9780470666715

Gannon, T. A., Rose, M. R., & Ward, T. (2008). A descriptive model of the offense process for female sexual offenders. *Sexual Abuse: A Journal of Research and Treatment, 20*(3), 352–374. doi: 10.1177/1079063208322495

Hanson, R. K., & Harris, A. J. R. (1998). *Dynamic predictors of sexual recidivism.* (User report 1998-1). Ottawa, Canada: Department of the Solicitor General Canada.

Hanson, R. K., Harris, A. J. R., Scott, T. L., & Helmus, L. (2007). *Assessing the risk of sexual offenders on community supervision: The Dynamic Supervision Project.* (User Report 2007-05). Ottawa, Canada: Public Safety Canada.

Hazlett, E. A., New, A. S., Newmark, R., Haznedar, M. M., Lo, J.N., Speiser, L.J., et al. (2005). Reduced anterior and posterior cingulated gray matter in borderline personality disorder. *Biological Psychiatry, 58*(8), 614–623. doi: 10.1016/j. biopsych.2005.04.029

Heatherton, T. F. (2011). Neuroscience of self-regulation. *Annual Review of Psychology, 62,* 363–390. doi: 10.1146/annurev.psych.121208.131616

Hill, S. Y., Wang, S., Kostelnik, B., Carter, H., Holmes, B., McDermott, M., et al. (2009). Disruption of orbitofrontal cortex laterality in offspring from multiplex alcohol dependence families. *Biological Psychiatry, 65*(2), 129–136. doi: 10.1016/j. biopsych.2008.09.001

Hirschi, T. (2004). Self-control and crime. In R. F. Baumeister & K. D. Vohs (Eds.), *Handbook of self-regulation* (pp. 537–552). New York: Guilford Press.

Hudson, S. M., Ward, T., & Marshall, W. L. (1992). The abstinence violation effect in sex offenders: A reformulation. *Behavior Research and Therapy, 30*(5), 435–441. doi: 10.1016/0005-7967(92)90027-E

Hull, J. G., & Slone, L. B. (2004). Alcohol and self-regulation. In R. F. Baumeister & K. D. Vohs (Eds.), *Handbook of self-regulation* (pp. 466–491). New York: Guilford Press.

Karoly, P. (1993). Mechanisms of self-regulation: A systems view. *Annual Review of Psychology, 44*(1), 23–52. doi: 10.1146/annurev.ps.44.020193.000323

Kingston, D. A., Yates, P. M., & Firestone, P. (2012). The self-regulation model of sexual offending: Relationship to risk and need. *Law & Human Behavior, 36*(3), 215–224. doi: 10.1037/h0093960

Langdon, P. E., Maxted, H., Murphy, G. H., & SOSTEC-ID Group (2007). An exploratory evaluation of the Ward and Hudson Offending Pathways model with sex offenders who have intellectual disability. *Journal of Intellectual and Developmental Disability, 32*(2), 94–105. doi: 10.1080/13668250701364686

Laws, D. R. (1989). *Relapse prevention with sex offenders.* New York: Guilford Press.

Laws, D. R., Hudson, S. M., & Ward, T. (2000). *Remaking relapse prevention with sex offenders: A sourcebook.* Thousand Oaks, CA: Sage.

Levenson, J. S., Willis, G. M., & Prescott, D. S. (2015). Adverse childhood experiences in the lives of female sex offenders. *Sexual Abuse: A Journal of Research and Treatment, 27*(3), 258–283. doi: 10.1177/1079063214544332

Lindsay, W. R., Steptoe, L., & Beech, A. T. (2008). The Ward and Hudson pathways model of the sexual offense process applied to offenders with intellectual disability. *Sexual Abuse: A Journal of Research & Treatment, 20*(4), 379–392. doi: 10.1177/1079063208323369

Linehan, M. M. (1993). *Cognitive-behavioral treatment of borderline personality disorder.* New York: Guilford Press.

Marlatt, G. A. (1982). Relapse prevention: A self-control program for the treatment of addictive behaviors. In R. B. Stuart (Ed.), *Adherence, compliance, and generalization in behavioral medicine* (pp. 329–378). New York: Brunner/Mazel.

Marlatt, G. A., & Gordon, J. R. (1985). *Relapse prevention: Maintenance strategies in the treatment of addictive behaviors.* New York: Guilford Press.

Marques, J. K., Day, D. M., Nelson, C., & Miner, M. H. (1989). The Sex Offender Treatment and Evaluation Project: California's relapse prevention program. In D. R. Laws (Ed.), *Relapse prevention with sex offenders* (pp. 247–267). New York: Guilford Press.

Marques, J. K., Wiederanders, M., Day, D. M., Nelson, C., & van Ommeren, A. (2005). Effects of a relapse prevention program on sexual recidivism: Final results from California's Sex Offender Treatment and Evaluation Project (SOTEP). *Sexual Abuse: Journal of Research & Treatment, 17*(1), 79–107. doi: 10.1177/107906320501700108

McGrath, R. J., Cumming, G. F., Burchard, B. L., Zeoli, S., & Ellerby, L. (2010). *Current practices and emerging trends in sexual abuser management: The Safer Society 2009 North American survey.* Brandon, VT: The Safer Society Press.

Miller, W. R., & Rollnick, S. (2013). *Motivational interviewing: Helping people change* (3rd ed.). New York: Guilford Press.

Miner, M. H., Marques, J. K., Day, D. M., & Nelson, C. (1990). Impact of relapse prevention in treating sex offenders: Preliminary findings. *Annals of Sex Research, 3*(2), 165–185. doi: 10.1007/BF00850869

Minzenberg, M. J., Fan, J., New, A. S., Tang, C. Y., & Siever, L. J. (2007). Fronto-limbic dysfunction in response to facial emotion in borderline personality disorder: An event-related fMRI study. *Psychiatry Research: Neuroimaging, 155*(3), 231–243. doi: 10.1016/j.pscychresns.2007.03.006

Minzenberg, M. J., Fan, J., New, A. S., Tang, C. Y., & Siever, L. J. (2008). Frontolimbic structural changes in borderline personality disorder. *Journal of Psychiatric Research, 42*(9), 727–733. doi: 10.1016/j.jpsychires.2007.07.015

Pithers, W.S. (1990). Relapse prevention with sexual aggressors: A method for maintaining therapeutic gain and enhancing external supervision. In W. L. Marshall, D. R. Laws & H. E. Barbaree (Eds.), *Handbook of sexual assault: Issues, theories, and treatment of the offender* (pp. 343–361). New York: Plenum Press.

Pithers, W. D., Marques, J. K., Gibat, C. C., & Marlatt, G. A. (1983). Relapse prevention with sexual aggressives: A self-control model of treatment and maintenance of change. In J. G. Greer & I. R. Stuart (Eds.), *The sexual aggressor: Current perspectives on treatment* (pp. 214–239). New York: Van Nostrand Reinhold.

Polaschek, D. L. L. (2003). Relapse prevention, offense process models, and the treatment of sexual offenders. *Professional Psychology: Research & Practice, 34*(4), 361–367. doi: 10.1037/0735-7028.34.4.361

Siegle, G. J. (2007). Brain mechanisms of borderline personality disorder at the intersection of cognition, emotion, and the clinic. *American Journal of Psychiatry, 164*(12), 1776–1779. doi: 10.1176/appi.ajp.2007.07091505

Stinson, J. D., & Becker, J. V. (2011). Sexual offenders with serious mental illness: Prevention, risk, and clinical concerns. *International Journal of Law and Psychiatry, 34*(3), 239–245. doi: 10.1016/j.ijlp.2011.04.011

Stinson, J. D., & Becker, J. V. (2012). *Treating sex offenders: An evidence-based manual*. New York: Guilford Press.

Stinson, J. D., Becker, J. V., & McVay, L. A. (2015). Treatment progress and behavior following two years of inpatient sex offender treatment: A pilot investigation of Safe Offender Strategies. *Sexual Abuse: A Journal of Research and Treatment*, online first. doi: 10.1177/1079063215570756

Stinson, J. D., Becker, J. V., & Sales, B. D. (2008). Self-regulation and the etiology of sexual deviance: Evaluating causal theory. *Violence and Victims, 23*(1), 35–52. doi: 10.1891/0886-6708.23.1.35

Stinson, J. D., McVay, L. A., & Becker, J. V. (in press). Post-hospitalization outcomes for psychiatric sex offenders: Comparing two treatment protocols. *International Journal of Offender Therapy and Comparative Criminology*.

Stinson, J. D., Robbins, S. B., & Crow, W. C. (2011). Self-regulatory deficits as predictors of sexual, aggressive, and self-harm behaviors in a psychiatric sex offender population. *Criminal Justice and Behavior, 38*(9), 885–895. doi: 10.1177/0093854811409872

Stinson, J. D., Sales, B. D., & Becker, J. V. (2008). *Sex offending: Causal theories to inform research, prevention, and treatment*. Washington, DC: American Psychological Association. doi: 10.107/11708-000

Ward, T. (2000). Relapse prevention: Critique and reformulation. *The Journal of Sexual Aggression, 5*(2), 118–133. doi: 10.1080/13552600008413303

Ward, T., & Brown, M. (2004). The good lives model and conceptual issues in offender rehabilitation. *Psychology, Crime & Law, 10*(3), 243–257. doi: 10.1080/10683160410001662744

Ward, T., & Gannon, T. A. (2006). Rehabilitation, etiology, and self-regulation: The comprehensive good lives model of treatment for sexual offenders. *Aggression and Violent Behavior, 11*(1), 77–94. doi: 10.1016/j.avb.2005.06.001

Ward, T., & Hudson, S. M. (1996). Relapse prevention: A critical analysis. *Sexual Abuse: A Journal of Research and Treatment, 8*(3), 177–200. doi: 10.1007/BF02256634

Ward, T., & Hudson, S. M. (1998). A model of the relapse process in sexual offenders. *Journal of Interpersonal Violence, 13*(6), 700–725. doi: 10.1177/088626098013006003

Ward, T., Hudson, S. M., & Keenan, T. (1998). A self-regulation model of the sexual offense process. *Sexual Abuse: A Journal of Research and Treatment, 10*(2), 141–157. doi: 10.1023/A:1022071516644

Ward, T., Hudson, S. M., & Siegert, R. J. (1995). A critical comment on Pithers' relapse prevention model. *Sexual Abuse: A Journal of Research and Treatment, 7*(2), 167–175. doi: 10.1007/BF02260203

Ward, T., Louden, K., Hudson, S. M., & Marshall, W. L. (1995). A descriptive model of the offense chain for child molesters. *Journal of Interpersonal Violence, 10*(4), 452–472. doi: 10.1177/088626095010004005

Ward, T., Mann, R. E., & Gannon, T. A. (2007). The Good Lives Model of offender rehabilitation: Clinical implications. *Aggression and Violent Behavior, 12*(1), 87–107. doi: 10.1016/j.avb.2006.03.004

Webster, S. D. (2005). Pathways to sexual offense recidivism following treatment: An examination of the Ward and Hudson self-regulation model of relapse.

Journal of Interpersonal Violence, 20(10), 1175–1196. doi: 10.1177/08862605052 78532

Yates, P. M., & Kingston, D. A. (2006). The self-regulation model of sexual offending: The relationship between offence pathways and static and dynamic sexual offence risk. *Sexual Abuse: A Journal of Research and Treatment, 18*(3), 259–270. doi: 10.1177/107906320601800304

Yates, P. M., Kingston, D. A., & Hall, K. (2003). Pathways to sexual offending: Validity of Hudson and Ward's self-regulation model and relationship to static and dynamic risk among treated high risk sexual offenders. Presented at the 22nd Annual Research and Treatment Conference of the Association for the Treatment of Sexual Abusers (ATSA). St. Louis, Missouri: October 2003.

7

Cognition, Emotion and Motivation

Treatment for Individuals who have Sexually Offended

Geris A. Serran

The purpose of this chapter is to integrate the concepts discussed in the previous chapters and provide recommendations on treatment for individuals who sexually offend with respect to the domains of cognition, emotion and motivation. As highlighted throughout this book, integration is required in our understanding of these domains. Too frequently, we read literature or theories that discuss one domain (e.g., cognition) without consideration of the impact of emotions or behaviours (or the interactional effect that each have on the other). Importantly, the chapters in this book make strong efforts to present a unified, integrated approach to the areas of cognition, emotion and motivation. The current chapter briefly summarizes research literature in these areas and emphasizes intervention, so that treatment providers can offer the most effective intervention to their clients. Based on my experience in treating sexual offenders, I also suggest that treatment efforts need to be dynamic and integrated. Focusing on separate 'modules', I argue, will be less successful than considering an overall approach based on an integrated conceptualization of the client.

Part 1: Attitudes and Cognitions, Coping and Emotion Management, Motivation

Cognition

In the sexual offender literature, since the 1980's there have been numerous references to the importance of 'cognitive distortions' that characterize men who have sexually offended. However, this term is rather broad, general and confusing in nature. One of the main problems is that there seems to be a 'distortion' that only offenders engage in distorted thinking; in reality we all engage in distorted thinking from time to time. Distortions include thoughts, beliefs, perceptions and attitudes as well as minimizations of the nature and detail of offences, and are discussed in some detail in Chapter 3 of this volume by Ó Ciardha, who very comprehensively addresses the topic of cognition, cognitive distortions, implicit

Sexual Offending: Cognition, Emotion and Motivation, First Edition.
Edited by Theresa A. Gannon and Tony Ward.
© 2017 John Wiley & Sons Ltd. Published 2017 by John Wiley & Sons Ltd.

theories and schemas. Thus, my discussion of this domain is brief and highlights some key areas that treatment providers need to consider.

Salter (1988) viewed denial, excuses or distorted thoughts as a means of justifying, minimizing or rationalizing offending (Bumby, 1996); these distortions were viewed as deliberate lies that must be vigorously challenged in order for intervention to be successful. This view did not appear unusual; many therapists viewed distortions as something that must be challenged with the assumption that the victim or police report represented the 'accurate' offence account. This view seemed to follow from the concept that the purpose of distortions was to facilitate or maintain sexual offending, or a means of justifying, minimizing or rationalizing offending (Bumby, 1996).

More recent discussions in the literature propose a more flexible view of cognition. This view appears to have been facilitated by Maruna's (2001) research on excuses. He challenged the 'problem' of distortions by noting that former offenders who offered excuses for their crimes were less likely to reoffend than those who admitted to being 'offenders'. This view is very important for treatment providers to consider because the term 'cognitive distortions' is rather negative and assumes that individuals who have offended are the only ones who might have patterns of thinking that are not healthy. In fact, we all make excuses, justify our actions or think in ways that might not be helpful. However, it is helpful to distinguish between ways of thinking that might contribute to offending behaviour.

In fact, the majority of cognitions displayed by individuals who have sexually offended are not criminogenic (Marshall, Marshall & Ware, 2009). Only a very limited set of cognitions (expression of attitudes reflecting a tolerance of sexual abuse and emotional identification with children) are predictive of recidivism. Various authors (Maruna & Mann, 2006; Marshall et al., 2009) have suggested that there is no value in focusing on non-criminogenic cognitions. Yet, many treatment programmes emphasize that accepting full responsibility results in treatment success (McGrath et al., 2009). It seems almost intuitive that somebody who accepts full responsibility and admits to his or her offending has more insight and is more likely to be successful. However, consider an individual who has numerous male and female child victims, experiences inappropriate arousal, has limited adult connections and uses sex to cope with stress and negative emotions. He fully admits to his offending, as compared to a man who denies offending against his daughter. Minimizing or denying does not predict recidivism (Hanson & Bussière, 1998; Hanson & Morton-Bourgon, 2005). In fact, Maruna and Mann suggest that making excuses or externalizing behaviours is in fact normative, and forcing an individual to admit to all details can in fact be counter-productive, leading them to believe that they are 'bad' and have no chance to change. Recent research examining well-known measures of cognition (i.e., RAPE and MOLEST scales; Bumby, 1996) used often to measure treatment success, suggests that these scales may well be measuring a variety of constructs which is why they do not predict sexual recidivism (see Nunes et al., 2014).

Importantly, Maruna and Mann (2006) and Mann and Hollin (2001) challenge the usefulness of the term 'cognitive distortion'. They point out that various forms of cognition are related to sexual offending. For example, many offenders provide explanations for their offending, which at times are viewed as blame shifting (e.g., 'I was drunk or high', or 'I was very depressed'). These statements are often viewed as distortions but can actually help clinicians identify key issues for intervention.

Mann and Shingler (2006), specifically looking at cognitive distortions in sexual offenders, note that these thoughts are typically the product of schemas, which are deep-rooted belief systems held by the clients as a result of early experiences. Simply challenging the distortions that arise will not be sufficient in changing the underlying structure; instead core beliefs must be addressed on an emotional level (see Langton & Marshall, 2000, 2001). Interestingly, Nunes and colleagues (2016) found that attitudes (evaluations) of rape were independent of cognitions assessed using the RAPE Scale (Bumby, 1996) and each played an independent role in predicting sexually aggressive behaviour. This recent research suggests that we need to broaden our understanding of attitudes and beliefs, and the role that these might play in sexual aggression. This research also suggests that much more attention needs to be paid to the content of items on scales measuring cognition, since it is sometimes unclear exactly what they are measuring. Clearly, accurate and clear measurement of cognitions is required to understand progression throughout treatment.

A schema-based theory of cognition in sexual offending proposes that certain dysfunctional cognitive schemas can influence the likelihood of sexual offending. Schemas originate from early life experiences and are not typically in conscious awareness. The schema becomes a framework for processing new information, importantly in this context social and personal information. An individual with a dysfunctional schema might interpret neutral or negative information as threatening. These thoughts could increase the likelihood of offending in the presence of other risk factors. Importantly, schemas, or deeply held dysfunctional beliefs, do increase emotions in that emotional awareness, expression or recognition might be strongly affected. If we consider domains where we have very strong beliefs, we are also more likely to be emotionally reactive when those beliefs are triggered.

Ó Ciardha (see Chapter 3 in this volume) highlights an important point; in the domain of sexual offending, therapists have been far too simplistic when focusing on cognition. Simply focusing on issues such as denial and minimization is not meaningful. Rather, professionals should address the deeper, underlying issues that contribute to our thought processes, such as attachment, perspective-taking ability, deviant sexual interests and cognitions associated with these interests and schemas.

Emotion

Ward (see Chapter 1 in this volume) offers a new way of considering the role of emotion. Anger is an emotion typically viewed as being 'unacceptable' when expressed by incarcerated clients. It is also common for clients who cry to be immediately referred to psychology. While any extreme emotion (either positive or negative) can be problematic (and therefore does need to be regulated) emotion is necessary to live a rich and fulfilling life and we should be encouraging, rather than discouraging, appropriate expression of emotion in clients. Helping clients to understand how their emotions affect the way they think and react is an important part of treatment. Clients should expect to experience anger, fear, guilt, sadness or loneliness. They need to learn what is triggering these emotions, what thoughts precede or are elicited and how they are tempted to react.

Blagden, Lievesley and Ware (Chapter 5 in this volume) emphasize the critical interplay between emotions, thoughts and resulting behaviours (in this case, sexual offending). Shame and guilt are two domains frequently visited in the assessment and treatment of clients who have sexually offended. In particular, the impact of shame on the client's view of self and ability to make changes cannot be ignored. Again, we cannot look at emotion in a vacuum since issues such as shame, deep-rooted feelings of insecurity or emotion management difficulties strongly influence thoughts and behaviours.

Howells, Day and Wright (2004) explored the literature detailing the importance of affect in sexual offending. Various researchers have demonstrated that negative affect is associated with offending; for example Pithers, Marques, Gibat and Marlatt (1983) revealed that 75% of re-offences were precipitated by situations that evoked negative moods (e.g., boredom, frustration, anger). Pithers and colleagues (1988) further examined the immediate precursors of sexual re-offending in 136 men who had sexual abused children and 64 men who had raped adults. Of the men who raped adults, 94% reported experiencing anger due to interpersonal conflict immediately before offending, while 46% of the men who abused children reported anxiety and 38% reported experiencing depression. This research, however, was conducted retrospectively which may have resulted in bias.

Negative emotional and interpersonal conflict have been associated with deviant sexual fantasies in sexual offenders (Proulx, McKibben & Lusignan, 1996). The tendency for sexual offenders to engage in self-denigration (Neidigh & Tomiko, 1991) and emotional rumination (Roger & Masters, 1997) suggests that emotion-focused strategies are detrimental.

Looman (1995) found that individuals who had sexually assaulted children were more likely to fantasize sexually about a child as opposed to an adult when feeling depressed, rejected or angry, or following an interpersonal argument. Both Looman and Proulx et al. (1996) suggest that sexual offenders may engage in deviant sexual fantasies as a means of reducing distress (i.e., as a means of coping with negative moods). Research inducing a negative mood using Velten's (1968) procedure with incarcerated men who had sexually offended produced interesting results (Marshall, Marshall & Moulden, 2000). Specifically, it was found that individuals who reported offending while in a negative mood state were more likely to be susceptible to a mood induction procedure, however, inducing negative mood did not necessarily affect specific areas of functioning (such as self-esteem, anxiety and coping using sex). It was concluded that those susceptible to mood induction were already struggling in those particular domains.

Importantly, Hanson and Harris (2000) determined that acute negative affect impacts reoffending, rather than a general negative mood state; thus, it is the change in mood prior to offence that is of concern. Therefore, an offender who is generally angry or depressed is apparently not at increased risk to reoffend, but if his mood shifts this could trigger offending. From a treatment perspective, monitoring mood with clients and integrating emotion management techniques to deal with crises 'in the moment' may be critical. Furthermore, some individuals might be motivated to maintain negative emotional states due to the attention or reinforcement they receive. For example, anger can be used to control others while depression can elicit attention. If we think about this issue in terms of sexual offending behaviour, anger could therefore be used to 'force' sexual activity where anxiety might lead someone to choose a child victim for acceptance and comfort. Individuals who struggle with emotion regulation might also be more likely to use problematic or 'quick fix' strategies because they are unable to tolerate negative emotional states. Therefore, aggression, sexual activity, substance use or other avoidance-based strategies might be used.

A major criticism of the majority of research and even intervention strategies in sexual offending is that they emphasize only negative mood states and emotions. Ward and Hudson (2000) addressed this issue to some degree in their self-regulation model of offending. According to this model, self-regulation consists of processes that allow an individual to engage in goal-directed behaviour, including inhibition as well as enhancement or maintenance of specific behaviours. In Ward and Hudson's model, two pathways are associated with avoidance goals (i.e., where the goal is to avoid offending), while the other two pathways are associated with approach goals (i.e., where sexual offending is the goal). The avoidant-passive pathway involves the inability to control sexually deviant behaviours. Individuals under regulate their behaviour and emotions, resulting in a loss of control over behaviour. Powerful negative affective states are typically involved in this pathway and individuals tend to be impulsive, experience low self-efficacy and lack effective coping strategies. The avoidant-active pathway involves misregulation, where the offender actively attempts to control deviant thoughts and behaviours, but the strategies employed are not effective. For example, the offender might use substances or pornography as a means of reducing deviant thoughts, with the opposite result. The predominant affective state is negative.

The approach-automatic pathway involves the use of overlearned behavioural scripts with behaviours appearing impulsive. The primary affective state differs; some individuals might experience a negative mood state while others experience positive mood. Positive emotions are associated with the anticipation of engaging in offending behaviour. The approach-explicit pathway involves intact self-regulation. In this pathway, the offender views his deviant sexual behaviour as acceptable (e.g., he believes that children are receptive to and not harmed by sexual activity or that women cannot refuse sexual activity). Affective state may be negative or positive in this case.

Motivation

The challenge in working with sexual offenders is that they are a heterogeneous group, and the factors that motivate one individual to offend might be completely different in another individual. Cognitions and deep-rooted schemas can impact motivation. For example, if individuals who have offended develop healthy, prosocial ways of thinking and are able to challenge offence-supportive thoughts they will be less motivated to follow through with an offence. Further, situational factors play into motivation such that if an offender is equipped with the skills, ability and means to meet his needs in a healthier manner, presumably he will be less motivated to offend and more motivated to choose a healthy pathway. It often appears that when examining motivation, treatment providers focus primarily on the 'offence-cycle' or 'offence pathways', which are very specific rather than more general in nature. The problem with this approach is that clients then develop 'tunnel vision' and notice only identified specific risk factors (e.g., seeking out a prostitute, going to bars) rather than general factors that might suggest they are slipping into an unhealthy lifestyle and placing them at risk.

Self-regulation is critical to motivation (see Stinson, Chapter 6 in this volume). Chapter 6 in this volume covers various theories that include self-regulatory processes, including the multi-modal self-regulation theory (Stinson, Sales & Becker, 2008), which examines the role of self-regulation from a developmental perspective. Carver (2004) found affective self-control is integral to behavioural regulation. Importantly, poor self-regulation predicts likelihood of reoffending (Hanson, 2006) which means that intervention needs to effectively address cognition and emotion, as we have seen that both of these aspects impact behaviour. Importantly, Stinson and colleagues' theory is comprehensive and considers developmental influences on thoughts, feelings and resulting behaviour. Taking a comprehensive approach and considering the impact of intact versus dysfunctional regulation allows treatment providers to better address client need areas. The next section details intervention strategies that address all of these domains in a comprehensive, flexible and integrated manner.

Part 2: Intervention

During the 1960s and 1970s, behavioural modification procedures aimed at reducing sexual interests in deviant behaviours were the main intervention utilized. In the 1970s, Marshall added a social skills component, and during the 1990s, relationship skills training was also considered relevant. Over the years various other components have been incorporated: empathy skills, coping skills, self-esteem enhancement, intimacy and healthy relationships.

Traditional cognitive-behavioural programmes for treating sexual offenders have generally focused excessively on cognition, to the exclusion of other important factors. In many programmes, most of the cognitive restructuring work either addresses factors that are not criminogenic, or does so in a very rational fashion (e.g., Socratic Method). However, a strictly rational approach does not lead to behavioural change. Pfafflin and colleagues (2005) note in treating men who have sexually offended, only when rational understanding is accompanied by an emotional response will we see behavioural change. Clients who express understanding or are able to effectively answer questions or complete homework, but have no emotional reaction or response, will typically not demonstrate behavioural change. Treatment providers need to be emotionally responsive and encourage clients to be emotionally expressive; this is related to successful outcomes for a range of problem areas (Cooley & Lajoy, 1980; Orlinsky & Howard, 1986). Little progress occurs when therapists are overly rational; appropriate emotional expressions allow for processing of issues. A validating, empathic, warm and encouraging relationship with the therapist is crucial to affect regulation; interpersonal validation is beneficial at increasing affect regulation.

Importance of Therapeutic Process

Therapists need to have the skills necessary to establish strong therapeutic rapport with these clients, who are often strongly stigmatized for their behaviour or behave in ways that make the development of a strong rapport challenging (i.e., express negative or inappropriate attitudes). Beech and Fordham (1997) and Beech and Hamilton-Giachritsis (2005) demonstrated that only treatment groups that functioned cohesively and encouraged expressiveness generated relevant treatment change on various measures of change. Beech and colleagues (Beech & Fordham, 1997; Beech & Hamilton-Giachritsis, 2005) found that scores on the Expressiveness subscale of Moos's (1986) Group Climate Scale were significantly associated with beneficial changes across a range of programmes for clients who had sexually offended.

Pfafflin, Bohmer, Cornehl and Mergenthaler (2005) found that emotional expressiveness was crucial in attaining beneficial treatment changes. The emotional responsivity of the therapist and his or her ability to evoke emotion in the session is a critical feature that can be lost in efforts to be rational and objective or in a more psychoeducational approach. Evoking emotion is critical to elicit relevant attitudes, beliefs and interpersonal schema. In the calming setting of a treatment group, when attitudes are being presented or discussed in a rational manner, it is easy for clients to express both positive and prosocial attitudes. At the time of offending, when in a different emotional state, individuals who have raped women, for example, might sexualize women's behaviour, while individuals who have abused children might misinterpret children's innocent behaviours as sexual.

Greenberg and Watson (2006) consider the therapeutic relationship as strongly facilitating emotional processing and regulation. Clients who have sexually offended might have difficulties regulating strong emotions, and failure to manage difficult emotions is considered a dynamic risk factor. Importantly, a validating relationship with the therapist is considered crucial in helping clients regulate affect (Greenberg, 2007). Clients with under regulated affect have been shown to benefit from interpersonal validation as much as they do from specific techniques aimed directly at emotion regulation and distress tolerance skills (Linehan, 1993). Research suggests that successful treatment outcome is related to the degree to which clients are given the opportunity to be emotionally expressive (Cooley & Lajoy, 1980; Orlinksy & Howard, 1986). Empathy and acceptance by the therapist contributes to affect regulation by providing interpersonal soothing and encourages the ability to regulate emotion. The therapist's communication of emotion (through facial and verbal expression) creates the emotional climate. Providing a safe and responsive emotional climate facilitates emotional processing.

Other researchers have also found that encouraging emotional expression facilitates treatment change (Orlinksy & Howard, 1986). Saunders (1999) demonstrated that expression of feelings by clients determines the impact each treatment session has and found these expressions were best facilitated by emotional expressiveness of the therapist. These various studies indicate that attitudes and beliefs are affected by emotional states, and interpersonal schemas are typically only accessed and ultimately changed when activated through emotional expression.

Furthermore, emotional experiences and emotional expressiveness during treatment are related to successful outcome with various disorders. Processing information while in an emotional state leads to change, while intellectualizing and analyzing issues is unlikely to do so (Klein, Mathieu-Couglan & Kiesler, 1986). In fact, Lietaier (1992) notes that little progress occurs when therapists are excessively rational.

Specific to clients who have sexually offended, Pfafflin et al. (2005) and Hunter, Pfafflin and Ross (2007) conducted two qualitative studies which demonstrated that the expression of emotion during therapy sessions is a significant predictor of treatment-induced change. Pfafflin and colleagues indicated these changes were greatest when emotional expression was also associated with an intellectual understanding of the issues.

Self-disclosure by therapists (to a degree) can be helpful in both evoking emotional states and in illustrating various points. Harmless examples provided by the therapist of instances where he/she has cognitively distorted information to serve his/her needs helps the client to understand that it is the content, not the tendency to distort that is problematic.

One important aspect of participation is the active elicitation and encouragement of prosocial attitudes and the prompt discouragement of antisocial views. An aggressive, confrontational approach has no place in treatment. Beech and Fordham (1997) demonstrated that confrontation is counter therapeutic; examining treatment groups using Moos's (1986) Group Environment Scale, they found that groups with the highest cohesiveness displayed high levels of change while those with low cohesiveness did not change at all. In the group having the lowest cohesiveness, the therapist employed an aggressively confrontational style. Equally problematic is an unconditionally supportive approach, where therapists fail to challenge any problematic behaviour or thoughts. Adopting a style that is warm and supportive, yet firm and non-confrontational is deemed the ideal therapeutic style. Importantly, Marshall and colleagues (2002) found that the influence of crucial therapist features (empathy, warmth, rewarding and directive) accounted for 60% of the variance in beneficial changes.

A Comprehensive Approach to Treatment

An example of a comprehensive, positive approach to treatment for individuals who have sexually offended has been developed by Marshall, Marshall, Serran and O'Brien (2011). This programme has evolved over 40 years and has been implemented in an outpatient community setting, various Canadian federal prisons and in a secure facility for those experiencing mental disorder.

In conducting treatment, we encourage a flexible approach. Highly detailed treatment manuals are contraindicated as clients are heterogeneous and evidence suggests that therapists who adhere to a detailed treatment manual work less effectively with these clients (Goldfried & Wolfe, 1996; Marshall, 2009). Many treatment approaches, especially those that emphasize a manualized approach, typically address various domains (e.g., victim empathy, cognitive distortions and offence analysis) as separate entities. Adopting a comprehensive treatment approach is more likely to help individuals who have offended understand the relationship between these domains.

For example, criminogenic cognitions should not be addressed in a separate 'module', in which these distortions are identified and challenged. Not only does this create an artificial atmosphere, but it is also unlikely that this approach will elicit true change. As much as possible, challenging distorted cognitions in the context in which they occur (e.g., naturally, during discussions) or during relational interactions or descriptions of relational interactions (e.g., discussion with parole officer or partner) is preferred. Various strategies can be used to help modify distorted cognitions. Cognitive restructuring (Murphy, 1990) involves exploring the reasoning and value behind a particular belief system followed by an alternative way of viewing the situation. Cognitive behavioural strategies, such as examining the pros the cons of particular attitudes and beliefs versus alternative ways of thinking, can be incorporated. A new twist on testing problematic beliefs is suggested in a recent article by Gannon (2016) which examines use of the behavioural experiment (BE) with forensic clients. This technique is recommended because it targets cognition at both the rational and experiential level; many other techniques, such as thought records or psychoeducation, remain solely at the rational level.

When detailed treatment manuals are involved, treatment becomes 'one size fits all' and psychoeducational (Green, 1995). Laws and Ward (2006) noted that this approach is problematic in that it virtually ignores the importance of responsivity of the therapist. This appears to be particularly the case when we consider the importance of emotion in psychotherapy. The use of a structured manual – whilst ensuring treatment integrity across sites – promotes more of a psychoeducational approach, which can serve to limit emotional expression and result in a lower likelihood of challenging and changing deep-rooted schemas. Our programme recognizes that an unstructured approach can also be problematic, in that therapists might struggle to remain focused on relevant issues and clients might become confused about what is expected of them. Therefore, having a treatment guide, which outlines key areas (such as the cognition, emotion and behavioural issues highlighted throughout this book) is helpful.

Our programme also encourages the use of cognitive, behavioural and emotion-focused techniques; many programmes are primarily cognitive since they focus almost exclusively on challenging cognitions. Some treatment professionals contend that individuals who have sexually offended should overcome cognitive distortions, minimization and denial in order for treatment to be successful.

However, neither denial nor minimization is related to the propensity to reoffend (Hanson & Bussière, 1998; Hanson & Morton-Bourgon, 2004).

In terms of treatment approach, the early stages of treatment should emphasize a motivational approach, which allows for development of trust. Our research has shown that treatment is more successful when the therapist displays support, empathy and warmth, reinforcement and directiveness (see Marshall et al., 2002). Other researchers have found that group cohesion and expressiveness facilitate the attainment of treatment goals (Beech & Fordham, 1997; Beech & Hamilton-Giachritsis, 2005).

Many cognitive behavioural/relapse prevention programmes explore the client's past offending behaviour in detail in order to develop an 'offence cycle', which assumes that a common chain of thoughts, feelings and behaviours characterizes all of the offences of each individual client. A relapse prevention plan can then be developed to help prevent future offending. Unfortunately, the plans generated are often avoidance-focused; substantial research indicates that avoidance goals are much more difficult to achieve and maintain. Mann, Webster, Schofield and Marshall (2004) demonstrated that clients encouraged to develop approach goals were fully engaged in treatment and completed their homework, were more open and communicative and presented with genuine motivation.

Approach goals fit well with developing plans to build a better life that does not include offending. In applying the Good Lives Model to the treatment of individuals who have sexually offended, the therapist works collaboratively with each client to develop a limited set of personalized goals consistent with his individual interests and abilities (Ward, 2002; Ward & Stewart, 2003). The client is helped to identify strategies to achieve these goals, including the development of skills, coping strategies, knowledge, self-confidence and ability to seek support.

Domains Targeted

Early in treatment clients prepare a life history that incorporates experiences from childhood, adolescence, early adulthood, mid-life and older age. This particular exercise can be used to identify patterns of cognition, deep-rooted belief systems or schemas and potential offence motivating factors (e.g., intimacy or relational problems, poor coping strategies, unhealthy lifestyle). Clients are encouraged to identify both successes and problems in relationships, sexual activities, education, work, leisure and health. Various issues might be identified, including problematic attachments with caregivers, trauma and abuse, low self-worth, poor coping strategies, relationship difficulties, a failure to accept responsibility for choices and poor self-regulation skills (behavioural and emotional). Importantly, the autobiography allows clients and therapists to identify client strengths, which can be utilized in the change process. Each of these areas is described in more detail below, but as has been emphasized throughout, we do not target these areas as separate modules in treatment.

In order for change to be viewed as a possibility, clients need to possess confidence in their ability to change and need to possess a positive sense of self. Clients are encouraged to identify their positive qualities, to participate actively in positive and healthy activities and are encouraged to view themselves as distinct from their offending behaviour. These strategies allow clients to be accountable, to express guilt rather than shame and to make constructive changes in their lives.

Some may argue that self-worth should not be addressed since it is not a dynamic risk factor. We view this as a mistake; low self-worth affects the entire person and impacts areas (which do contribute to risk) such as relationship stability, emotion management and coping/problem-solving ability, to name a few. A strong sense of shame and lack of self-worth often contributes to the tendency of clients to deny or minimize personal responsibility. Clients are assisted in identifying the perceptions, attitudes and beliefs, as well as the underlying schema that have contributed to the domains that increase risk of offending behaviour. In doing so, clients have the opportunity to establish a sense of power and control over themselves and their decisions.

The specific offence details are far less important than the factors that contribute to offending. Thus, rather than asking clients to develop an 'offence cycle' we instead encourage an understanding of their offending, in that clients individually identify background factors that resulted in a vulnerability to offending behaviour as well as offence-specific factors that ultimately led to the offence. These 'dynamic risk factors' often include issues such as relationship dysfunction, anger, acute mood states, intoxication, lack of self-regulation (behavioural or emotional), poor coping skills and sexual issues (such as inappropriate sexual interests, sexual preoccupation, coping using sex). Offence specific factors might include seeking a potential victim, fantasizing about the victim and rationalizing or justifying an attempt to offend.

Coping Skills

Individuals who have sexually offended have been shown to have both ineffective coping styles and deficiencies in their capacity to problem-solve in specific situations (Cortoni & Marshall, 2001; Marshall, Serran & Cortoni, 2000; Neidigh & Tomiko, 1991; Serran, Firestone, Marshall & Moulden, 2007). Clients often identify difficulties dealing with issues such as conflict, relationship difficulties and general stress and might employ strategies such as avoidance, aggressive behaviour, substance use or emotional suppression. Poor coping can be affected by rigid thinking styles, experiences such as early childhood abuse (which affects information processing) and emotional expression or regulation difficulties. In treatment, we help clients to understand the development of their coping strategies and through role-plays and practice, to develop skills such as communication, mindfulness, distraction techniques where necessary, problem-solving skills and stress management techniques.

Intimacy Deficits

In order to help clients develop healthier relationships, we commence by exploring attachment styles; often attachments are insecure and clients have experienced some form of physical, emotional or sexual abuse or neglect which has affected their ability to establish healthy intimacy (Marshall & Marshall,

2000; Starzyk & Marshall, 2003). As a result, it is critical that clients develop the skills, attitudes and self-confidence necessary to function effectively in adult relationships. Importantly, a secure relationship with the therapist helps clients explore these domains. It may be important to help clients come to terms with their parental relationships or early childhood trauma in order to help heal some of these issues and address underlying relationship schema. Also, exploring patterns in later adult relationships can help clients understand their relationship style and determine ways of relating differently. In close relationships, clients are encouraged to communicate, address conflict and express emotion in healthy ways.

Emotional Issues

As noted earlier in the section on motivation there is evidence that individuals who sexually offended experience deficits in self-regulation (Ward & Hudson, 2000). In the general psychological literature, control over emotions is essential to the development of effective self-regulation (Baumeister & Vohs, 2004). Deficits in both behavioural and emotional self-regulation are linked to criminal behaviour, poor sexual self-regulation, substance abuse and intimacy deficits. Acute emotional states have been found to predict sexual reoffending (Hanson & Harris, 2000). Targeting emotional regulation in treatment, therefore, is critical; emotional regulation is necessary for general self-regulation, individuals who have sexually offended have problems recognizing emotions in others (Hudson et al., 1993) and often in identifying their own emotions. Importantly, the expression of emotions during therapy is significantly predictive of positive gains being derived from treatment for sexual offending (Pfafflin et al., 2005). When the therapist and client maintain their interactions at a strictly cognitive level, the desired changes do not occur; it is only when cognition and emotion are targeted simultaneously that change can occur. This highlights the importance of allowing emotional expression, discussing emotionally charged topics and addressing underlying schemas. That said, in cases where clients are overly emotionally expressive (i.e., become highly distressed or express high levels of anger), they need to regulate emotions through more calming methods such as relaxation, meditation or other regulatory techniques. Techniques from Linehan's Dialetical Behaviour Therapy can be very useful in this regard, as she highlights many strategies to assist in emotional regulation and acceptance. Other strategies include helping clients identify and put feelings into words, helping them feel and recognize the value in all emotion, helping them accept emotional experiences and helping them tolerate difficult emotions. Given that the expression of emotion is important for progress in therapy (Howells & Day, 2006) and that strong emotions have been found to play a role in the offence cycles of both violent and sexual offending (Howells et al., 2004), it is critical that therapists are able to integrate emotional expression into treatment. In order to effectively address deep-rooted schemas (e.g., distrust of women) it is essential to elicit emotion (which will facilitate expression of these schemas). Incorporating some of the work of Jeffrey Young (Young, Klosko & Weishaar, 2003) can be particularly effective with personality-disordered clients.

Sexual Interests

Early behavioural approaches to the treatment of sexual offending focused almost exclusively on the modification of deviant sexual interests. Some clients display deviant sexual arousal when phallometrically assessed or acknowledge sexual interest in an inappropriate age group or in non-consenting sexual activity. Furthermore, some clients report high levels of sexual preoccupation or admit to using sexual activity or masturbation to cope with stress or difficult emotions. Modifying deviant interests, increasing comfort with sexuality in general, establishing and respecting sexual boundaries and enhancing the skills, behaviours and attitudes that facilitate sexual satisfaction are goals of treatment. At times, medication might be recommended (for example, in instances where clients are sexually compulsive or so preoccupied they find it difficult to manage their thoughts, or in the case of sadism).

Self-management Plans

We do not employ classic 'relapse prevention' plans in treatment for reasons described above; instead the Good Lives Model is used as a template for helping clients develop appropriate goals. Some limited avoidance strategies are employed; for example, with respect to men who have abused children, part of their self-management plan would be to avoid being in situations where they might be alone with children. Some clients might also need to avoid substance use, or avoid certain peers or risky areas. Excessive restrictions, however, are seen to place individuals who have sexually offended at greater risk for re-offence because they will not only believe they are incapable of success but will also find it next to impossible to build a healthy life. Our goal in self-management is to help clients use effective coping strategies to manage risks such as acute moods (i.e., anger, loneliness, jealousy) and to develop a Good Life plan. When the goals of a good life are not met, at least to a reasonable degree, the person will have a poorly integrated sense of self, experience frustration, feel unsatisfied, helpless and hopeless, and are likely to seek satisfaction in maladaptive ways (Ward & Stewart, 2003).

Clients do not need to remain in treatment until they are 'perfect'; rather we assist them in establishing the skills necessary to help them effectively navigate their lives. The therapist helps the client develop their own individualized good life plan. Clients are encouraged to identify the domains that are most important to them, and to identify goals to enhance that domain, in line with their level of functioning. We then help clients break down their goals into short- and long-term goals, and help them to be specific in what they want to achieve.

Summary

The goal of this chapter has been to integrate some key domains often explored in sexual offending (cognition, motivation and emotion) and discuss an intervention approach that integrates all of these domains. The overall approach described here is designed to comprehensively address key issues relevant to sexual offending in an integrated manner. Importantly, our approach has been deemed effective in reducing recidivism, which is the overall ultimate goal (Marshall et al., 2011).

Those who work with men who have sexually offended need to be flexible in their approach and to keep in mind that clients struggle with many of the same issues we do; they have patterns of thinking that cause lifestyle problems, they struggle to effectively manage emotions and they are at times motivated to make decisions with negative consequences. Developing a good case conceptualization, where we understand some of the background dynamics that might result in our clients being less able to effectively manage these aspects of their lives is helpful in addressing the role of cognition, emotion and motivation to offend. Ultimately, we want to help our clients cease offending behaviour but we should not forget that they are also human beings trying to navigate many life challenges. Helping them come to terms with their issues, address need areas and establish a healthy approach to life will ultimately reduce the likelihood of further offending. As highlighted throughout this chapter, we are more likely to succeed with respect to this goal if the cognitive, emotional and motivational aspects are integrated throughout treatment.

References

Baumeister, R. F., & Vohs, K. D. (2004). *Handbook of self-regulation: Research, theory, and applications.* New York: Guilford Press.

Beech, A. R., & Fordham, A. S. (1997). Therapeutic climate of sexual offender treatment programs. *Sexual Abuse: A Journal of Research and Treatment, 9,* 219–237. doi: 10.1177/107906329700900306

Beech, A. R., & Hamilton-Giachritis, C. E. (2005). Relationship between therapeutic climate and treatment outcome in group-based sexual offender treatment programs. *Sexual Abuse: A Journal of Research and Treatment, 17,* 127–140. doi: 10.1177/107906320501700204

Bumby, K. M. (1996). Assessing the cognitive distortions of child molesters and rapists: Development and validation of the MOLEST and RAPE scales. *Sexual Abuse: A Journal of Research and Treatment, 8,* 37–54. doi: 10.1007/bf02258015

Carver, C. S. (2004). Self-regulation of action and affect. In R. F. Baumeister & K. D. Vohs (Eds.), *Handbook of self-regulation: Research, theory, and applications* (pp. 13–39). New York: Guilford Press.

Cooley, E. J., & Lajoy, R. (1980). Therapeutic relationship and improvements as perceived by clients and therapists. *Journal of Clinical Psychology, 36,* 562–570.

Cortoni, F., & Marshall, W. L. (2001). Sex as a coping strategy and its relationship to juvenile sexual history and intimacy in sexual offenders. *Sexual Abuse: A Journal of Research and Treatment, 13,* 27–43. doi: 10.1177/107906320101300104

Gannon, T. A. (2016). Forensic psychologists should use the behavioral experiment to facilitate cognitive change in clients who have offended. *Aggression and Violent Behavior [Online First].* doi: 10.1016/j.avb.2016.02.008

Goldfried, M. R., & Wolfe, B. (1996). Psychotherapy practice and research: Repairing a strained alliance. *American Psychologist, 51,* 1007–1016. doi: 10.1037?0003-066X.51.10.1007

Green, R. (1995). Psycho-educational modules. In B. K. Schwartz & H. R. Cellini (Eds.), *The sex offender: Corrections, treatment and legal practice* (pp. 13.1–13.10). Kingston, NJ: Civic Research Institute.

Greenberg, L. S. (2007). Emotion in the therapeutic relationship in emotion focused therapy. In P. Gilbert & R. L. Leahy (Eds.), *The therapeutic relationship in the cognitive behavioural psychotherapies* (pp. 43–62). New York: Routledge.

Greenberg, L. S., & Watson, J. (2006). *Emotion-focused therapy of depression.* Washington, DC: American Psychological Association Press.

Hanson, R. K. (2006). Stability and change: Dynamic risk factors for sexual offenders. In W. L. Marshall, Y. M. Fernandez, L. E. Marshall & G. A. Serran (Eds.), *Sexual offender treatment: Controversial issues* (pp. 17–31). Chichester, UK: John Wiley & Sons.

Hanson, R. K., & Bussière, M. T. (1998). Predicting relapse: A meta-analysis of sexual offender recidivism studies. *Journal of Consulting and Clinical Psychology, 66,* 348–362. doi: 10.1037/0022-006x.66.2.348

Hanson, R. K., & Harris, A. J. R. (2000). Where should we intervene? Dynamic predictors of sex offender recidivism. *Criminal Justice and Behavior, 27,* 6–35. doi: 10.1177?0093854800027001002

Hanson, R. K., & Morton-Bourgon, K. E., (2004). The characteristics of persistent sexual offenders: A meta-analysis of recidivism studies. *Journal of Consulting and Clinical Psychology, 73,* 1154–1163. doi: 10.1037?0022-006X.73.6.1154

Howells, K., & Day, A. (2006). Affective determinants of treatment engagement in violent offenders. *International Journal of Offender Rehabilitation and Comparative Criminology, 50,* 174–186. doi: 10.1177/0306624x05281336

Howells, K., Day, A., & Wright, S. (2004). Affect, emotions and sex offending. *Psychology, Crime & Law, 10,* 179–195. doi: 10.1080/10683160310001609988

Hudson, S. M., Marshall, W. L., Wales, D. S., McDonald, E., Bakker, L. W., & McLean, A. (1993). Emotional recognition skills of sex offenders. *Annals of Sex Research, 6,* 199–211. doi: 10.1007?BF00849561

Hunter, J. C., Pfafflin, F., & Ross, T. (2007). Patient, bezugspflege und therapeut: Ein empirischer untersuchungsansatz fur forensische therapieverlaufe [Patient, primary nurse, and therapist: An empirical approach for evaluating forensic treatment]. *Forensische Psychiatrie und Psychotherpie: Werkstattschriften, 14,* 23–35.

Klein, M. H., Mathieu-Couglan, P., & Kiesler, D. (1986). The experiencing scales. In L. S. Greenberg & W. Pinsoff (Eds.), *The psychotherapeutic process: A research handbook* (pp. 21–71). New York: Guilford Press.

Langton, C. M., & Marshall, W. L. (2000). The role of cognitive distortions in relapse prevention programs. In D. R. Laws, S. M. Hudson & T. Ward (Eds.), *Remaking relapse prevention with sex offenders: A sourcebook* (pp. 167–186). Newbury Park, CA: Sage.

Langton, C. M., & Marshall, W. L. (2001). Cognition in rapists: Theoretical patterns by typological breakdown. *Aggression and Violent Behavior, 6,* 499–518. doi: 10.1016/S1359-1789(00)00029-X

Laws, D. R., & Ward, T. (2006). When one size doesn't fit all: The reformulation of relapse prevention. In W. L. Marshall, Y. M. Fernandez, L. E. Marshall & G. A. Serran (Eds.), *Sexual offender treatment: Controversial issues* (pp. 241–254). Chichester, UK: John Wiley & Sons.

Lietaier, G. (1992). Helping and hindering processes in client-centered/experiential psychotherapy: A content analysis of client and therapist postsession perceptions. In S. G. Toukmanian & D. L. Rennie (Eds.), *Psychotherapy process research: Paradigmatic and narrative approaches* (pp. 134–162) Newbury Park, CA: Sage.

Linehan, M. (1993). *Skills training manual for treating borderline personality disorder*. New York: Guilford Press.

Looman, J. (1995). Sexual fantasies of child molesters. *Canadian Journal of Behavioural Science, 27*, 321–332. doi: 10.1037/0008-400x.27.3.321

Mann, R. E., & Hollin, C. R. (2001, November). Schemas: A model for understanding cognition in sexual offending. Paper presented at the 20th Annual Research and Treatment Conference of the Association for the Treatment of Sexual Abusers, San Antonio, TX.

Mann R.E., and Shingler, J. (2006). Collaboration in clinical work with offenders: Treatment and risk assessment. In W.L. Marshall, Y.M. Fernandez, L.E. Marshall, and G.A. Serran (Eds.), *Sexual offender treatment: controversial issues* (pp. 225–239). New York: John Wiley and sons.

Mann, R. E., Webster, S. D., Schofield, C., & Marshall, W. L. (2004). Approach versus avoidance goals in relapse prevention with sexual offenders. *Sexual Abuse: A Journal of Research and Treatment, 16*, 65–75.

Marshall, W. L. (2009). Manualization: A blessing or a curse? *Journal of Sexual Aggression, 15*, 109–120. doi: 10.1080/13552600902907320

Marshall, W. L., & Marshall, L. E. (2000). The origins of sexual offending. *Trauma, Violence & Abuse, 1*, 250–263. doi: 10.1177?1524838000001003003

Marshall, L. E., Marshall, W. L., & Moulden, H. A. (2000, October). Mood induction with sexual offenders. Paper presented at the 21st Annual Research and Treatment Conference of the Association for the Treatment of Sexual Abusers. Montreal, Canada.

Marshall, W. L., Marshall, L. E., Serran, G. A., & O'Brien, M. D. (2011). *Rehabilitating sexual offenders: A strengths-based approach*. Washington, DC: American Psychiatric Association Press.

Marshall, W. L., Marshall, L. E., & Ware, J. (2009). Cognitive distortions in sexual offenders: Should they all be targets? *Sexual Abuse in Australia and New Zealand: An Interdisciplinary Journal, 2*, 70–78.

Marshall, W. L., Serran, G. A., & Cortoni, F. A. (2000). Childhood attachments, sexual abuse, and their relationship to adult coping in child molesters. *Sexual Abuse: A Journal of Research and Treatment, 12*, 17–26. doi: 10.1177/107906320 001200103

Marshall, W. L., Serran, G. A., Moulden, H., Mulloy, R., Fernandez, Y. M., Mann, R. E., et al. (2002). Therapist features in sexual offender treatment: Their reliable identification and influence on behavior change. *Clinical Psychology and Psychotherapy 9*, 395–405. doi: 10.1002/cpp.335

Maruna, S. (2001). *Making good: How ex-convicts reform and rebuild their lives.* Washington, DC: American Psychological Association Press. doi: 10.1037? 10430-000

Maruna, S., & Mann, R. E. (2006). A fundamental attribution error? Rethinking cognitive distortions. *Legal and Criminological Psychology, 11,* 155–177. doi: 10.1348/135532506X114608

McGrath, R. J., Cumming, G. F., Burchard, B. L., Zeoli, S., & Ellerby, L. (2010). *Current practices and emerging trends in sexual abuser management. The Safer Society 2009 North American Survey.* Brandon, VT: Safer Society Press.

Moos, R. H. (1986). *Group environment scale manual* (2nd ed.). Palo Alto, CA: Psychology Consulting Press.

Murphy, W. D. (1990). Assessment and modification of cognitive distortions in sex offenders. In W. L. Marshall, D. R. Laws & H. E. Barbaree (Eds.), *Handbook of sexual assault: Issues, theories and treatment of the offender* (pp. 331–342). New York: Plenum Press.

Neidigh, L. W., & Tomiko, R. (1991). The coping strategies of child sexual abusers. *Journal of Sex Education and Therapy, 17,* 103–110.

Nunes, K., Hermann, C., White, K., Petterson, C., & Bumby, K. (2016). Attitude may be everything, but is everything an attitude? Cognitive distortions may not be evaluations of rape. *Sexual Abuse: A Journal of Research and Treatment* [Online First]. doi: 10.1177/1079063215625489

Nunes, K., Petterson, C., Hermann, C., Looman, J., & Spape, J. (2014). Does change on the MOLEST and RAPE scales predict sexual recidivism? *Sexual Abuse: A Journal of Research and Treatment, 1–21.* doi: 10.1177/1079063214540725

Orlinsky, D. E., & Howard, K. I. (1986). Process and outcome in psychotherapy. In S. L. Garfield & A. E. Bergin (Eds.), *Handbook of psychotherapy and behavior change* (3rd ed., pp. 311–384). New York: John Wiley & Sons.

Pfafflin, F., Bohmer, M., Cornehl, S., & Mergenthaler, F. (2005). What happens in therapy with sexual offenders? A model of process research. *Sexual Abuse: A Journal of Research and Treatment, 17,* 141–151. doi: 10.1177?1079063205017 00205

Pithers, W. D., Marques, J. K., Gibat, C. C., & Marlatt, G. A. (1983). Relapse prevention with sexual aggressors: A self-control model of treatment and maintenance of change. In J. G. Greer & I. R. Stuart (Eds.), *The sexual aggressor: Current perspectives on treatment* (pp. 214–239). New York: Van Norstrand Reinhold.

Pithers, W. D., Kashima, K. M., Cumming, G. F., Beal, L. S., & Buell, M. M. (1988). Relapse prevention of sexual aggression. In R. A. Prentky & V. L. Quinsey (Eds.), *Human sexual aggression: Current perspectives* (pp. 244–260). New York: New York Academy of Sciences.

Proulx, J., McKibben, A., & Lusignan, R. (1996). Relationship between affective components and sexual behaviors in sexual aggressors. *Sexual Abuse: A Journal of Research and Treatment, 8,* 279–289. doi: 10.1177/107906329600800404

Roger, D., & Masters, R. (1997). The development and evaluation of an emotional control training program for sexual offenders. *Legal and Criminological Psychology, 2,* 51–64. doi: 10.1111/j.2044-8333.1997.tb00332.x

Salter, A. C. (1988). *Treating child sex offenders and victims? Assessment and treatment of child sex offenders: A practical guide.* Beverly Hills, CA: Sage.

Saunders, M. (1999). Clients' assessments of the affective environment of the psychotherapy session: Relationship to session quality and treatment effectiveness. *Journal of Clinical Psychology, 55,* 597–605. doi: 10.1002/(SICI)1097-4679(199905)55:5<597::AID-JCLP7>3.0.CO;2-M.

Serran, G. A., Firestone, P., Marshall, W. L., & Moulden, H. (2007). Changes in coping following treatment for child molesters. *Journal of Interpersonal Violence, 22,* 1199–1210. doi: 10.1177/0886260507303733

Starzyk, K. B., & Marshall, W. L. (2003). Childhood family and personological risk factors for sexual offending. *Aggression and Violent Behavior, 8,* 93–105. doi: 10.1016/S1359-1789(01)00053-2

Stinson, J. D., Sales, B. D., & Becker, J. V. (2008). *Sex offending: Causal theories to inform research, prevention, and treatment.* Washington, DC: American Psychological Association Press. doi: 10.1037/11708-000

Velten, E. (1968). A laboratory task for induction of mood states. *Behaviour Research and Therapy, 6,* 473–482.

Ward, T. (2002). Good lives and the rehabilitation of offenders: Promises and problems. *Aggression and Violent Behavior, 7,* 513–528. doi: 10.1016/S1359-1789(01)00076-3

Ward, T., & Hudson, S. M. (2000). A self-regulation model of relapse prevention. In D. R. Laws, S. M. Hudson & T. Ward (Eds.), *Remaking relapse prevention with sex offenders: A sourcebook* (pp. 79–101). Thousand Oaks, CA: Sage.

Ward, T., & Stewart, C. A. (2003). Good lives and the rehabilitation of sexual offenders. In T. Ward, D. R. Laws & S. M. Hudson (Eds.), *Sexual deviance: Issues and controversies* (pp. 21–44). Thousand Oaks, CA: Sage.

Young, J. E., Klosko, J. S., & Weishaar, M. E. (2003). *Schema therapy: A practitioner's guide.* New York: Guilford Press.

8

Cognition, Emotion and Motivation

Future Directions in Sexual Offending

Theresa A. Gannon and Tony Ward

In this closing chapter we consider future research priorities for the sexual offending literature in the areas of cognition, emotion and motivation (CEM). In pursuit of this aim, we examine historical and contemporary research and treatment trends in this area. Fortunately, the preceding chapters have already examined key developments across theory, research and treatment for the key constructs of CEM applied to sexual offending. In this chapter, we identify many of the key developments in our theoretical and research-based understanding of CEM with reference to the literature discussed in previous chapters. We also highlight how these developments should be used to inform contemporary treatment practices with clients who have sexually offended. Following this, again referring to previous chapters, we identify key aspects of CEM research and theorizing that require future consideration and advancement in order to facilitate state of the art treatment for clients who have sexually offended.

Key Developments in Theoretical and Research-Based Understanding of CEM

Without doubt, significantly more is known about CEM in relation to sexual offending than was known three to four decades ago. In the 1970s and 1980s, for example, CEM research was largely neglected since much of the literature focused on behaviourist principles and the associated constructs of inappropriate sexual preferences and interests (Marshall, Laws & Barbaree, 1990). As a result, treatment programmes for individuals who had sexually offended focused predominantly on the assessment and 'normalization' of inappropriate sexual preferences, in which behaviourist principles were preferred as a means to modify such preferences (Laws & Marshall, 2003; Marshall, 1996; Marshall et al., 1990; Quinsey & Earls, 1990). In the 1970s, however, treatment programmes for individuals who had sexually offended began to adopt more of a cognitive stance in line with mainstream cognitive behavioural approaches (see Marshall & Laws, 2003).

Sexual Offending: Cognition, Emotion and Motivation, First Edition.
Edited by Theresa A. Gannon and Tony Ward.

For example, programmes began to focus on developing clients' social skills (Marshall & Williams, 1975), since it was hypothesized that clients lacked the necessary skills to facilitate and maintain age-appropriate intimate relationships (Marshall & Laws, 2003).

In reviewing the historical literature on CEM applied to sexual offending it appears that the 1980s was a critical time. In the forthcoming sections, we examine the key milestones for each CEM subcomponent separately before examining historical conceptualizing of CEM as a more holistic entity.

Cognition

Cognition, as a concept, appears to have received a huge amount of attention in correctional psychology. In 1984, Abel, Becker and Cunningham-Rathner provided the first published account of cognition characterizing men who sexually abuse children. Previous to this account, the only reference to sexual offence supportive beliefs was associated with feminist literature on cultural rape myths (e.g., Burt, 1980). Thus, it is no exaggeration to state that Abel and colleagues' account, and later accounts (e.g., Abel et al., 1989), revolutionized theory, research and treatment efforts (Gannon & Polaschek, 2006). Abel and colleagues (1984) highlighted a series of 'cognitive distortions' or beliefs common to individuals with sexual offence histories and developed a questionnaire measure of these beliefs for use with clients who had abused children (see the Abel and Becker Cognitions Scale; Abel et al., 1989). On the face of it, Abel and colleagues' conceptualization of cognition appeared simple: the beliefs described supported sexual offending. In other words, such beliefs required assessment and cognitive restructuring to bring about reductions in offending behaviour and this is something that was readily grasped by the treatment community (see Gannon & Polaschek, 2006; Murphy, 1990). In fact, using cognitive restructuring, therapists provided clients with a rationale of how their faulty thinking contributed to their offending and educated clients how to identify and challenge such distortions using cognitive therapy approaches (Becker & Murphy, 1998; Gannon & Polaschek, 2006).

However, a closer examination of Abel and colleague's works highlighted numerous conceptual problems (Gannon & Polaschek, 2006; Ó Ciardha, Chapter 3 in this volume; Ward, 2000). Abel and colleagues presented cognitive distortions as representing varying constructs interchangeably (e.g., beliefs and justifications), which made it difficult for researchers and treatment professionals to adequately conceptualize the term 'cognitive distortion'. In a series of later articles, Ward and colleagues (Drake, Ward, Nathan & Lee, 2001; Ward, 2000; Ward & Keenan, 1999) provided a much more concrete account of 'cognitive distortions' by proposing that such distortions represented the product of underlying implicit theories or schemas. Similarly to Beck (1976, 1987), they argued that distorted implicit theories develop in response to unusual developmental experiences (e.g., child abuse) that become explained by the development of maladaptive views about the world (Drake et al., 2001). Such theories were hypothesized to influence social information processing so that congruent information was readily assimilated and incongruent information either disregarded or reinterpreted to fit the pre-existing distorted theory. Ward (2000) identified five implicit theories to account for documented post-offence explanations of sexual offending: *children as sexual beings* (core beliefs that children seek out and enjoy sexual relations with adults), *nature of harm* (core beliefs that sexual abuse is only harmful when characterized by physical violence), *dangerous world* (core beliefs regarding the world being hostile and rejecting), *uncontrollability* (core beliefs in which one's behaviour is deemed to be externally controlled) and *entitlement* (core beliefs upholding an inherent 'right' to sexually abuse). Ward and colleagues' conceptualizations appeared revolutionary and were quickly adapted to explain adult rape (Polaschek & Gannon, 2004; Polaschek & Ward, 2002). Numerous researchers designed studies to collect evidence for each of the implicit theories using questionnaire, interview and indirect measures (see Ó Ciardha, Chapter 3 in this volume or Gannon, Ward & Collie, 2007). As noted in Chapter 3, however, the evidence base for implicit theories has not been reliably established although there is some convincing evidence that men who have sexually abused children sexualize children (Babchishin, Nunes & Hermann, 2013) and that sexually aggressive men objectify women (Rudman & Mescher, 2012). Nevertheless, Ward and colleagues' implicit theories have played a significant role in the development of treatment initiatives with clients who have sexually offended. Many treatment programmes and providers began to introduce the concept of social-cognition and social-information processing within programmes (see Drake et al., 2001; Gannon et al., 2011) to guide clients on the automatic and implicit effects of schema in relation to contextual, environmental and internal triggers. What was missing, however, was a more complex and fluid account of cognition in relation to sexual offending.

In the mid 2000s, theorists and researchers began to grapple with the complexity of sexual offence related cognition (Gannon & Polaschek, 2006; Maruna & Mann, 2006; Ward, Gannon & Keown, 2006). A landmark manuscript by Maruna and Mann (2006) prompted professionals to differentiate offence-supportive beliefs from other forms of cognition regarded to be appropriate and normal (i.e., justifications and excuse-making). In particular, Maruna and Mann argued that research and treatment professionals were conflating these constructs resulting in confusion and inappropriate responses to cognition within treatment. Maruna and Mann highlighted that excuse-making in other contexts (see Snyder & Higgins, 1988) was largely viewed as appropriate and normative, and helped individuals to maintain a healthy level of self-esteem. Consequently, treating such excuses as criminogenic was at odds with the wider criminological literature. Furthermore, it threatened to undermine the therapeutic relationship by causing a number of problematic affective states such as shame and distrust (see Blagden, Lievesley & Ware, Chapter 5 in this volume). The consequences of such conceptualizations for treatment were clear. Practitioners needed to engage with cognition in a much more complex manner through detecting differences in cognitions across individuals (i.e., some individuals might hold a series of offence-supportive schemas while others might be characterized by excuse-making) and taking into consideration time in treatment (i.e., excuses might be more likely to occur early in the treatment process) (Gannon, 2009; Marshall, Marshall, Serran & O'Brien, 2011). Indeed, meta-analyses support the view that beliefs and attitudes (measured using questionnaires) are related to sexual reoffending whilst denial and minimization are not (Hanson & Morton-Bourgon, 2005; Helmus, Hanson, Babchishin & Mann, 2013). However, questionnaire assessments of sexual offence related beliefs vary hugely regarding scope and content of items (see Hermann et al., 2012; Nunes et al., 2016). Consequently, it can be difficult to identify exactly which types of cognition are related to sexual offence recidivism.

It has taken some time for multi-factor theories of sexual offending to grapple with offence-related cognition in a sophisticated manner (see Bartels, Chapter 2 in this volume). Early theorists (e.g., Finkelhor, 1984; Hall & Hirschmann, 1991; 1992; Marshall & Barbaree, 1990) were not informed by knowledge regarding offence-supportive cognition and its complexity due to the lack of research and single-factor theorizing in this area. Consequently, professionals treating clients who have sexually abused should be mindful of this when choosing theory to guide their practice. More contemporary theories (e.g., Ward & Beech's *Integrated Theory of Sexual Offending [ITSO]*, 2006) approach the concept of cognition in a multi-faceted manner and include elements of neuropsychology as well as excuse-making. However, given research advances in the area of neurodevelopmental cognitive deficits (see Ó Ciardha, Chapter 3 in this volume), this aspect of the model could be further developed. Furthermore, as Bartels (Chapter 2 in this volume) notes, the elucidation of how such cognition interacts with the concepts of emotion – in particular positive emotion – and motivation requires further consideration.

A clear problem highlighted by authors of the preceding chapters (see Ó Ciardha, Chapter 3 or Brown, Chapter 4 in this volume) is the lack of research attention paid to the cognition of females who have sexually offended. A handful of studies have been conducted examining sexual offence-supportive beliefs or empathy and these studies suggest – on balance – that women who offend alone are most likely to hold deficits in these areas (see Gannon & Alleyne, 2013). Furthermore, the sexual offence-supportive beliefs noted in women appear to be qualitatively different from those documented in men (Gannon & Alleyne, 2013). Nevertheless, there is still much work to be conducted before any definitive conclusions can be made.

Emotion/Affect

Correctional psychology appears to have conceptualized cognition as being the primary construct of significance. Consequently, affect has received less attention in theory, research and treatment. Furthermore, in practice, correctional psychology has viewed affect unilaterally; negative emotions overpower clients, facilitate crime and need to be contained (Serran, Chapter 7 in this volume; Ward, Chapter 1 in this volume). There is no doubt that such conceptualizations of emotion/affect have been driven by traditional CBT approaches that began pervading the sexual offending field in the 1980s. Traditional CBT approaches tend to view cognition as the primary mechanism facilitating and maintaining problematic symptoms and behaviour. Emotion is conceptualized as representing the *consequence* or downstream effect of problematic cognitive appraisals; a direct precursor for problematic behaviour that requires containment and modification through cognitive directed change or restructuring (Dobson & Craig, 1996; Samoilov & Goldfried, 2000). It is not difficult to find examples of such traditional CBT conceptualizations in the sexual offence or general offence treatment literatures (Ireland, Ireland & Birch, 2009; Layton MacKenzie, 2006; Morin & Levenson, 2002). What is clear, however, is that mainstream research knowledge about the relationship between cognition and affect is progressing significantly (see Ward, Chapter 1 in this volume), and informing CBT approaches. Yet, interestingly, many of the preceding chapter authors call for more focus on affect in theory, research and treatment. We believe that the developing nature of forensic-clinical psychology means that we are constantly playing catch up with mainstream clinical psychology. In this sense, we must be swift to analyze broader developments, yet critical and thoughtful in our adaptation and development of techniques and conceptualizations. So, what are the key developments regarding affect that forensic-clinical psychologists should consider? Across this book some general themes have evolved that reflect mainstream CBT developments. First, emotion needs to be conceptualized as an important concept *alongside* cognition. Second, effective therapy requires the *in vivo* facilitation of emotion. Finally, two further themes, more specific to sexual offending, have evolved concerning developments in our understanding of shame and guilt and positive affect. All four of these themes apply to both male and female perpetrators of sexual abuse.

Emotion Conceptualized Alongside Cognition

Reconceptualizing emotion and placing greater importance on this construct in the sexual offence field is a key priority. Cognitive neuroscience research strongly suggests that the experience of emotion does not always require cognitive input (LeDoux, 1996) and that emotion and cognition overlap to a large degree using shared neural pathways (Pessoa, 2013). Ward (Chapter 1 in this volume) calls upon researchers to desist from viewing cognition as the key driver of inappropriate behaviour and to reconceptualize emotion as a more important concept in the aetiology and treatment of clients who have sexually offended. Using research and theory from philosophy and neuroscience, as well as contemporary psychology, Ward argues that emotions are highly important and biologically adaptive cues that – through interaction with cognitive constructs – enable individuals to assess goal progress and make sense of the social world. In other words, emotions are evolutionary adaptive and the key motivators of action since they enable us to quickly identify threats to our goals or opportunities for goal attainment. The implications of this reconceptualization are important for the future generation of multi-factor theories of sexual offending as well as treatment. None of the theories outlined by Bartels (Chapter 2 in this volume) adequately account for the theoretical and research developments associated with emotion and its relationship with cognition. Consequently, practitioners require a significant amount of flexibility and creativity to incorporate these conceptualizations into their everyday practice.

In Vivo **Facilitation of Emotion**

Longstanding research and theory suggests that although emotion and cognition are linked, they may be differentiated along information processing subtypes (i.e., propositional or implicational; Teasdale, 1997; Teasdale & Barnard, 1993). The rational verbal system is associated with propositional processing (i.e., knowing something to be true), whereas the holistic emotional and non-verbal system is associated with implicational processing (i.e., feeling something to be true). Various authors in this book (e.g., Blagden et al., Chapter 5 and Serran, Chapter 7) have outlined the importance of activating emotion within therapeutic contexts. The reasons for this stem from therapeutic outcomes associated with propositional versus implicational processing. In short, in order to tackle problematic emotions (and cognitions) associated with problem behaviours, therapeutic techniques must target *meaning* at both the propositional and implicational level (Bennett-Levy et al., 2004; Samoilov & Goldfried, 2000; Gannon, 2016). Thus, in order to bring about meaningful change (i.e., feeling something to be significant), clients' emotion (and associated cognition) may only be altered when affective and cognitive restructuring tasks are presented during emotional activation (Samoilov & Goldfried, 2000). What this means for sexual offence work is that therapists must be skilled practitioners who are able to manage affective episodes in treatment and identify key opportunities for affective restructuring. In short, sexual offending therapists need to possess a complete repertoire of therapy skills and no longer should be considered to be simply behavioural technicians. In mainstream CBT approaches, guided imagery is one technique used by practitioners to address emotionally difficult memories. Here, adults revisit their memories and are instructed in intervene in ways that essentially 'rescript' the memory (Holmes, Arntz & Smucker, 2007). The emotional activation associated with reliving the memory is hypothesized to bring about experiential change in distressing memories (Samoilov & Goldfried, 2000). Clearly, such a technique could be adapted for use with clients who have sexually offended, not only to restructure distressing and traumatic memories but also perhaps to restructure experiences of inappropriate sexual arousal and intense negative emotional states. Again, then, the message is that we must not ignore emotional states and processes within sexual offence treatment. Emotional activation within therapy is not strongly emphasized within sexual offence treatment (see Marshall et al., 2011 for an exception) and yet it represents a very promising evidence based avenue for bringing about effective change in behaviour (Gannon, 2016). It may even explain some current anomalies within the sexual offence field. For example, is it possible that clients' report the victim empathy aspects of treatment (which often involves perspective taking and emotion inducing chair work) to be successful precisely because of the activation of emotion? As Brown (Chapter 4 in this volume) highlights, it may be that our methods of measurement are not yet sophisticated enough to measure improvements brought about by the use of this experiential method.

Shame and Guilt

There is no doubt that significant gains have been made in our understanding of these concepts in recent years (see Blagden et al., Chapter 5 in this volume).

Shame and guilt have largely been understood in relation to how they might impede the therapeutic process (see Serran, Chapter 7 in this volume), or facilitate relapse (see Stinson, Chapter 6 in this volume). However, it is likely that they play an integral role in offence maintenance as well (see LeBel, Burnett, Maruna & Bushway, 2008; Ward, Louden, Hudson & Marshall, 1995). For example, the individual who offends sexually against a child and experiences internalized shame may well try to fight future urges to offend and yet experience hopelessness and depression that results in further entrenchment of offending behaviour. Interestingly, however, although negative affect – in a general sense – is often cited in multi-factor theories of sexual offending as both potential offence triggers and causal mechanisms, they do not specifically cite shame or guilt as important affective experiences, despite the focus on these concepts within the wider desistence literature (LeBel et al., 2008). We view this as being one key area for future multi-factor theoretical work in the field of sexual offending. Much more satisfactory, however, has been the focus that professionals have taken on the impact that shame and guilt might have within the treatment room. As Blagden et al. (Chapter 5 in this volume) have highlighted, shame is viewed as a problematic emotional experience within therapy since the *self* is evaluated highly negatively engendering negative affect, low self-esteem, self-focus and poor empathy (see also Marshall et al., 2011). Guilt, on the other hand, is considered to be a more helpful emotional experience since it involves a negative focus on the *behaviour* rather than the person as a whole. Consequently, guilt is likely to be associated with positive engagement with therapy whereas shame will obstruct a client's ability to engage meaningfully in the change process. As Marshall and colleagues (2011) have noted (see also Serran, Chapter 7 in this volume), although self constructs associated with shame such as self-esteem can be enhanced by therapists using specific tasks within therapy, strong experiences of shame are likely to require intense schema focused work. Consequently, intensive schema work might most helpfully be identified and undertaken prior to any referral for sexual offence work. However, it must be stressed that the skill level of therapists required to effectively engage in this type of work is much higher than that typically required by correctional services.

Positive Affect

The authors of the preceding chapters note that positive affect has received very little attention in theory, research and treatment (see in this volume Bartels, Chapter 2; Blagden et al., Chapter 5; Stinson, Chapter, 6; Ward, Chapter 1). For example, positive affect only began to appear in multi-factor theories in the early 2000s when Ward and Siegert (2002) proposed their Pathways Model of sexual offending. In the most recent multi-factor model (Ward & Beech's ITSO, 2006), although positive affect is acknowledged, Bartels (Chapter 2 in this volume) argues that much more emphasis is needed on elucidating varying types of affect and how it interacts with other factors to facilitate and maintain sexual offending. We view this as a critical area of research and theory that requires attention. As Ward (Chapter 1 in this volume) notes, emotions and their expression are a requirement of a meaningful life (see Christensen, 2012; Maiese, 2011). As such, emotion should be viewed as a critical part of therapy. Therapists may feel uncomfortable engaging with positive affect associated with offending and mistakenly believe that by doing so they are colluding in some way. However, offence-process model research shows clearly that some males and females who sexually offend experience positive affect pre-, peri- and post-offence (see Gannon, Rose & Ward, 2008; Ward et al., 1995). Thus, engaging with and reflecting on positive affect will be critical for uncovering the values and goals underlying sexual offending. For example, the client who boasts about his sexually aggressive behaviour with peers or who feels excited about planning his next sexual encounter with a child hold values, cognitions and goals that are clearly signalled by their affective descriptions.

Motivation

Motivations are conceptualized as directing decision-making, subsequent goals and actions (Bartels, Chapter 1 in this volume). In practice, a whole network of factors can work together at any given time to motivate an individual to sexually offend. Consequently, key motivators underlying sexual offences can sometimes be difficult to ascertain even though they represent an important component for understanding and treating sexual offending. A large number of general theories outside of the sexual offending domain exist in relation to motivation (e.g., Atkinson & Birch, 1970; Deci & Ryan, 2008; Maslow, 1943) some of which have permeated the sexual offence literature. For example, Bartels (Chapter 1 in this volume) highlights the importance of the Good Lives Model of rehabilitation (Ward & Stewart, 2003) in understanding the human needs (e.g., relatedness) and associated values (i.e., beliefs around importance of needs; 'Any partner is better than no partner') that might ultimately underlie a person's decision (conscious or unconscious) to sexually offend. However, the sexual offending research field has not always been particularly forthcoming with clear definitions of motivation or values as concepts (see Ward et al., 2006 and Ward & Hudson, 2000 for exceptions). In the 1970s and 1980s, it was the more simplistic conceptualization of sexual offence motivators that dominated theory, research and subsequent treatment efforts (i.e., power, control, anger, sexual gratification; Groth & Burgess, 1977; Laws & Marshall, 1990). More recently, professionals have been able to highlight four main groups of motivators or criminogenic needs that are related to sexual offending: inappropriate sexual interests, offence-supportive cognition, self-regulation problems and intimacy deficits (Craig, Beech & Harkins, 2009; Hanson & Harris, 2000; Hanson & Morton Bourgon, 2005; Thornton, 2013). However, the single biggest predictor or motivator of repeat sexual offending appears to be inappropriate sexual interests, clearly an appetitive factor (Hanson & Morton Bourgon, 2005).

The degree to which theorists have incorporated motivation within multi-factor theories of sexual offending has varied significantly (Bartels, Chapter 2 in this volume). For example, Finkelhor (1984) incorporated a somewhat simplistic view of motivation to sexually offend against children. In his theory, an individual could be motivated by emotional congruence with children, and/or sexual arousal, and/or blockage of age appropriate relationships. Given only one motivator was hypothesized to be required for a sexual offence to occur, it is unclear how, for example, emotional congruence with children might translate into sexual abuse (Ward & Hudson, 2001). Hall and Hirschmann (1991, 1992) provided an explicit focus on four primary motivators (i.e., sexual arousal, cognitive distortions, affective dyscontrol and personality issues). However, their conceptualization of cognition as a motivator was problematic, appearing to contrast sharply with their conceptualizations of cognition as a mediator (see Bartels, Chapter 2 in this volume). In other theories of sexual offending (e.g., Marshall & Barbaree, 1990; Ward & Siegert, 2002) motivation has not been clearly conceptualized (Bartels, Chapter 2 in this volume). Consequently, professionals have been left with significant guesswork regarding the form and function of motivators underlying sexual offending. Ward and Beech's (2006) theory represents an improvement in this respect since motivational goals are conceptualized in line with the Good Lives Model (Ward & Stewart, 2003), and motivation is conceptualized as stemming from the motivational/emotional neuropsychological system. However, as Bartels (Chapter 2 in this volume) notes, there is still work to be done since this theory requires further clarification of how problematic motivators and goals are initially formed.

Although an understanding of sexual offence motivation has not been fully actualized in multi-factor models of sexual offending, work on the offence process has brought about some detailed conceptualizations of motivators in relation to sexual offending. A key concept incorporated in all of these latter theories is that of self-regulation (i.e., 'the ability to modulate and control emotion, cognition and behaviour' in line with one's goals and aspirations; Stinson, Chapter 6 p. 89 in this volume). In other words, such models attempt to more specifically clarify the links between CEM. Initially, such theories were imported from the addictions literature (Laws, 1989; Pithers, 1990; Pithers, Marques, Gibat & Marlatt, 1983) and focused on the individual's pathway to sexual offence risk (i.e., Relapse Prevention [RP]) as well as their cognitive and emotional response to this risk (e.g., hopelessness 'I can't do this, it's too hard'). RP theory has been subject to significant conceptual critique over the last few years (see Laws et al., 2000; Polaschek, 2003; Ward & Hudson, 1996) since its key concepts do not directly translate to sexual offending behaviour (see Stinson, Chapter 6 in this volume). This was particularly problematic for practitioners since many of the clients that they came across during therapy did not neatly fit into RP theory as they demonstrated a huge variation of motivation and self-regulatory styles. In fact, a large-scale follow up of RP treatment failed to show robust treatment effects casting doubt over the clinical utility of the RP approach (Marques et al., 2005).

Of significance in this area was the theoretical development of self-regulation explanations of the offence and relapse processes (Ward & Hudson, 1998; Ward, Hudson & Keenan, 1998). Ward and his colleagues described three types of self-regulation associated with sexual offending: self-regulatory failure (i.e., the inability to suppress emotions and behaviours facilitating sexual offending), misregulation (i.e., the inappropriate use of regulation such as using alcohol to 'block out' inappropriate thoughts) and intact regulation (i.e., strong self-regulation skills used improperly in the service of inappropriate goals and values such as sexual interest in children or revenge). Thus, men who sexually offend were conceptualized as demonstrating different reasons for relapse. Men who failed to regulate or misregulated appeared motivated – at least to some degree – to avoid further reoffending and yet relapsed due to poor self-regulation. For men who effectively regulated, however, it was the motivators and associated values driving offending that required amendment in order to maintain desistence. Self-regulatory theory has gained an impressive amount of empirical evidence, is consistent with general theories of self-regulation (see Stinson, Chapter 6 in this volume), and is also able to account for the sexual offence process of females who have sexually abused (see Gannon et al., 2008; Gannon et al., 2014). Self-regulation theory has also been combined with the Good Lives Model (Ward & Stewart, 2003) to provide practitioners with the motivational tools necessary to motivate long-term desistence (Yates & Prescott, 2011; Yates, Prescott & Ward, 2010).

A recent conceptualization of self-regulation applied to sexual offending, that is best viewed as a single factor theory, has been proposed by Stinson and colleagues (Stinson & Becker, 2013; Stinson, Sales & Becker, 2008) in the form of the Multi-Modal Theory of Self-regulation. This theory conceptualizes dysregulation and dysregulation reinforcement as being key factors that motivate a person to sexually offend. In particular, this theory emphasizes the childhood factors underlying the development of poor self-regulatory styles (i.e., biological, social and environmental developmental factors) and focuses almost exclusively on four self-regulatory problems (emotional, cognitive, interpersonal and behavioural dysregulation). Within this theory, dysregulation across these domains is viewed as being a relatively normative experience. However, for individuals who sexually offend, the perceived reinforcement of dysregulating (e.g., feeling powerful, loved or sexually gratified) motivates them towards sexual offending. A particularly useful aspect of the theory is the links made between self-regulatory problems and cognitive, emotional and personality factors documented in the sexual offending literature. The framework is also able to explain more generally problematic behaviours rather than focusing solely on sexual offending. Some empirical support is already available for treatment implemented in line with this model (Stinson, Becker & McVay, 2015). However, this theory represents a relatively new perspective on motivation and self-regulation applied to sexual offending.

A key focus of self-regulatory accounts of relapse is on the cognitive, emotional and behavioural elements associated with the dichotomous goals of: (1) being motivated to reoffend or; (2) being motivated to avoid reoffending. Such conceptualizations have been imported from the general self-regulation literature (e.g., Baumeister & Heatherton, 1996; Carver & Scheier, 1990) and – whilst helpful – can at times focus so much on the mechanism of self-regulation that the key motives underlying sexual offending may be poorly conceptualized or even missed. Aspects of self-regulation are informative, should be used in place of basic RP, and could be better integrated in multi-factor theories of sexual offending. However, we believe the most important aspects of treatment for both male and female clients revolve around the basic pinpointing of motivation (i.e., What ultimately motivated the person to sexually offend? Were they originally trying to avoid or facilitate offending? Were some motivators chronically accessible or unleashed due to strong emotion and poor self-regulation? Why were these motivators chronically accessible? Does the individual hold problematic motivators, goals and values that lead them to seek out explicit opportunities to offend?). Once the key motivators underlying offending have been identified and formulated, practitioners can then examine how these motivators have developed and assign therapy targets using Good Lives language. Utilizing the Good Lives Model (Ward & Stewart, 2003) practitioners can then work on motivating the person to engage in therapy meaningfully and to desist from offending through appealing to that person's personal interests and life values. As noted earlier, these aspects can be relatively easy to unpick if therapists use affect as an indicative tool. What is of key importance is that treatment is targeted at each individual's motivational system. Presumably, some motivations and goals will be easier to reframe than others. For example, work is desperately needed to understand how best to motivate individuals who have sexually inappropriate interests. While some theorists suggest that inappropriate sexual interest can be reconditioned (Laws & Marshall, 1991; Marshall, 2006), more recent conceptualizations view paedophilia, for example, as a sexual preference which is unlikely to respond successfully to reconditioning principles (Seto, 2012). Thus, there can be great variation across treatment programmes as to how this key motivator is dealt with. Given inappropriate sexual interest represents the biggest predictor of reoffending (Hanson & Morton-Bourgon, 2005), it is important that the field is able to develop best practice methods for working with this underlying motivator.

Concluding Comments: The Whole Picture of CEM

In this chapter, we have examined theorizing, research and treatment associated with each component of CEM separately. Although this has enabled us to put forward a detailed account of developments in each individual area, we are also aware that in doing so we have artificially separated out constructs that are inextricably entwined and operate in unison (Crocker et al., 2013). It is this conundrum that consistently permeates the research literature. In order to understand key concepts and processes we must study them – and write about them – in depth; often focusing on one topic at a time. However, we must also understand exactly how these concepts interrelate and this can be challenging for researchers (who cannot possibly test a multitude of mechanisms in single studies) as well as theorists who are tasked with the role of demonstrating how CEM factors interrelate. As we have seen, not one of the multi-factor theories available to explain sexual offending can grapple with and extrapolate the links between CEM sufficiently to guide therapists unfalteringly. Ward and Beech's (2006) ITSO goes some way, however, there is much room for improved clarity of how CEM operates to facilitate and maintain sexual offending. Furthermore, the preceding chapters show that research and mainstream CBT conceptualizations have developed considerably since

2006. Thus, professionals treating clients who have sexually abused should be mindful of this when examining theory to guide their practice. Even the latest multi-factorial theory will not adequately address the CEM constellation. And, in the area of female perpetrated sexual abuse there is currently no multi-factor theory available.

Consequently, in order to treat CEM in an evidence-based manner, practitioners must adhere to the three central principles of evidence-based practice (EBP): (1) ensuring that the best research evidence is used to guide practice; (2) using clinical expertise and decision making to apply research to clinical practice; and (3) considering client individuality in terms of values and preferences when allocating interventions (Lilienfeld et al., 2013; Spring, 2007). Thus, in order to treat CEM according to EBP, a significant amount of practitioner experience and competence is required. Treatment professionals themselves (see Marshall, 2009; Marshall et al., 2011; Serran, Chapter 7 in this volume; Stinson & Becker, 2013; Ward, Chapter 1 in this volume) have stressed that in order to bring about positive change in clients who have sexually offended, examining constructs in a sophisticated and unified manner *throughout* treatment is paramount. In other words, it is a mistake to include modules solely focused on any of the CEM concepts since they all interrelate. Thus, concentrating on them separately can be unduly restrictive and only tap into the rational and logical propositional processing system. Such a strategy is unlikely to fully engage individuals in treatment and also represents an old fashioned and unfruitful approach to CEM.

A key message that has arisen from many of the preceding chapters in this book is that cognition – although important – should no longer be viewed as the key construct driving sexually inappropriate behaviour. Instead, it is affect that requires our attention. What is needed is fluidity, dynamism and therapists who are able to elicit emotion skilfully in sessions to bring about meaningful change. Unfortunately, high levels of clinical skill are not always available in large mainstream translations of sexual offence treatment where paraprofessionals lead groups (see Gannon & Ward, 2014). Given the considerable clinical skills that would be needed to translate CEM research into effective practice we find this trend to be exceedingly worrying.

In terms of moving the CEM field forward there are some obstacles that need to be overcome. Ward and Beech (2015) argue that a key problem has been researchers' focus on data to the expense of developing overarching theoretical explanations. A solution they put forward is one of integrative pluralism in which researchers work in a much more coordinated manner to examine their topic of expertise across varying explanatory domains; creating links between different areas of explanation. For example, if a researcher develops an explanation of empathy, then they would keep in mind previous existing research on cognition and emotional recognition within sexual offending and across mainstream psychology. They would then seek to link these areas conceptually. This is a laudable aim. However, a key problem relates to the overlap inherent across many of the constructs used to explain sexual offending (Ó Ciardha, Chapter 3 in this volume). Ó Ciardha, for example, highlights how beliefs about the sexuality of children overlap with the construct of sexual interest in children and yet these two constructs are often discussed and researched 'independently'. Ó Ciardha notes that, in some cases, it appears that theorizing about sexual offence related cognition has become isolated from pre-existing high quality background research and theorizing outside of the sexual offence field. Thus, it seems there is a fine line between integrative pluralism and more problematic recreation of isolated knowledge. Researchers and theorists simply must be aware of each other and acknowledge each other for integrative pluralism to work well.

Understanding the reasons why individuals intentionally act in sexually abusive ways requires a sophisticated grasp of psychological systems and the way they dynamically interact in social contexts. Clinicians need to be theoretically literate as well as therapeutically versatile, a demanding and yet necessary expectation. There are simply no shortcuts to effective practice.

References

Abel, G. G., Becker, J. V., & Cunningham-Rathner, J. (1984). Complications, consent and cognitions in sex between children and adults. *International Journal of Law and Psychiatry, 7*, 103–189. doi: 10.1016/0160-2527(84)90008-6

Abel, G. G., Gore, D. K., Holland, C. L., Camps, N., Becker, J. V., & Rathner, J. (1989). The measurement of the cognitive distortions of child molesters. *Annals of Sex Research, 2*, 135–152. doi: 10.1007/bf00851319

Atkinson, J. W., & Birch, D. (1970). *The dynamics of action*. New York: John Wiley & Sons.

Babchishin, K. M., Nunes, K. L., & Hermann, C. A. (2013). The validity of Implicit Association Test (IAT) measures of sexual attraction to children: A meta-analysis. *Archives of Sexual Behavior, 42*(3), 487–499. doi: 10.1007/s10508-012-0022-8

Baumeister, R. F., & Heatherton, T. F. (1996). Self regulation failure: An overview. *Psychological Inquiry, 7*, 1–15. doi: 10.1207/s15327965pli0701_1

Beck, A. T. (1976). *Cognitive therapy and the emotional disorders*. New York: International Universities Press.

Beck, A. T. (1987). Cognitive models of depression. *Journal of Cognitive Psychotherapy, 1*, 5–37.

Becker, J. V., & Murphy, W. D. (1998). What we know and do not know about assessing and treating sex offenders. *Psychology, Public Policy, and Law, 4*, 116–137. doi: 10.1037/1076-8971.4.1-2.116

Bennett-Levy, J., Westbrook, D., Fennell, M., Cooper, M. Rouf, K., & Hackmann, A. (2004). Behavioural experiments: Historical and conceptual underpinnings. In J. Bennett-Levy, G. Butler, M. Fennell, A. Hackmann, M. Mueller & D. Westbrook (Eds.), *Oxford guide to behavioural experiments in cognitive therapy* (pp. 1–20). Oxford, UK: Oxford University Press.

Burt, M. R. (1980). Cultural myths and supports for rape. *Journal of Personality and Social Psychology, 38*(2), 217–230. doi: 10.1037/0022-3514.38.2.217

Carver, C. S., & Scheier, M. F. (1990). Origins and functions of positive and neagative affect: A control-process view. *Psychological Review, 97*, 19–35. doi: 10.1037/0033-295x.97.1.19

Christensen, W. (2012). Natural sources of normativity. *Studies in the History and Philosophy of Biological and Biomedical Sciences, 43*, 104–112. doi: 10.1016/j.shpsc.2011.05.009

Craig, L. A., Beech, A. R., & Harkins, L. (2009). The predictive accuracy of risk factors and frameworks. In A. R. Beech, L. A. Craig & K. D. Browne (Eds.), *Assessment and treatment of sex offenders: A handbook* (pp. 53–74). Chichester, UK: John Wiley & Sons.

Crocker, L. D., Heller, W., Warren, S. L., O'Hare, A. J., Infantolino, Z. P., & Miller, G. A. (2013). Relationships among cognition, emotion, and motivation: Implications for intervention and neuroplasticity in psychopathology. *Frontiers in Human Neuroscience, 7*, 1–19. doi: 10.3389/fnhum.2013.00261

Deci, E. L., & Ryan, R. M. (2008). Self-determination theory: A macrotheory of human motivation, development, and health. *Canadian Psychology, 49*, 182–185. doi: 10.1037/a0012801

Dobson, K. S., & Craig, K. S. (Eds.). (1996). *Advances in cognitive-behavioral therapy*. Thousand Oaks, CA: Sage.

Drake, C., Ward, T., Nathan, P., & Lee, J. (2001). Challenging the cognitive distortions of child molesters: An implicit theory approach. *Journal of Sexual Aggression, 7*, 25–40. doi: 10.1080/13552600108416165

Finkelhor, D. (1984). *Child sexual abuse: New theory and research*. New York: The Free Press.

Gannon, T. A. (2009). Current cognitive distortion theory and research: An internalist approach to cognition. *Journal of Sexual Aggression, 15*(3), 225–246. doi: 10.1080/13552600903263079.

Gannon, T. A. (2016). Forensic psychologists should use the behavioral experiment to facilitate cognitive change in clients who have offended. *Aggression and Violent Behavior, 27*, 130–141. doi: 10.1016/j.avb.2016.02.008

Gannon, T. A., & Alleyne, E. K. A. (2013). Female sexual abusers' cognition: A systematic review. *Trauma, Violence, and Abuse, 14*(1), 67–79. doi: 10.1177/1524838012462245

Gannon, T. A., King, T., Miles, H., Lockerbie, L., & Willis, G. (2011). Good Lives sexual offender treatment for mentally disordered offenders. *British Journal of Forensic Practice, 13*(3), 153–168. doi: 10.1108/14636641111157805

Gannon, T. A., & Polaschek, D. L. L. (2006). Cognitive distortions in child molesters: A re-examination of key theories and research. *Clinical Psychology Review, 26*, 1000–1019. doi: 10.1016/j.cpr.2005.11.010

Gannon, T. A., Rose, M. R., & Ward, T. (2008). A descriptive model of the offense process for female sexual offenders. *Sexual Abuse: A Journal of Research and Treatment, 20*(3), 352–374. doi: 10.1177/1079063208322495

Gannon, T. A., & Ward, T. (2014). Where has all the psychology gone? A critical review of evidence-based psychological practice in correctional settings. *Aggression and Violent Behavior, 19*(4), 435–446. doi: 10.1016/j.avb.2014.06.006

Gannon, T. A., Ward, T., & Collie, R. (2007). Cognitive distortions in child molesters: Theoretical and research developments over the past two decades. *Aggression and Violent Behavior: A Review Journal, 12*(4), 402–416. doi: 10.1016/j.avb.2006.09.005

Gannon, T. A., Waugh, G., Taylor, K., Blanchette, K., O'Connor, B., & Ó Ciardha, C. O. (2014). Women who sexually offend display three main offense styles: A re-examination of the descriptive model of female sexual offending. *Sexual Abuse: A Journal of Research and Treatment, 26*(3), 207–224. doi: 10.1177/1079063213486835

Groth, A. N., & Burgess, A. W. (1977). Rape: A sexual deviation. *American Journal of Orthopsychiatry, 47*, 400–406. doi: 10.111/j.1939-0025.1977.tb01246.x

Hall, G. C. N., & Hirschman, R. (1991). Toward a theory of sexual aggression: A quadripartite model. *Journal of Consulting and Clinical Psychology, 59*, 662–669. doi: 10.1037/0022-006X.59.5.662

Hall, G. C. N., & Hirschman, R. (1992). Sexual aggression against children: A conceptual perspective of etiology. *Criminal Justice and Behavior, 19*, 8–23. doi: 10.1177/0093854892019001003

Hanson, R. K., & Harris, A. J. R. (2000). Where should we intervene? Dynamic predictors of sex offender recidivism. *Criminal Justice and Behavior, 27*, 6–35. doi: 10.1177/0093854800027001002

Hanson, R. K., & Morton-Bourgon, K. E. (2005). The characteristics of persistent sexual offenders: A meta-analysis of recidivism studies. *Journal of Consulting and Clinical Psychology, 73*, 1154–1163. doi: 10.1037/0022-006X.73.6.1154

Helmus, L., Hanson, R. K., Babchishin, K. M., & Mann, R. E. (2013). Attitudes supportive of sexual offending predict recidivism: A meta-analysis. *Trauma, Violence, & Abuse, 14*, 34–53. doi: 10.1177/1524838012462244

Hermann, C. A., Babchishin, K. M., Nunes, K. L., Leth-Steensen, C., & Cortoni, F. (2012). Factor structure of the Bumby RAPE scale: A two factor model. *Criminology and Penology, 39*, 869–886. doi: 10.1177/0093854812436802

Holmes, E. A., Arntz, A., & Smucker, M. R. (2007). Imagery rescripting in cognitive behavior therapy: Images, treatment techniques and outcomes. *Journal of Behavior Therapy and Experimental Psychiatry, 38*, 297–305. doi: 10.1016/j.jbtep.2007.10.007

Ireland, J. L., Ireland, C. A., & Birch, P. (2009). *Violent and sexual offenders: Assessment, treatment and management.* Cullompton, UK: Willan.

Laws, D. R. (1989). *Relapse prevention with sex offenders.* New York: Guilford Press.

Laws, D. R., Hudson, S. M., & Ward, T. (2000). *Remaking relapse prevention with sex offenders: A sourcebook.* Thousand Oaks, CA: Sage.

Laws, D. R., & Marshall, W. L. (1990). A conditioning theory of the etiology and maintenance of deviant sexual preference and behavior. In W. L. Marshall, D. R. Laws & H. E. Barbaree (Eds.), *Handbook of sexual assault: Issues, theories and treatment of the offender* (pp. 209–229). New York: Plenum Press.

Laws, D. R., & Marshall, W. L. (1991). Masturbatory reconditioning: An evaluative review. *Advances in Behaviour Research and Therapy, 13*, 13–25. doi: 10.1016/0146-6402(91)90012-Y

Laws, D. R., & Marshall, W. L. (2003). A brief history of behavioral and cognitive behavioral approaches to sexual offenders: Part 1. Early developments. *Sexual Abuse: A Journal of Research and Treatment, 15*, 75–92. doi: 10.1177/107906320 301500201

Layton MacKenzie, D. (2006). *What works in corrections: Reducing the criminal activities of offenders and delinquents.* New York: Cambridge University Press.

LeBel, T. P., Burnett, R., Maruna, S., & Bushway, S. (2008). The 'chicken and egg' of subjective and social factors in desistance from crime. *European Journal of Criminology, 5*(2), 131–159. doi: 10.1177/1477370807087640

LeDoux, J. E. (1996). *The emotional brain.* New York: Simon and Schuster.

Lilienfeld, S. O., Ritschel, L. A., Lynn, S. J., Cautin, R. L., & Latzman, R. D. (2013). Why many clinical psychologists are resistant to evidence-based practice: Root causes and constructive remedies. *Clinical Psychology Review, 7*, 883–900. doi: 10.1016/j.cpr.2012.09.008

Maiese, M. (2011). *Embodiment, emotion and cognition.* Basingstoke, UK: Palgrave Macmillan.

Marques, J. K., Wiederanders, M., Day, D. M., Nelson, C., & van Ommeren, A. (2005). Effects of a relapse prevention program on sexual recidivism: Final results from California's Sex Offender Treatment and Evaluation Project (SOTEP). *Sexual Abuse: Journal of Research & Treatment, 17*(1), 79–107. doi: 10.1177/107906320501700108

Marshall, W. L. (1996). Assessment, treatment, and theorizing about sex offenders: Developments during the past twenty years and future directions. *Criminal Justice and Behavior, 23*, 162–199. doi: 10.1177/0093854896023001011

Marshall, W. L. (2006). Olfactory aversion and directed masturbation in the modification of deviant preferences. A case study of a child molester. *Clinical Case Studies, 5*, 3–14. doi: 10.1177/1534650103259754

Marshall, W. L. (2009). Manualization: A blessing or a curse? *Journal of Sexual Aggression, 15*, 109–120. doi: 10.1080/13552600902907320

Marshall, W. L., & Barbaree, H. E. (1990). An integrated theory of the etiology of sexual offending. In W. L. Marshall, D. R. Laws & H. E. Barbaree (Eds.), *Handbook of sexual assault: Issues, theories, and treatment of the offender* (pp. 257–275). New York: Plenum Press.

Marshall, W. L., & Laws, D. R. (2003). A brief history of behavioral and cognitive behavioral approaches to sexual offenders: Part 2. The modern era. *Sexual Abuse: A Journal of Research and Treatment, 15*, 93–120. doi: 10.1177/107906320301500202

Marshall, W. L., Laws, D. R., & Barbaree, H. E. (1990). Issues in sexual assault. In W. L. Marshall, D. R. Laws & H. E. Barbaree (Eds.), *Handbook of sexual assault: Issues, theories, and treatment of the offender* (pp. 3–7). New York: Plenum Press.

Marshall, W. L., Marshall, L. E., Serran, G. A., & O'Brien, M. D. (2011). *Rehabilitating sexual offenders: A strength-based approach.* Washington, DC: American Psychological Association Press.

Marshall, W. L., & Williams, S. (1975). A behavioural approach to the modification of rape. *Quarterly Bulletin of the British Association for Behavioural Psychotherapy, 4*, 78.

Maruna, S., & Mann, R. E. (2006). A fundamental attribution error? Rethinking cognitive distortions. *Legal and Criminological Psychology, 11*(2), 155–177. doi: 10.1348/135532506X114608

Maslow, A. H. (1943). A theory of human motivation. *Psychological Review, 50*, 370–396. doi: 10.1037/h0054346

Morin, J. W., & Levenson, J. S. (2002). *The road to freedom.* Oklahoma City, OK: Wood'N'Barnes.

Murphy, W. D. (1990). Assessment and modification of cognitive distortions in sex offenders. In W. L. Marshall, D. R. Laws & H. E. Barbaree (Eds.), *Handbook of sexual assault: Issues, theories, and treatment of the offender* (pp. 331–342). New York: Plenum Press.

Nunes, K. L., Hermann, C. A., White, K., Pettersen, C., & Bumby, K. (2016). Attitude may be everything, but is everything an attitude? Cognitive distortions may not be evaluations of rape. *Annals of Sex Research* [Online First]. doi: 10.1177/1079063215625489

Pessoa, L. (2013). *The cognitive-emotional brain: From interactions to integration.* Cambridge, MA: MIT Press.

Pithers, W. S. (1990). Relapse prevention with sexual aggressors: A method for maintaining therapeutic gain and enhancing external supervision. In W. L. Marshall, D. R. Laws & H. E. Barbaree (Eds.), *Handbook of sexual assault: Issues, theories, and treatment of the offender* (pp. 343–361). New York: Plenum Press.

Pithers, W. D., Marques, J. K., Gibat, C. C., & Marlatt, G. A. (1983). Relapse prevention with sexual aggressives: A self-control model of treatment and maintenance of change. In J. G. Greer & I. R. Stuart (Eds.), *The sexual aggressor: Current perspectives on treatment* (pp. 214–239). New York: Van Nostrand Reinhold.

Polaschek, D. L. L. (2003). Relapse prevention, offense process models, and the treatment of sexual offenders. *Professional Psychology: Research & Practice, 34*(4), 361–367. doi: 10.1037/0735-7028.34.4.361

Polaschek, D. L. L., & Gannon, T. A. (2004). The implicit theories of rapists: What convicted offenders tell us. Sexual Abuse: A Journal of Research and Treatment, *16*(4), 299–315. doi: 10.1023/B:SEBU.0000043325.94302.40

Polaschek, D. L. L., & Ward, T. (2002). The implicit theories of potential rapists: What our questionnaires tell us. *Aggression and Violent Behavior, 7*(4), 385–406.

Quinsey, V. L., & Earls, C. M. (1990). The modification of sexual preferences. In W. L. Marshall, D. R. Laws & H. E. Barbaree (Eds.), *Handbook of sexual assault: Issues, theories, and treatment of the offender* (pp. 279–295). New York: Plenum Press.

Rudman, L. A., & Mescher, K. (2012). Of animals and objects: Men's implicit dehumanization of women and likelihood of sexual aggression. *Personality and Social Psychology Bulletin, 38*, 734–746. doi: 10.1177/0146167212436401

Samoilov, A., & Goldfried, M. R. (2000). Role of emotion in Cognitive-Behavior Therapy. *Clinical Psychology: Science and Practice, 7*, 373–385. doi: 10.1093/clipsy.7.4.373

Seto, M. C. (2012). Is pedophilia a sexual orientation? *Archives of Sexual Behavior, 41*, 231–236. doi: 10.1007/s10508-011-9882-6

Snyder, C. R., & Higgins, R. L. (1988). Excuses: Their effective role in the negotiation of reality. *Psychological Bulletin, 104*, 23–35. doi: 10.1037//0033-2909.104.1.23

Spring, B. (2007). Evidence-based practice in clinical psychology: What is it; why it matters; what you need to know. *Journal of Clinical Psychology, 63*, 611–631. doi: 10.1002/jclp.20373

Stinson, J. D., & Becker, J. V. (2013). *Treating sex offenders: An evidence-based manual.* London: Guilford Press.

Stinson, J. D., Becker, J. V., & McVay, L. A. (2015). Treatment progress and behavior following two years of inpatient sex offender treatment: A pilot investigation of Safe Offender Strategies. *Sexual Abuse: A Journal of Research and Treatment,* online first. doi: 10.1177/1079063215570756

Stinson, J. D., Sales, B. D., & Becker, J. V. (2008). *Sex offending: Causal theories to inform research, prevention, and treatment.* Washington, DC: American Psychological Association Press. doi: 10.107/11708-000

Teasdale, J. D. (1997). The relationship between cognition and emotion: The mind-in-place in mood disorders. In D. M. Clark & C. G. Fairburn (Eds.), *The science and practice of cognitive behaviour therapy* (pp. 67–93). Oxford, UK: Oxford University Press.

Teasdale, J. D., & Barnard, P. J. (1993). *Affect, cognition and change: Remodelling depressive thought.* Hove, UK: Lawrence Erlbaum.

Thornton, D. (2013). Implications of our developing understanding of risk and protective factors in the treatment of adult male sexual offenders. *International Journal of Behavioral Consultation and Therapy, 8,* 62–65. doi: 10.1037/h0100985

Ward, T. (2000). Sexual offenders' cognitive distortions as implicit theories. *Aggression and Violent Behavior, 5,* 491–507. doi: 10.1016/s1359-1789(98)00036-6

Ward, T., & Beech, A. (2006). An integrated theory of sexual offending. *Aggression and Violent Behavior, 11,* 44–63. doi: 10.1016/j.avb.2005.05.002

Ward, T., & Beech, A. R. (2015). Dynamic risk factors: A theoretical dead-end? *Psychology, Crime & Law, 21,* 100–113. doi: 10.1080/1068316x.2014.917854

Ward, T., Gannon, T. A., & Keown, K. (2006). Beliefs, values, and action: The judgment model of cognitive distortions in sexual offenders. *Aggression and Violent Behavior, 11*(4), 323–340. doi: 10.1016/j.avb.2005.10.003

Ward, T., & Hudson, S. M. (1996). Relapse prevention: A critical analysis. *Sexual Abuse: A Journal of Research and Treatment, 8*(3), 177–200. doi: 10.1007/BF02256634

Ward, T., & Hudson, S. M. (1998). A model of the relapse process in sexual offenders. *Journal of Interpersonal Violence, 13*(6), 700–725. doi: 10.1177/088626098013006003

Ward, T., & Hudson, S. M. (2000). A self-regulation model of relapse prevention. In W. L. Marshall, D. R. Laws & H. E. Barbaree (Eds.), *Handbook of sexual assault: Issues, theories and treatment of the offender* (pp. 79–101). New York: Plenum Press.

Ward, T. & Hudson, S. M. (2001). Finkelhor's precondition model of child sexual abuse: A critique. *Psychology, Crime and Law, 7,* 291–307. doi: 10.1080/10683160108401799

Ward, T., Hudson, S. M., & Keenan, T. (1998). A self-regulation model of the sexual offense process. *Sexual Abuse: A Journal of Research and Treatment, 10*(2), 141–157. doi: 10.1023/A:1022071516644

Ward, T., & Keenan, T. (1999). Child molesters' implicit theories. *Journal of Interpersonal Violence, 14,* 821–838. doi: 10.1177/088626099014008003

Ward, T., Louden, K., Hudson, S. M., & Marshall, W. L. (1995). A descriptive model of the offense chain for child molesters. *Journal of Interpersonal Violence, 10*(4), 452–472. doi: 10.1177/088626095010004005

Ward, T., & Siegert, R. J. (2002). Toward a comprehensive theory of child sexual abuse: A theory knitting perspective. *Psychology, Crime & Law, 8,* 319–351. doi: 10.1080/10683160208401823

Ward, T., & Stewart, C. A. (2003). Criminogenic needs and human needs: A theoretical model. *Psychology, Crime, & Law, 9*, 125–143. doi: 10.1037/0735-7028.34.4.353

Yates, P. M., & Prescott, D. S. (2011). *Building a better life: A good lives and self-regulation workbook.* Brandon, VT: Safer Society Press.

Yates, P. M., Prescott, D. S., & Ward, T. (2011). *Applying the good lives and self-regulation models to sex offender treatment: A practical guide for clinicians.* Brandon, VT: Safer Society Press.

Index

Sexual Offending: Cognition, Emotion and Motivation, First Edition.
Edited by Theresa A. Gannon and Tony Ward.
© 2017 John Wiley & Sons Ltd. Published 2017 by John Wiley & Sons Ltd.

women (as offenders)
  childhood environment factors 101
  dangerousness of men/males
    perception 45
  dearth of research on 60, 130
  emotional dysregulation 77
  empathy 60, 77
  multi-factor theory, lack of 138
  self-regulation model 101–102, 136
  treatment 77–78

women (as victims)
  dangerous world theory 45
  desire to understand 24
  distorted cognitions about 20–21, 28
  hostile attitudes towards 22, 23–24
  rape myths 42
  see also rape
Wright, S. 17, 112

Yoder, J. R. 37